NO FARMS
NO FOOD

Hauser Family Cookbook 2022
© Kristi Bright 2022
Camp Verde, Arizona, USA
KDP ISBN 9798818173702
4rd Edition
Printed in United States of America
Copyright data available on file.
Bright, Kristi, 1964-
Hauser Family Cookbook 2022/Kristi Hauser Bright
Includes biographical reference
1. Cookbook   2. Title

www.hauserandhauserfarms.com
www.gloryboundpublishing.com

Hauser Family Cookbook
BLACK AND WHITE
VERSION

All of our family recipes for 2022
Compiled by Kristi Hauser Bright

Glorybound Publishing
Camp Verde, Arizona
Released 2022

Dedicated to our beloved son,
brother, husband, father and pops.

Forever in our hearts.
Your legacy will always be present.

Kevin Wayne Hauser

November 29,1960 - December 27, 2019

A Poem for Kevin

And, on the 8th day, God looked down on the Verde Valley and said, "I need a caretaker." So, God made a farmer.

God said, "I need somebody who has the patience to learn how to do things the right way; who will honor his father and mother through hard work and a lot of mischief; put a smile on their faces and pride in their hearts." So, God made a farmer.

God needed somebody who could bale alfalfa with baling twine, and bind a family together with laughter and love; who always encouraged others to do the right thing, but was quick to forgive when they didn't." So, God made a farmer.

God said, "I need somebody strong enough to clear trees and heave bales, yet patient enough to teach his children how to fish. It had to be somebody who'd plow deep and straight without cutting corners; somebody to seed, weed, feed, rake, disc and plow while still having the tenderness to bait a hook for his youngins'." So, God made a farmer.

God said, "I need somebody to care for the crop, fix broken tractors, and share strawberry milk with the grandkids before mom comes to pick them up." So, God made a farmer.

God said, "I need someone who will teach the world hard work with a handshake means something; someone to drive fast down the rut, to beat the rain as he bales and hauls his friend's alfalfa field when his friend is busy saying goodbye to his beloved wife." So, God made a farmer.

God said, "I need somebody with arms strong enough to plow a field and yet patient enough to let his grandkids drive the combine even when he's in a hurry." So, God made a farmer.

God said, "I need somebody who can turn an empty field into food, change a tire in the mud; who can make a harness out of haywire, feed sacks and shoe scraps...and who, during the busy harvest, will always make time to watch the Packers." So, God made a farmer.

God said, "I need someone who will still run his tired hands through his little girl's hair after a long day of clearing ditches; someone who will stop by the house every morning to welcome those he loves, into the day...and, who will always make room at La Fonda's so they can sit down and have a hot meal." So, God made a farmer.

God said, "I need a man who will do his best; someone who will do things that no one else can; someone who will bring life into the world and sow seeds of adventure and joy everywhere he goes; someone who understands how important time is, and how much more important it is to use his time here to make the world a better place; leaving the world better than when he found it."

And so, on November 29th 1960, God made Kevin Wayne Hauser.

I would like to thank my mom, Brenda Hauser, for compiling 2 cookbooks over the years and keeping our recipes popular with family and friends--any one who came to the table. I am happy to introduce book number 4.

Mom,
Thanks for all of your help with the 2022 Edition. You inspired me to treasure the recipes, keeping them sacred while adding the new generation's favorites to the book. Cooking has brought us together in our everyday lives, celebrations and holidays; and, our family has been soo blessed with some of the GREATEST cooks ever!

BRENDA HAUSER

I have many memories of going to my grandma's houses, excited for what was coming out of the oven. Learning how to cook, bake, can and preserve food from the finest women I know, is a blessing I have always cherished. It brings me joy to share special recipes from my family and friends with others.   Kristi Hauser Bright

EVA HAUSER

NAOMA MOORE

The Hauser Family has deep roots in Iowa, starting in the late 1800's and early 1900's. In 1950, Lester and Eva Hauser decided to sell their farm in Iowa and move to Arizona. They loaded up their belongings and their 5 children, Jimmy, Dick, Patty, Mary and Donny. They settled in Phoenix, AZ, where they continued farming and eventually, Jimmy, Dick and Donny all established their own farms throughout Arizona.

FARM AUCTION!

As I have decided to quit farming and will go to Arizona for my health, I will sell the following property at Public Auction on my farm located four miles South of the Shell Rock Diagonal and a mile and a quarter West, or a mile South and mile East of Norton's Corners and seven miles North of New Hartford and 9 miles West of Janesville, Iowa,

Thursday, Feb. 15

BEGINNING AT 1.00 O'CLOCK IN THE AFTERNOON

The Lester Hauser Property

1943 M Farmall, comletely overhauled; 238 Cultivator, heat houser and chains; 2 P McD Corn Picker; 3 14 in McD Plow; Case Baler with new motor and auger; 7 ft McD tractor Mower; 2 row McD mounted tractor Planter; 4-wheel McD Spreader on rubber; . 14 ft Western Cultipacker; 11 ft Weed Hog spring tooth Harrow; 2 20 ft Harrows with folding drawbars; 7 ft Case Tandem Disc; 8 ft McD Stalk Cutter; Coats Manure Loader; 8 ft JD Grain Binder; McD endgate Seeder Mc D No 10 Hammermill with several extra screens; 3 Rubber Tired Wagons; 2 flared Wagon Boxes; 1 flat rack; Tractor Wood Saw; Sandwich Elevator with Hoist and Speed Jack; 18 ft Bale Elevator; McD Portable Milker; McD Cream Separator; 300 gal Gas Barrel with hoze and nozzle; 2 80 gal Hog Waterers; 4 Hog Feeders; Several Hog Troughs & Pens; 32 foot Extension Ladder; 50 ft Rubber Endless Belt; 3 Stone Boats; loading chute; 10 Rolls Cribbing New 6 ft Galvanized Tank; Tank Heater; 11 Pig Brooder and Heat Lamps; set Harness & Collars; 2 Chicken Brooder Stoves; Cream Cans; 3 sets Steel Nests; Several Chicken Feeders, Tools, & other articles too numerous to mention:

150 BALES ALFALFA 2nd CROP: 350 BALES ALFALFA 1st CROP 400 BALES 1st Crop CLOVER;

700 BUSHEL GOOD CORN; 1200 BUSHEL RESELECT CLINTON OATS;50 BU BARLEY from Cert: Seed

15 BUSHEL CLOVER SEED, Ames TESTED 400 BALES STRAW 5 BUSHEL ALFALFA SEED

200 LAYING HENS THREE FOOT MALL CHAIN SAW 1935 FORD V 8 PICKUP

Eighteen 24 foot POLES, Several hundred feet of native lumber and posts SOME FURNITURE Goods

Lester Hauser, Owner

OSCAR TOSTLEBE, Auctioneer   SECURITY STATE BANK, Clerk
USUAL TERMS   NO PROPERTY TO BE REMOVED UNTIL SETTLED FOR

Table of Contents

CORN

APPETIZER

SOUP

BREAD

MAIN DISH

VEGETABLE

CAKES

COOKIES

CANNING

INDEX

THE SWEET CORN STORY

In the early 1970s, armed with a tin box, an old wood table, a folding chair and an umbrella, 1 set up at the two-acre sweet corn patch. It sold for fifty cents a dozen, but of course you had to pick your own. Dick had planted it for me, but I had to water and hoe it and pay him back for the seed from my profits. A neighbor used to help me hoe before and after we got off work. It was fun to see people come down the dusty road in their clean white cars and high heels to pick corn. The next year he planted five acres and it became quite a popular summer project as the years went by. It has now been passed on to the next generation of farmers and is very successful. They plant about 50 acres and have machinery to plant, cultivate and pick. It is still fun to

visit with old-timers from all parts of the country who appreciate farming and to hopefully educate the young about where their food comes from.

Thank You,
Brenda Hauser

BRENDA HAUSER
SELLING CORN
1980's

CLAUDIA HAUSER
2021

COOKING WITH CORN

Fresh corn is pure summer. It's sweet flavor makes it easy to love. Corn is versatile and can easily go from a quick and easy side dish to a show stopping main. Corn is typically treated like a vegetable in cooking, however, it's actually a healthy whole grain. It's also a rich source of antioxidants, and whether you enjoy it on or off the cob, it has a rightful spot in a healthy diet. Many people ask our family what our favorite way to cook corn on the cob is. Our little ones eat it right off the cob, raw. When gathering for a large family celebration, we simply take the corn, husk and all, and put in a large bucket of water. Soak for about 30 minutes, then throw it right on the grill, turning often. The husk will brown after about 30 minutes on the grill. Simply peel back the shuck and enjoy!! Of course we also enjoy the traditional shucking and boiling for 8 minutes also.

Interesting fact about corn silk: Silks capture the pollen grains which then begin traveling through the silk and into the ear of corn. Every silk is attached to a single ovule inside the ear which will form into a kernel upon successful pollination.

4-H Corn Special

Mitchell Ferguson

1 Lb. ground beef
1 sm. onion, finely chopped
1 1/2 c. cooked rice
2 c. seeded, chopped fresh tomatoes,
or 1 can diced tomatoes
2 c. fresh, frozen or canned sweet corn

Salt & pepper, to taste
1 T. Worcestershire sauce
1 c. crushed saltine crackers
1/4 c. butter or margarine, melted
Dash of red pepper sauce

In a large skillet, brown beef and onion; drain. Stir in rice, tomatoes, corn, salt, pepper, Worcestershire sauce and red pepper sauce. Pour into a greased 9x13-inch baking dish. Combine cracker crumbs and butter; sprinkle on top. Bake at 350° for 30 minutes.

Bacon Wrapped Corn

Kristi Hauser Bright

8 ears sweet corn, husks removed
8 bacon strips, uncooked
2 T Chili powder

Wrap each ear of corn with a bacon strip. Place on a piece of heavy-duty foil. Sprinkle with chili powder. Wrap securely, twisting ends to make handles for turning. Grill corn, covered, over medium heat for 20 to 25 minutes, turning once.

Beefy Cornbread

June Thompson

1 Lb. ground beef
1 sm. onion
2 or 3 jalapeno peppers, seeded & chopped
1 (8 1/2 oz.) pkg. cornbread mix
3/4 tsp, salt
1/2 tsp. baking soda

1 can creamed corn
1 c. milk
1/2 c. vegetable oil
2 eggs, beaten
3 c. shredded Cheddar cheese, divided

In a large skillet, brown beef, onion and peppers over medium heat until no longer pink. Drain and set aside. In a small bowl, combine cornbread mix, salt, baking soda, corn, milk, oil and eggs. Pour half into a greased 9x13-inch baking dish. Layer with half of cheese and all of beef mixture. Top with remaining cheese and CAREFULLY spread remaining batter over top. Bake, uncovered, at 350° for 40 to 45 minutes, or until a toothpick inserted comes out clean.

Cheesy Corn Spoonbread

Kevin Hauser

1 med. onion, chopped
1/4 c. butter or margarine
2 eggs
2 c. (16 oz.) sour cream
1 (15 1/4 oz.) can whole kernel corn, drained
1 (14 3/4 oz.) can cream-style corn
1/4 tsp. salt
1/4 tsp. pepper
1 (8 1/2 oz.) pkg. cornbread/muffin mix
1 med. jalapeno pepper, minced*
2 c. (8 oz.) shredded Cheddar cheese, divided

When cutting or seeding hot peppers, use rubber or plastic gloves to protect your hands. Avoid touching your face or eyes. In a skillet, saute onion in butter until tender; set aside. In a bowl, beat the eggs; add sour cream, both cans of com, salt and pepper. Stir in cornbread mix just until blended. Fold in sautéed onion, jalapeno and 1 1/2 cups of cheese. Transfer to a greased shallow 3-quart baking dish. Sprinkle with the remaining cheese. Bake, uncovered, at 375° for 35 to 40 minutes, or until a toothpick inserted near the center comes out clean; cool slightly. Yield: 12 to 15 servings.

Chicken Tortilla Soup

Kristi Hauser Bright

2 cartons chicken broth
1 container of fresh salsa
1 can black beans
1 ½ cup corn kernels (fresh or canned)
1 can chicken or
1 to 2 cups cooked, shredded chicken

Pour all ingredients in pot and simmer for 30 minutes.
Top with any or all of the following:

Cheese
Cilantro
Sour Cream
Avocado

Colorful Corn Salad

Banning Cantarini

2 (10 oz.) pkg. frozen com, thawed
2 c. diced green pepper
2 c. diced sweet red pepper
2 c. diced celery
1 c. minced fresh parsley
1 c. chopped green onions
1/2 c. shredded Parmesan cheese
2 tsp. ground cumin

11/2 tsp. salt
3/4 tsp. pepper
1/2 tsp. hot pepper sauce
1/8 tsp. cayenne pepper
3 T. olive or vegetable oil
2 garlic cloves, minced
6 T. lime juice

In a large bowl, combine the first 12 ingredients. In a microwave-safe dish, combine oil and garlic. Microwave, uncovered, on HIGH for 1 minute. Cool. Whisk in lime juice. Pour over the corn mixture and toss to coat. Cover and refrigerate until serving. Yield: 16 to 18 servings. For the record, we only use our own Hauser sweet corn, which we freeze and can in the summer.

Confetti Corn Salad

Pat Boler

2 c. fresh com kernels
3/4 c. water
1 (14 1/2 oz.) can black beans, rinsed & drained
1/2 c. sliced green onions
1/2 c. chopped red bell pepper
1 sm. cucumber, seeded & chopped
2 cloves garlic, minced

1/4 c. chopped fresh cilantro
1 tsp. sweet red pepper flakes
1/4 tsp. ground ginger
1/4 tsp. salt
2 T. com oil
2 T. rice vinegar
1 T. sesame oil
1 T. lime juice

Combine corn kernels and 3/4 cup water in a saucepan; bring to a boil. Cover, reduce heat, and simmer 7 to 8 minutes, or just until tender. Drain. Combine corn kernels and the next 6 ingredients in a large bowl. Whisk together red pepper flakes and the next 6 ingredients until blended; pour over corn mixture. Cover salad and chill at least 2 hours. Yield: 4 to 6 servings.

Cold Corn Salad

Lois Baldwin

1 pkg. frozen corn, almost thawed
6 to 8 slices bacon, fried crispy & crumbled
2 to 3 fresh garlic cloves (more, to taste)
2 to 3 chopped fresh jalapeno peppers, with membrane & seeds removed

Chopped olives, black or green (opt.)
2 to 3 stems chopped green onion
1 c. grated Colby-Jack cheese, marbled
Original Hidden Valley Ranch dressing

In a large mixing bowl, combine all chopped vegetables with com. Stir in enough dressing to coat vegetables (1/2 bottle will do). Then stir in grated cheese and crumbled bacon on top. If you are going to serve immediately, let the com thaw completely. If you have a long way to go, mix the salad with the com slightly thawed, so it will still be cold when you get there. This is a good replacement for potato salad at cookouts.

Corn and Zucchini Fritters

Brenda Hauser

1 1/2 c. all-purpose flour
1/2 tsp. baking powder
Coarse salt & freshly-ground pepper
2 T. unsalted butter, melted
2 Lg. eggs
1/2 c. + 2 T. milk
1/2 c. finely-chopped, cooked ham (opt.)

1 1/2 c. grated zucchini (about 8 oz.)
2 c. fresh corn kernels (3 to 4 ears)
Vegetable oil, for frying
Cooked bacon, sliced Cheddar cheese, avocado & tomato for serving (opt.)

Whisk together flour, baking powder, 2 teaspoons salt and 1/4 teaspoon pepper in a large bowl. In a separate bowl, stir together butter, eggs and milk; add to flour mixture and stir until just combined. Add ham (if desired), zucchini and corn; stir until well blended. Heat 1 inch of oil in a large cast-iron skillet over medium heat until it registers 350° on a deep-fry thermometer. Working in batches of 4 or 5, gently drop 2 tablespoons batter into skillet for each fritter, pressing gently with a spatula to flatten. Cook, turning once, until golden brown, about 2 minutes per side. Transfer with a spatula or slotted spoon to paper towels to drain. Season fritters with salt and pepper while still hot. Make sandwiches with fritters using bacon, cheese, avocado and tomato, if desired.

Corn Casserole

Deanna Vaux

1/2 stick butter or margarine
1 c. sour cream
1 can whole kernel corn
1 can cream-style corn

2 beaten eggs
1 box Jiffy corn muffin mix
Salt & pepper, to taste
1 T. chopped onion

350°. Adapts well to home-canned or frozen corn. Even the picky eaters in our family love this.

Corn Chow Chow

Edith Jones

18 to 20 med. ears of Hauser's corn
11/2 qt. shredded cabbage 1/2 c. dry
mustard
2 c. chopped sweet red pepper
5 T. canning salt
1 qt. white vinegar

3 T. mustard seed
2 T. celery seed
1 T. whole cloves, tied in cheesecloth
bag
1 tsp. turmeric

Husk corn and remove silk. Blanch ears of corn 5 minutes in boiling water; plunge into cold water. Drain and cut corn from cob to about 2/3 of their depth to yield 2 quarts kernels. Put a layer of vegetables in an enameled pan, stone jar or glass bowl; sprinkle with salt. Repeat until all vegetables and 3 tablespoons salt are used. Let stand overnight. Drain well. Heat vinegar and all remaining ingredients (including 2 tablespoons salt) to boiling; add vegetables and cook slowly until tender, about 20 minutes. Pack hot, into hot jars, leaving 1/2-inch headspace. Adjust caps. Process pints 10 minute and quarts 15 minutes in boiling water bath. Yield: about 6 pints.

Corn Chowder

Pat Boler

3/4 c. chopped onion
2 T. butter or margarine
1 c. diced, cooked, peeled potatoes
1 c. diced, fully-cooked ham
2 c. fresh, frozen or canned sweet corn

1 c. cream-style corn
1 can cream of mushroom soup
2 1/2 c. milk
Salt & pepper, to taste
1 T. chopped fresh parsley

In a heavy saucepan, cook the onion in butter until tender. Add all remaining ingredients and bring to a boil. Simmer a few minutes to blend the flavors. So good on a cold day served with warm bread.

Corn Chowder

Teddy Whitaker

2 med. red potatoes
1 c. cubed cooked ham
1/2 c. diced bell pepper
1/2 c. chopped celery
1 tsp, butter
2 T. flour

1 (14 oz.) can chicken broth
1 (12 oz.) can evaporated milk
1 (15 oz.) can creamed-corn
1 (15 oz.) can kernel corn
Salt & pepper, to taste

Cut potato and ham into 1/2-inch cubes. Heat butter; add celery and bell pepper. Cook until tender. Stir in flour; heat until bubbly. Gradually add broth, milk and corn; whisk until blended. Add potatoes; bring to a boil. Reduce heat; cook, uncovered, 12 minutes. Stir in ham. Remove from heat. Optional: Top chowder with crisp crumbled bacon, chopped green onions and shredded cheese. Serve with bread or rolls and salad.

Corn Medley

Brenda Hauser

2 c. fresh-cut sweet corn (3 to 4 ears)
2 T. butter or margarine
1/4 c. chopped onion
1/4 c. chopped green pepper
1/2 tsp. salt (opt.)
1/4 tsp. ground cumin
1 Lg tomato, chopped & seeded
2 T. sugar or sugar substitute

Combine the first 6 ingredients in a medium saucepan; cook and stir over medium heat until butter is melted. Cover and cook over low heat for 10 minutes. Stir in tomato and sugar or sugar substitute; cook, covered, 5 minutes longer.

Corn Oysters

Sue Hauser

1 3/4 c. all-purpose flour
1 T. sugar
1 tsp. baking powder
1/2 tsp. salt
1 (17 oz.) can whole kernel corn, undrained
1 egg, beaten
2 T. milk
1 1/2 c. shortening

Combine flour, sugar, baking powder and salt; mix well. Combine corn, egg and milk; stir into dry ingredients. Heat shortening in a large skillet over medium heat to 375°; drop corn mixture by tablespoonfuls into skillet. Cook until golden, turning once. Drain on paper towels. Serve hot. Yield: about 2 dozen.

Corn Relish

Grandma Naoma Moore

1 doz. ears corn, cut off cob
1 sm. head cabbage, chopped fine
1 bunch celery, chopped
2 med. onions, chopped
2 red peppers, chopped
2 c. sugar
1/4 tsp. salt
1 tsp. dry mustard
1 qt. apple cider vinegar

Boil all ingredients for 25 minutes and put into jars. Process in hot water bath for 15 minutes. We sometimes leave out the cabbage and dilute the vinegar if it seems too tangy.

Corn Stuffing

Pam Oxendale

4 strips bacon, diced
1/2 c. onion, diced
3 c. collard or mustard greens, stemmed
& chopped (I use spinach)
2/3 c. fresh corn (I use 1 c.)
1/2 c. red bell pepper, diced

3 T. chicken broth
1 jalapeno, seeded & minced
1 c. purchased prepared cornbread,
crumbled
1/4 tsp. cayenne pepper
Salt, to taste
4 chicken breasts

Saute bacon until crisp, about 10 minutes. Add onion and greens; cook until tender. Stir in bell pepper and jalapeno. Cook 2 minutes. Add corn and broth. Cook 2 more minutes. Off heat, add cornbread and spices. At this point, it can be cooled and saved for another day, or on a foil- wrapped baking sheet. Spoon stuffing into 4 mounds. Lay a chicken breast over each mound (I pound the breasts in a gallon Ziploc bag to 1/2-inch thickness to shorten cooking time.) Bake at 350º for 20 to 40 minutes, depending on thickness of chicken. Yield: 4 servings. It takes quite a bit of chopping, but otherwise is very easy and tasty.

Corn-Bacon Chowder

Nettie Eurom

1/4 c. margarine
1/2 lb. bacon, cut small
1 med. onion, chopped
4 unpeeled, diced potatoes
1 stalk celery, chopped

3 (8 1/2 oz.) cans creamed corn
2 (16 oz.) cans whole kernel corn
1 to 1 1/2 c. milk
1 c. chicken broth
Pepper, to taste

Melt margarine in heavy 4-quart pan over medium heat. Add bacon and cook until just crisp. Add onion and saute until translucent, about 12 minutes. Add creamed com, broth, potatoes and celery. Simmer for 20 minutes. Add drained whole kernel corn and simmer for 12 more minutes. Add enough milk for desired consistency. Season to taste.

Corny Cake

Pat Boler

1 (17 oz.) can creamed corn
1/2 c. brown sugar
3/4 c. sugar
3 eggs
1 c. vegetable oil
1 T. baking powder

2 1/4 c. flour
1 tsp. baking soda
1 tsp. salt
1 tsp. cinnamon
1/2 c. raisins
1/2 c. nuts, chopped

CARAMEL FROSTING:

4 T. butter
1/2 c. brown sugar

1/4 c. milk
2 to 3 c. powdered sugar

In a mixing bowl, combine corn and sugars; add eggs and oil. Beat well. Combine dry ingredients; add to batter. Mix well. Stir in raisins and nuts. Bake at 350° for 30 to 35 minutes in a 9x13-inch pan. Frosting: Bring butter, sugar and milk to a boil, then stir in confectioners' sugar. Cool and frost cake.

Corny Tomato-Dumpling Soup

Zach Hauser

1 Lb. ground beef
3 c. fresh or frozen corn
1 (28 oz.) can diced tomatoes
2 (14 1/2 oz.) cans beef broth 1 c. chopped onion

1 garlic clove, minced
1 1/2 tsp. dried basil
1 1/2 tsp. dried thyme
1/2 tsp. dried rosemary, crushed
Salt & pepper, to taste

CORN DUMPLINGS:

1 c. all-purpose flour
1/2 c. cornmeal
2 1/2 tsp. baking powder
1/2 tsp. salt
1 egg

1/2 c. cornmeal
2/3 c. milk
1/2 tsp salt
1 c. fresh or frozen corn
1 T minced fresh parsley

In a large saucepan or Dutch oven over medium heat, cook beef until no longer pink; drain. Stir in corn, tomatoes, broth, onion, garlic and seasonings. Bring to a boil. Reduce heat; cover and simmer for 30 to 45 minutes.
Dumplings: Combine flour, cornmeal, baking powder and salt in a bowl. In another bowl, beat egg; stir in milk, corn, cheese and parsley. Stir into dry ingredients just until moistened. Drop by tablespoonfuls onto simmering soup. Cover and simmer for 15 minutes, or until a toothpick inserted in a dumpling comes out clean (do not lift cover while simmering). Yield: 8 servings (about 2 quarts).

CORN

Creamy Corn Salad

Pat Boler

6 c. frozen corn, thawed
3 c. chopped seeded tomatoes
1 c. cubed avocado

2/3 c. julienned sweet red pepper
2/3 c. julienned green pepper
1/2 c. chopped onion

DRESSING:

1 c. mayonnaise
2 T. red wine vinegar
2 T. Dijon mustard

1 tsp. salt
1/8 tsp. pepper

In a large bowl, combine the corn, tomatoes, avocado, peppers and onion. In a small bowl, whisk the dressing ingredients. Pour over salad and toss to coat. Cover and refrigerate for 30 minutes, or until chilled. Yield: 12 servings.

Fiesta Tamale Pie

Brenda Hauser

1 sm. onion, minced
1 clove garlic, minced
3 T. butter
3 T. olive oil
1 1/2 lb. ground beef
1 (No. 2 1/2) can tomatoes
1 (No. 2 1/2) can whole kernel corn

2 tsp. salt
2 tsp. chili powder
20 to 24 pitted ripe olives
1 c. cornmeal
1 c. milk
2 eggs, well beaten
1 1/2 c. grated American cheese

Heat oven to 350°. Saute onion and garlic in butter and oil until yellow. Add ground beef; cook until brown. Simmer tomatoes, corn, salt and chili powder in saucepan 20 minutes; add meat mixture. Pour into 7 1/2 x 11 1/2 x 1 1/2" pan. Press olives into mixture. Mix cornmeal, milk and eggs and cook until thick. Spread over filling. Sprinkle with grated cheese. Bake 1 hour. Yield: 8 to 10 servings.

Freezer Sweet Corn

Brenda Hauser

4 qt. fresh-cut sweet corn (18 to 20 ears)
1 qt. hot water

2/3 c. sugar
1/2 c. butter or margarine
2 tsp. salt

Combine all ingredients in a large kettle; simmer for 5 to 7 minutes, stirring occasionally. Pour into large shallow containers to cool; stir occasionally. Spoon into freezer bags or containers; freeze. Yield: 3 quarts.

Fresh Corn Salad

Pat Boler

8 ears fresh corn
1 tomato, chopped
1 zucchini, chopped
1 cucumber, peeled & chopped

1 red onion, chopped
1 red bell pepper, chopped
1/2 c. Italian-style salad dressing

Husk the corn and slice the kernels from the cob. In a large bowl, mix together the corn, tomato, zucchini, cucumber, onion and red bell pepper. Pour dressing over vegetables and toss to coat. Refrigerate until chilled, at least 1 hour.

Glorified Corn

Patty Fox

In a greased casserole, put:
3 eggs, beaten
Salt, to taste
1 can whole kernel corn
1 can cream-style corn
1 tsp. garlic salt

6 T. melted butter
1/4 c. cornmeal
1 can diced chilies
1 c. grated cheese

Top with more cheese. Bake for 45 minutes or more at 350°

Green Chili-Corn Tamales

Teddy Whitaker

5 Lb. masa
1 lb. lard
1 stick butter
2 cans white kernel corn
2 cans white creamed corn
Salt

About 2 lb. finely-chopped roasted green chilies (depends on how hot it is)
2 to 2 1/2 lb. grated Cheddar & Monterey Jack cheese
1 pkg. corn husks (Hojas)
Deli wrap (the grocery store has it in the meat department)

Whip lard and butter until smooth and creamy. Add masa, a little bit at a time, adding creamed corn (depending on the size of you mixer, you may have to do 2 batches). Beat about 3 minutes. Transfer to a large bowl and add the 2 cans of the kernel corn. Mix well and add salt to taste. Add chili and cheese. Mix well. Corn Husk: Clean the corn silks off, then put them in warm water to clean them and this softens them so they are pliable; drain. You may want to do this before you do your dough. To Assemble: Take a husk and drop a heaping tablespoon of corn masa on the left side of the husk and roll to the right side and fold up the end. Wet the ends of the deli wrap; put the tamale on one corner and roll in, then fold the 2 corners in and roll to the end and the wet corner should seal the tamale in (hope this makes sense), then cook them or freeze in freezer bags. To Cook: Steam for about 45 minutes, or when you test one, that it is firm. If frozen, cook for about 11/2 minutes, or until done. I usually take them out of the freezer and let them thaw out some before cooking and it doesn't take as long. This batter can be refrigerated the night before and made the next day.

Green Chili Cornmeal Casserole

Connie Steyaert

1 c. yellow cornmeal
1/4 tsp. baking soda
1 tsp. salt
1 can cream-style corn
2 eggs

1/3 c. melted shortening or oil
3/4 c. buttermilk
1 (4 oz.) can green chilies, diced
2 c. grated Longhorn cheese

Beat well, except for chilies and cheese. Pour 1/3 of the batter into a greased casserole dish, then half of chilies and cheese. Then another 1/3 of batter, then remaining cheese and chilies. Top with final 1/3 of the batter. Bake for 40 to 45 minutes at 350°. This is good hot or cold, with salsa. A great potluck dish.

Grilled Corn, The Hauser Way

Kristi Hauser Bright

Grilling corn in the husks is so easy. There's no need to remove the silk and tie the husk closed before grilling. Just soak the corn in water for about 30 minutes, grill, turning often, for about 30 minutes, and add your favorite flavored butter.

Herbed Corn

Claudia Hauser

12 c. frozen corn
1 c. water
1/2 c. butter or margarine, cubed
2 T. minced fresh parsley
2 tsp. salt

1 tsp. dill weed
1/2 tsp. garlic powder
1/2 tsp. Italian seasoning
1/4 tsp. dried thyme

In a large saucepan, combine corn and water. Bring to a boil. Reduce heat; cover and simmer for 4 to 6 minutes, or until corn is tender. Drain; stir in the remaining ingredients. Yield: 10 to 12 servings.

Layered Fiesta Casserole

Lois Baldwin

1 Lb. extra-lean ground beef
1 green pepper, chopped
1 red pepper, chopped
1 (16 oz.) jar chunky salsa
1 can diced tomatoes, undrained
1 pkg. (about 2 c.) frozen corn
12 corn tortillas
1 1/2 c. shredded Cheddar or
Longhorn cheese

Preheat oven to 375°. Brown meat with peppers in a large skillet, stirring frequently; drain. Stir in salsa, tomatoes and corn; bring to a boil. Spoon 1 cup meat mixture onto bottom of a 9x13-inch baking dish. Top with 6 tortillas, overlapping as necessary. Spoon half of the remaining meat mixture over tortillas; top with 3/4 cup of cheese. Top with remaining 6 tortillas and meat mixture. Cover with foil. Bake for 25 to 30 minutes, or until heated through. Remove from oven; uncover. Sprinkle with remaining 3/4 cup cheese. Let stand 5 minutes, or until cheese is melted.

Mississippi Cornbread Salad

Betty Black

1 (8 oz.) pkg. cornbread/muffin mix
1 (1 oz.) envelope ranch dressing
1 c. sour cream
1 c. mayonnaise
1/2 c. red pepper, chopped
8 Lg. tomatoes, chopped
1/2 c. green pepper, chopped
1/2 c. green onion, chopped
2 (15 oz.) cans whole kernel corn
2 c. shredded cheese
10 slices bacon, cooked & crumbled
2 c. shredded lettuce

Prepare cornbread according to directions. Stir together salad dressing mix, sour cream and mayonnaise. Gently toss vegetables; crumble half of cornbread into a trifle bowl. Top with half each ingredient and repeat layers. Cover and chill.

Mom's Corn Soup

Ken McKnight

2 doz. ears of com (Hauser's of course)
1 can evaporated milk
2 or 3 c. whole milk
1 c. butter or margarine
Salt & pepper, to taste

Use slicer to cut tops of kernels, then scrape cobs with back of a knife to remove the corn. Place in large pan and add the evaporated milk and enough milk to make a soup consistency. Add butter or margarine, salt and pepper. Bring to a boil slowly, stirring frequently to prevent sticking. Boil 15 to 20 minutes, stirring frequently. Remove from stove and enjoy, or freeze for later use.

One Pot Wonder

Kristi Hauser Bright

16 cups water
1 lg onion
3 T seafood seasoning
2 medium lemons, halved
1 lb small red potatoes
1 lb smoked kielbasa or fully cooked hot links, cut into 1 inch pieces

4 medium ears of corn, cut into thirds
2 lbs uncooked medium shrimp, peeled and deveined
Seafood cocktail sauce
Melted butter

In a stockpot, combine water, onion, seafood seasoning and lemons. Bring to a boil. Add potatoes, cook, uncovered, 10 minutes. Add kielbasa and corn, return to boil. Reduce heat and simmer, uncovered for 10 to 12 minutes or until potatoes are tender. Add shrimp, cook 2 to 3 minutes, until shrimp turn pink. Drain and transfer to a bowl. Service with cocktail sauce, butter and additional seafood seasoning.

Oven-Cooked Corn for Freezing

Brenda Hauser

22 c. fresh corn, cut off cob
Salt & pepper

1 Lb. Butter (we use 1/2 Lb.
1 qt. half & half

Mix all together in large oven proof pan and bake at 325° for 1 hour. Cool well and put about 2 cups in freezer bags or containers. This is so good straight from the freezer and into the microwave.

Potato-Corn Chowder

Kay Hauser

1 Lb. or so red potatoes, diced
Com, fresh, frozen or canned cream-style
1 onion, chopped
2 or more cans chicken broth
Instant mashed potatoes, for thickening

Salt & pepper, to taste
Basil, to taste
1/2 c. or so celery, chopped
1/2 c. grated carrot
2 c. or so milk
1/4 c. butter

Cook the potatoes, onion and celery in water until potatoes are tender. Add remaining ingredients and stir in a little instant mashed potatoes until thickened slightly. Cut-up ham can be added to make it a yummy main dish. Measurements aren't exact, as this is my sister-in-law, Kay's, recipe and she is such a good cook that she just doesn't see the need. This is so good served with her homemade bread.

Quick Corn Relish

Betty Haywood

1 can whole kernel corn, undrained
2 T. onion, chopped
3 tsp. sugar
3 T. pimentos, chopped

1 T. mustard seed
1/4 tsp. mustard seed
1/4 tsp. salt
1/4 tsp. dry mustard

Combine all ingredients, except corn, and cook for about 3 minutes. Add corn and cook 3 minutes more. Pour into jars and refrigerate. Yield: 1 pint.
Betty is Dick's Iowa cousin and such an inspirational cook. Her Mom used to make pies for a little restaurant in Union, Iowa.

Quick Frozen Corn

Brenda Hauser

15 c. corn (whole kernel - do not scrape cob)
3/4 c. sugar

1/4 c. salt, or to taste
5 c. ice water

Mix this all together. Pack in freezer bags and freeze immediately. When you prepare it for the table, remember it is already seasoned. May need a little more water as it cooks. Tastes almost as good as fresh.

Rosemary Corn Soup

Claudia Hauser

2 c. chopped onions
1/2 c. diced carrots
1/2 c. diced celery
3 T. butter or margarine, divided
7 1/2 c. fresh or frozen corn, divided
6 c. chicken broth

1 T. minced fresh rosemary, or 1 tsp. dried rosemary, crushed
2 garlic cloves, minced
1/4 tsp, cayenne pepper
1 med. sweet red pepper, chopped
1 c. half & half cream
Salt & pepper, to taste

In a large saucepan, saute onions, carrots and celery in 2 tablespoons butter until tender. Add 3 1/2 cups corn, broth, rosemary, garlic and cayenne pepper. Bring to a boil. Reduce heat; simmer, uncovered, for 30 minutes, stirring occasionally, Cool; process in batches in a blender or food processor until pureed. Return to the pan. In a small skillet, saute red pepper in remaining butter until tender. Add to corn mixture. Stir in cream and remaining corn; heat through, stirring occasionally. Season with salt and pepper. Yield: 8 servings.

Salsa Corn Cakes

Brenda Hauser

1 1/2 c. all-purpose flour
1/2 c. cornmeal
1 tsp. baking powder
1 tsp. salt
2 (3 oz.) pkg. cream cheese, softened
6 eggs
1 c. milk

1/4 c. butter or margarine, melted
1 (15 1/4 oz.) can whole kernel corn, drained
1/2 c. salsa, drained
1/4 c. minced green onions
Sour cream & additional salsa

Combine flour, cornmeal, baking powder and salt; set aside. In a mixing bowl, beat cream cheese and eggs; add milk and butter. Add the dry ingredients just until moistened. Fold in the corn, salsa and onions. Pour batter by 1/4 cupfuls onto a greased hot griddle. Turn when bubbles form on top; cook until the second side is golden brown. Serve with sour cream and salsa. Yield: 6 to 8 servings.

Seven-Layer Salad

Pat Boler

1 or 2 heads lettuce, shredded
1/2 c. celery, chopped
1 bell pepper, chopped
1 onion, chopped

1 pkg. frozen peas, cooked & cooled
3 T. sugar
1 T. salad dressing
1 or 2 c. shredded Cheddar cheese

In an 8x12-inch dish, layer lettuce, then celery, pepper, onion and peas. Mix the sugar with salad dressing and pour over entire salad, sealing edges well. Cover with cheese. Cover with plastic wrap and refrigerate overnight. Can add fresh com kernels to this, also.

Sharon's Corn Rolls

Kay Hauser

1/2 c. cornmeal
1/3 c. sugar
1/3 c. oil
2 eggs, well beaten
5 to 6 c. flour

2 tsp, salt
1 1/2 c. milk
1 pkg. yeast
1/4 c. water
3/4 c. creamed corn

In a heavy pan, cook cornmeal, sugar, oil, salt and milk until thick. Cool until luke-warm and add creamed corn, eggs and the yeast, which has been dissolved in 1/4 cup water. Mix well. Add enough flour to handle well. Knead until smooth and elastic. Let rise until double; form into rolls and let rise a second time for about 30 minutes. Bake for 15 minutes at 400°. Yield: about 30 rolls.

Spicy Corn and Cabbage

Jane Moore

1 head cabbage
1 Lg. onion
1 or 2 jalapenos (or 1 red bell pepper
if you don't like spicy)

3 ears corn (or 1 c. frozen)
6 to 8 cloves garlic
1/2 to 1 bunch cilantro
1 to 2 T. olive oil

You will need a large, deep skillet with tight-fitting lid. Cut onion in 1/4-inch slices; quarter the cabbage, then cut into 1-inch slices. Finely chop pepper and garlic; saute and stir for 1 to 2 minutes, then tum heat to medium and add 1 or 2 tablespoons of water (just enough to keep from burning) and put lid on. Cook a few minutes; add com and replace lid. Cook until all is tender-crisp, stir in cilantro and salt to taste. Serve! The combination of colors is fabulous.

Tamale Pie with Elk Burger

Kristi Hauser Bright

1 T oil
1 Onion
1 Clove garlic
1 Green Bell Pepper
1 ½ pounds elk burger (or regular burger)
½ cups corn kernels (fresh or canned)

14.5 ounce can crushed tomatoes
2 T cumin
T Chili powder
2 tsp salt
1 cup shredded cheddar cheese

For the Cornbread Topping:

1 box or package of corn bread (I use Marie Calendars)

Preheat oven to 375 degrees.

To make the filling: In a large skillet over medium high, heat the oil and add the onion, green pepper, garlic and meat. Cook, stirring occasionally, breaking up the meat, until meat is brown, approximately 15 to 20 minutes. Stir in the corn, crushed tomatoes, and spices. Bring to a simmer on low and simmer for 20 minutes. Remove from heat and let sit while you prepare the topping. Prepare the topping per instructions on box or package to make a batter. Pour the filling into a 13 x 9 baking pan and top with corn bread batter. Sprinkle with cheese. Bake for 30 to 40 minutes, until top is golden brown. let rest for 15 minutes before serving.

Appetizers & Beverages

KEVIN, DICK, KERRI, KIM, KRISTI, BRENDA HAUSER

Apple Pie Moonshine

Jennifer Fuller

1 64 Oz. Bottle Of Apple Juice
1 64 Oz. Bottle Of Apple Cider
3 C Sugar
2-6 Cinnamon Sticks (I Use 2)

1/2 Tsp Ground Nutmeg
1/2 Tsp Ground Cinnamon
1 750ml Bottle Of 190 Proof Everclear Grain Alcohol

Bring The Apple Juice, Cider, Sugar, Nutmeg, Ground Cinnamon And 2 Cinnamon Sticks To A Boil. Takes About 20-30 Minutes. Cover And Simmer 1 Hour. Remove From Heat And Let Cool To Room Temperature. Add Alcohol To Mixture. **Caution: Do Not Add Alcohol Near A Flame Or Heat Source. It Is Highly Flammable. Make Sure Mixture Is Completely Cool Before Adding Alcohol. Strain The Cinnamon Sticks Out Using Cheesecloth Or A Coffee Filter And Pour Into Sterile Jars. You Can Put A Cinnamon Stick In Each Jar If You Like. I Never Do Because They Can Make The Moonshine A Little Murky. Place Lids On Jars And Allow To Sit In A Cool, Dry Place For 1 Month. I Never Do This Part And No One Has Complained About The Taste. Makes 9 Quarts

Artichoke Dip

Kim Gioia

1 (15 oz.) can quartered artichoke hearts, drained
1 (3 oz.) can diced mild green chilies or diced jalapenos

1 c. grated Parmesan cheese
1 c. mayonnaise
3 to 4 chopped green onions
1 (8 oz.) pkg. cream cheese, softened

Preheat oven to 350°. Combine artichokes, chilies, cheese, mayonnaise and green onions. Mix in cream cheese. Spoon into a 9-inch square baking dish. Bake about 45 minutes. Serve with slices of French bread or toast. Yield: 8 servings.

Banana Slush Punch

Pat Boler

4 c. sugar
6 c. water
1 lg. can frozen orange juice
1 (2 qt.) can pineapple juice

1 c. lemon juice
5 ripe bananas, mashed
5 (1 qt.) btl. 7-up

Mix and freeze all ingredients, except 7-Up. Take it out 1 1/2 hours before serving, then add 7-Up. Yield: 5 gallons.

Beaver Nuggets

Jennifer Fuller

4.5 - 5 Oz Pkg. Of Puffed Corn (Found With Potato Chips)
1/2 Cup Butter
1/2 Cup Brown Sugar

1/4 Cup Light Corn Syrup
1/2T Baking Soda

Put Puffed Corn In Very Large Roaster Pan, Sprayed With Cooking Oil (Bigger Than A 9x 13) In 2 Qt Sauce Pan Bring Butter, Corn Syrup And Brown Sugar To A Boil Then Cook For 2 Minutes Longer. Add Baking Soda - It Will Foam Up. Stir Well And Remove From Heat. Pour Over Corn & Stir Really Well. Lift And Turn Works Best. Bake At 250 For 45 Minutes, Turning Every 15 Minutes. Remove From Oven & Spread On Waxed Paper To Cool, Breaking Up Clumps. If It Doesn't Coat All The Corn, That's Ok, It Still Tastes Really Good.

Best Garden Salsa

Kristi Hauser Bright

3 large tomatoes
1 large jalapeno
1 small yellow onion
3 cloves garlic

Cilantro
Lime
Salt and pepper

Combine first 5 ingredients in a large food processor and squeeze lime on top. Pulse until combined and a bit chunky. Add salt and pepper to taste.

Bourbon Slush Grandma

Sue Hauser

1 c. sugar
7 c. water
2 cans lemonade
1 can orange juice

2 c. boiling water
4 tea bags in boiling water
1 1/4 c. bourbon whiskey

Mix all ingredients in large plastic container and freeze until slushy.

Candied Jalapenos

Jennifer Fuller

1/2 C White Sugar
4 T Honey
6-10 Jalapenos, Sliced To Desired Thickness

4 T Honey
1 C Apple Cider Vinegar
Pinch of Salt

Add Sugar, Honey, Apple Cider Vinegar And Salt To Small Saucepan. Bring To A Boil Over High Heat, Stirring Often To Dissolve Sugar. Add Jalapenos And Cook 1 Minute Longer Then Remove From Heat. Allow Mixture To Cool And Then Store In A Glass Jar In Refrigerator. These Keep Almost Forever In The Refrigerator And Are Great On Sandwiches Too.

Cheese Ball

Lisa Enright

2 (8 oz.) pkg. cream cheese, softened
2 c. shredded Cheddar cheese
1 T. pimentos
1 T. chopped onion

1 T. chopped green pepper
2 tsp, Worcestershire sauce
1 tsp. lemon juice
1/4 tsp. salt

Mix cream cheese until soft, then add remaining ingredients (hands work best). Form into a ball, cover, and refrigerate. You can use more vegetables, if desired, and roll in chopped pecans before serving with crackers or vegetables.

Cheese Ball Teddy

Teddy Whitaker

2 (8 oz.) pkg. cream cheese, softened
1 (8 oz.) can crushed pineapple, drained
2 c. chopped pecans

1/4 c. chopped green bell pepper
2 T. finely-chopped green onion
1 tsp. salt

Beat cream cheese with fork until soft and smooth. Gradually stir in crushed pineapple, 1 cup pecans, green pepper, onion and salt. Shape into a ball. Roll in remaining nuts. Wrap in foil and refrigerate to harden. Serve with crackers.

Cheese Roll

Kay Hauser

1 (8 oz.) pkg. cream cheese
3 or 4 chopped green onions
Pecans, chopped fine
2 or 3 slices bacon, fried & crumbled
Dash of hot sauce
Dollop of mayonnaise
1/2 c. grated cheese

Combine all ingredients, except nuts, and form into 2 rolls on waxed paper. Roll in chopped nuts until well covered. Serve with crackers or vegetables. May substitute 1 (4-ounce) can green chilies for the green onions.

Chex Mix

Aymee Wilson

9 c. Chex brand cereals (pick one kind or mix Corn, Rice, etc.)
1 c. semi-sweet chocolate chips
1/2 c. peanut butter
1/4 c. (1/2 stick) butter
1/4 tsp. vanilla extract
1 1/2 c. powdered sugar

Combine chocolate chips, peanut butter and butter in 1 quart microwave-safe bowl. Microwave on HIGH for 1 to 11/2 minutes, or until smooth, stirring after 1 minute. Stir in vanilla. Put cereal in a large bowl. Pour chocolate mixture over cereal until pieces are evenly coated. Pour cereal mixture into large resealable plastic bag with powdered sugar. Shake until all pieces are well coated; spread on waxed paper to cool. Store leftovers in airtight container.

Connie's Punch

Connie Steyaert

2 pkg Kool-Aid, raspberry or cherry
2 c. sugar
2 qt. water
1 qt. ginger ale
1 (46 oz.) can pineapple juice
2 to 3 pt. raspberry sherbet

Mix all ingredients in punch bowl (all chilled). Add ginger ale. Add sherbet just before serving.

APPETIZER

Corn and Bacon Dip

Brenda Hauser

1 (8 oz.) pkg. cream cheese, softened
1 c. (8 oz.) sour cream
1/4 c. mayonnaise
2 garlic cloves, minced
1/4 tsp. hot pepper sauce
1 (15 1/4 oz.) can whole kernel corn, drained
8 bacon strips, cooked & crumbled
Assorted raw vegetables &/or crackers

In a mixing bowl, combine the first 5 ingredients. Stir in com and bacon. Cover and refrigerate for several hours. Serve with vegetables and/or crackers. Yield: 3 cups.

Crazy Crunch

Doris Runk

1 1/3 c. sugar
1 c. butter or margarine
1/2 c. corn syrup
1 tsp. vanilla
3/4 tsp. salt

CEREAL:

5 c. Crispix
5 c. Rice Chex
3 c. corn flakes

Mix the first 5 ingredients together in a medium saucepan. Cook to hard ball stage on candy thermometer. Pour over cereal mixture. Cool on cookie sheets. Store in covered container. Yield: 1 gallon of yummy treats.

Creamy Crock Pot Hot Chocolate

Christine Hauser

1.5 cups heavy cream
1 can (14oz) sweetened condensed milk
2 cups milk chocolate chips
6 cups milk
1 tsp vanilla extract

Mix all ingredients in crock pot and heat until warm.

Eggnog

Aunt Lucille Edwards

6 eggs
1/2 c. sugar
2 c. light cream or whipping cream
2 c. milk

1/8 tsp. salt
2 tsp. vanilla
Nutmeg, for garnish

Beat egg yolk until thick and lemon-colored. Beat in cream and milk, salt and vanilla. Beat egg whites until stiff peaks. Fold into egg yolk mixture. Yield: 2 1/2 quarts. Serve in chilled punch bowl. Sprinkle with nutmeg A Christmas favorite, but don't forget the bourbon.

Eggnog

Connie Steyaert

2 eggs, beaten
1 can Eagle Brand milk
1 tsp. vanilla

1/4 tsp. salt
1 or 2 qt. milk
1/2 pt. cream, whipped

Mix all ingredients in large punch bowl, except whipped cream. Add this when ready to serve. Looks pretty floating on top. Add brandy or Jim Beam to taste.

Embarrassingly Simple Corn Dip

Jennifer Fuller

8 Oz. Softened Cream Cheese
1 Medium Can Mexican Style Corn, Drained

2 Chipotle Chiles In Adobo Sauce, Diced
2-3 T Adobo Sauce

Combine All Of The Above And Enjoy. 2 Chiles Will Make This Dip Really Hot. Usually Use The Sauce And A Little Of The Chiles And It's Still Hot For Me.

Fajita Marinade

Jacob Gould

1 Lb Chicken, shrimp or steak
4-6 T canola oil
2 T lemon juice
1 1/2 tsp salt
1 1/2 tsp dried oregano

1 1/2 tsp cumin
1 tsp garlic powder
1/2 tsp chili powder
1/2 tsp paprika (I used smoked paprika)
1/2 tsp red pepper flakes

Combine all ingredients n a large ziplock bag or container and marinate for 2-6 hours.

Fire Crackers

Jennifer Fuller

1 # Wheat Saltine Crackers
1 Pkg Hidden Valley Fiesta Dip Mix
1 1/2 Cups Canola Oil

2 Tsp Crushed Red Pepper

Put Dry Dip Mix, Oil And Red Pepper Into A Large Baggie (Bigger Than A Gallon Size) Or Cut Recipe In Half And Repeat. Add Crackers And Gently Toss To Coat. Toss And Turn Every. 15 Minutes For 2 Hours. They Start Out Looking Very Wet But As Time, Tossing & Turning Goes By They Become Drier. I Put Them On Paper Towels To Dry Them A Little Also. You Can Cut This Recipe In Half So It Will Fit In A 1 Gallon Zip Lock.

Fruit Dip

Bonnie Nyce

8 oz. cream cheese
1/4 c. sugar

3/4 c. brown sugar
1 tsp. vanilla

Mix softened cream cheese with rest of ingredients.
Serve with apple slices, bananas or any fruit.
I make this before we leave on a road trip and take some apples. Easy road snack.

Homemade Granola

Kim Gould

2, ½ cups old-fashioned rolled oats
½ cup sliced unsalted almonds
½ cup coarsely chopped unsalted pecans
½ cup coarsely chopped unsalted walnuts
½ cup unsalted sunflower seeds
2 T sesame seeds
½ cup toasted wheat germ

1 cup shredded sweetened coconut
½ tsp cinnamon
1/8 tsp salt
½ cup vegetable oil
2/3 cup honey
1 cup dried fruits (such as cranberries, raisons, cherries, apricots, currants, etc)

Preheat oven to 325 degrees. Line a 13 x 18" rimmed baking sheet with foil. Combine oats, almonds, pecans, walnuts, sunflower seeds, wheat germ coconut, cinnamon and salt in large bowl. In a small bowl, whisk together honey and oil until combined. Pour over dry ingredients and mix well. Spread the granola mixture evenly onto the prepared baking sheet and bake for 25 to 30 minutes, stirring and re-spreading a few times with a spatula, until entire mixture is golden brown.

Green Chili Salsa

Marlin Johnson

6 To 8 Large Tomatillos
1 Head Garlic (Cut The Top Off add a
Tsp Of Olive Oil.)

Bake At 350 Degrees For 30 Minutes
Roast, Sweat And Peel:

3 Or 4 Green Chilies
1 Large Pablano Pepper

1 Jalapeno Pepper
Add Juice Of 1 Lime
Handful Of Cilantro

Put In Blender With 3 T. Of Olive Oil. Blend Well And Enjoy

Guacamole

Bertie Lightfoot

6 Lg. ripe avocados
8 oz. cream cheese
1 (4 oz.) can jalapenos, chopped
1 tsp. salt

1 1/2 tsp. garlic powder
Pinch of oregano
4 T. lemon Juice

Peel and remove pit from avocados and place in bowl. Add remaining
ingredients and mash with a potato masher until smooth.
Serve with tortilla chips and margaritas.

Homemade Kahlua

Kristi Hauser Bright

2 cups strong and hot fresh brewed coffee
4 cups sugar (I use organic)

2 cups rum (dark or light)
1 inch vanilla bean, cut in half lengthwise

Stir sugar into hot coffee and stir until sugar is dissolved. let cool. Add the rum and
vanilla pieces and stir. Place in a glass jar, covered, and let sit for 2 to 3 weeks in a
cool, dark place. Strain, removed vanilla beans and bottle.

Kahlua

Susan Welch

1 (2 oz.) jar good instant coffee
4 c. sugar
2 c. boiling water
1 vanilla bean
1 pt. brandy

Add boiling water to instant coffee and sugar. Cut up vanilla bean into small pieces and add to boiling water and coffee. Cool, then add brandy. Shake well and let stand for 30 days. Strain and put into pretty containers. We usually make a double batch.

Kahlua

Kim Gould

1 qt. vodka
2 vanilla beans
4 c. sugar
4 c. water
2 oz. Yuban coffee (any kind works)

Add sugar and water together and boil for 7 minutes. Slowly add coffee and stir until dissolved. After it cools, add vodka and pour over vanilla beans, which have been split lengthwise. Cover and put into a dark place to age for 2 weeks. Strain and pour into bottles. Great for Christmas gifts.

Lemonade Syrup

Grandma Naoma Moore

2 c. sugar
1 c. water
Rind of 2 lemons, cut into strips
1/4 tsp. salt
1 1/2 to 2 c. lemon juice

Boil sugar, water, lemon rind and salt for 5 minutes. Cool and add lemon juice. Strain; store in covered jars in freezer. To serve, add 1/4 cup syrup to 1 glass ice water or carbonated water. We freeze this in quart jars in lemon season and enjoy in the summer.

Margaritas

Kathy Hauser

6 ox. frozen limeade (Minute Maid)
6 ox. LaPaz Margarita mix
6 oz. tequila
Dash of triple sec

Blend all ingredients with lots of ice at high speed in the blender. Dip rim of glasses very slightly in foam, then in margarita salt. Corn chips and salsa are a must with these.

Munchies

Krystal Hollamon

1 (16 oz.) pkg. oat cereal (oat squares)
3 c. pecan pieces
1/2 c. light corn syrup
1/2 c. brown sugar, packed
1/4 c. butter or margarine
1 tsp. vanilla
1/2 tsp. baking soda

Heat oven to 250°. Combine cereal and pecans in a large pan (approximately 9x13 inches, fairly deep so can stir without contents falling out). Set aside. Combine corn syrup, brown sugar and margarine in a 2-cup microwave bowl and microwave 1 1/2 minutes; remove and stir. Microwave 1 1/2 minutes (make sure it boils a little). Stir and add the vanilla and baking

Nona's Shrimp Salsa

Jennifer Fuller

1 Medium Sized Medium Hot Pace Picante Sauce
1 Medium Sized Cocktail Sauce
Shrimp, Cut Into Small (Not Tiny) Pieces
Avocado, Cut Into Small" Pieces

Amount Of Shrimp And Avocado Depends On What You Want (Maybe 2 Cups Shrimp And 1-2 Avocados) Combine And Enjoy. This Is A 5 Star Recipe

Orange Julius

Kerri Hauser

1 (6 oz.) can orange juice concentrate
1 c. milk
1/2 c. sugar
2 tsp. vanilla
15 to 20 ice cubes

Place all ingredients in blender and blend until smooth and frothy.

Party Meat Balls

Marlys Hauser

2 lb. ground beef
1 med. onion, diced
1/2 c. ketchup
2 eggs, beaten
1 sleeve saltine crackers, crushed
1/3 c. milk
2 c. pineapple juice

1 c. ketchup
1/2 c. brown sugar
1/4 c. vinegar
1 T. soy sauce
1 T. Worcestershire sauce
1/2 c. onion, diced

Mix together the first 6 ingredients and form into 1- or 2-inch balls. Put into a 9x13-inch pan sprayed with nonstick cooking spray and bake at 350° for 30 minutes, or until juices run clear. Turn often. Put in crock-pot. While meat balls cook, put the next 7 ingredients into a saucepan and bring to a simmer. Pour this over the meat balls in crock-pot and keep warm to serve.

Party Mix

Bonnalyn Nyce

1 Lb. margarine
1 T. seasoned salt
1/4 c. Worcestershire sauce

5 boxes Chex cereals (Cheerios, Kix or Crispix work also)
3 c. mixed nuts
1 Lb. pretzel sticks

Melt margarine, salt and Worcestershire sauce together and pour over cereal, nuts and pretzels until all is coated. Bake at 250° for 1 hour. Stir every 15 minutes. Pour out on paper towels to cool and store in airtight containers.

Pink Punch

Karin Hauser

1 Lg. bottle cranberry juice
1/2 c. sugar

1 Lg. can pineapple juice
1 Lg. btl. ginger ale

Mix all ingredients together in a punch bowl, except ginger ale. Garnish with citrus slices. I usually fill a milk carton with water and cherries and freeze. This has been used for 30 years at every family celebration.

Popsicles

Grandma Sue Hauser

1 (3 oz.) pkg. Jello, any flavor
1 pkg. unsweetened Kool-Aid, any flavor

2/3 c. sugar

Mix together and add 3 cups boiling water. Stir until dissolved. Add 3 cups cold water or fruit juice. Pour into molds and freeze. Paper cups work well. Partially freeze, then add stick.

Raspberry Cheese Dip

Teddy Whitaker

1 c. chopped pecans
1 c. shredded Mozzarella cheese
1 c. shredded Cheddar cheese

1 c. mayonnaise
1/2 c. chopped green onions

Mix all together and spread in dish. When ready to serve, spread a thin layer of seedless raspberry jam over the top. Enjoy! I also use raspberry chipotle sauce.

Salsa

Donna Schwab

2 1Lg.. cans whole tomatoes
2 sm. cans diced green chilies
2 bunches green onions, finely chopped

2 T. diced jalapeno pepper
1 tsp, minced garlic
Salt or garlic salt, to taste

Drain juice from 1 can of tomatoes and discard. Place both cans in bowl and squeeze with hands until tomatoes are broken up into small pieces. (Do not put in blender - too soupy.) Add chilies, green onion, jalapeno pepper, minced garlic and salt. Mix well. Keep refrigerated. Yield: 1/2 gallon. Serve with chips, over eggs, over meat or over potatoes. Also makes a great Bloody Mary.

Sangria

Kristi Hauser Bright

1 bottle red wine, rose
1 1/2 c. club soda
1/2 c. sugar
1/2 c. lemon juice

2 oz. triple sec
Squeeze in chopped oranges, lemon, limes or grapefruit

Mix all ingredients and enjoy.

Seven-Layer Dip

Kristi Hauser Bright

1 (16 oz.) can refried beans
1 c. sour cream
1 c. diced tomatoes
2 cans diced green chilies, drained
1 can sliced black olives, drained

1 or 2 c. Jack & Longhorn cheeses, shredded
Avocados, chopped & mixed with lemon juice (opt.)

Spread beans on 10 inch serving platter. Spread sour cream over beans and layer remaining ingredients. Yield: 8 to 10 servings. Serve with tortilla chips.

Smoked Ice Cubes

Cody Cantarini

Put a pot of water in your Traeger or smoker, and smoke for at least 30 minutes. Let cool and pour into ice cube trays. Freeze. Serve over your favorite whiskey for a unique smoky flavor.

Sombrero Dip

Linda German

1 Lb. ground beef
1/4 c. chopped onion
1 tsp. salt
1 can refried beans

1 clove garlic, chopped, or 1 tsp. garlic salt
2 cans green chili salsa

Brown beef and drain. Add onion and garlic; cook until onion is soft. Add remaining ingredients. Cook until hot and bubbly. Garnish with 1/2 cup grated cheese and black olives. Serve warm with tortilla chips.

Stuffed Jalapeno Peppers

Patty Hauser Ink

22 Jalapeno peppers cut in half and cleaned
1 Lb. Sausage, regular or hot which ever you like.

18 Ounce cream cheese
1 Cup grated Parmesan cheese

Preheat oven to 425 degrees Cook sausage until browned. Mix cream cheese with Parmesan cheese add cooked sausage. Mix well. Stuff peppers and bake for 20 minutes or until golden brown.

Tortilla Roll-Ups

Lois Baldwin

4 or so Lg. flour tortillas
8 oz. cream cheese, softened
1 c. sour cream
1 (4 oz.) can chopped green chilies

3 T. chopped green onion
2 T. finely-chopped red bell pepper
12 oz. sharp Cheddar cheese, grated

In a medium bowl, combine cream cheese, sour cream, chilies, onion, pepper and Cheddar cheese. Mix thoroughly and spread onto tortillas. Roll up. Cover with Saran Wrap and chill for 2 hours or overnight. Cut each roll into I/2-inch slices. Serve with salsa.

Taco Wheels

Donna Schwab

4 (8 oz.) pkg. cream cheese
1 sm. jar pimentos
1 sm. can green chilies, diced
1/2 lb. sausage
1/2 c. grated Longhorn cheese

1/2 c. grated Jack cheese
1 sm. can chopped black olives
1 bunch finely-chopped green onions
1 doz. flour tortillas

Brown and crumble sausage; drain. Soften cream cheese; add all ingredients, except tortillas. Mix well. Spread tortillas with mixture and roll up jellyroll style. Cut in bite-size pieces; place on platter, cut-side down and serve. May be left whole and wrapped in plastic wrap; store in refrigerator. Cut as needed and serve.

APPETIZER

Soup

Dick Hauser and King

Avgolemono - Greek chicken lemon soup

Christine Hauser

1 whole chicken
1 box chicken stock
-2 liters water

1 box orzo noodles
Salt
3-5 lemons

Add water and chicken stock to large pot. Add chicken and simmer until chicken pulls apart easily from the bone. Remove chicken, debone and cut into bite size chunks. Place chicken to the side. Add orzo to simmering chicken stock. Cook pasta about 12-15 minutes, stirring periodically. When pasta is al dente, remove from heat. Add chicken back into pasta. Salt to taste. Once soup is slightly cooled, add juice of lemons to taste.

Cabbage Soup

Nettie Eurom

2 lb. ground turkey or beef, browned & drained
1 diced head cabbage
1 can cheese soup

1 can cream of mushroom soup
1 can cream of chicken soup
1 can RoTel tomatoes (any tomato green chili)

Put all in crock-pot and cook on low for 6 to 8 hours. I sometimes add a large can of diced tomatoes if it is a little thick.

Cantaloupe Soup

Sherry Aldtrin

1 1/2 c. orange juice
3 c. diced cantaloupe
3 T. lemon juice

1/4 tsp. salt
1 T. sugar (opt.)

Put all ingredients into blender and blend until smooth. Put in freezer until slushy, then stir and put into refrigerator. There have been many conversations at the com stand about recipes and this is one that became a favorite way to use that extra cantaloupe in the summer.

Chicken Tortilla Soup

Kristi Hauser Bright

2 cartons chicken broth
1 container of fresh salsa
1 can black beans
1 ½ cup corn kernels (fresh or canned)
1 can chicken or
1 to 2 cups cooked, shredded chicken

Pour all ingredients in pot and simmer for 30 minutes.
Top with any or all of the following:

Cheese
Cilantro
Sour Cream
Avocado

Corn-Bacon Chowder

Nettie Eurom

1/4 c. margarine
1/2 lb. bacon, cut small
1 med. onion, chopped
4 unpeeled, diced potatoes
1 stalk celery, chopped
3 (8 1/2 oz.) cans creamed corn
2 (16 oz.) cans whole kernel corn
1 to 1 1/2 c. milk
1 c. chicken broth
Pepper, to taste

Melt margarine in heavy 4-quart pan over medium heat. Add bacon and cook until just crisp. Add onion and saute until translucent, about 12 minutes. Add creamed com, broth, potatoes and celery. Simmer for 20 minutes. Add drained whole kernel corn and simmer for 12 more minutes. Add enough milk for desired consistency. Season to taste.

Corn Chowder

Teddy Whitaker

2 med. red potatoes
1 c. cubed cooked ham
1/2 c. diced bell pepper
1/2 c. chopped celery
1 tsp, butter
2 T. flour
1 (14 oz.) can chicken broth
1 (12 oz.) can evaporated milk
1 (15 oz.) can creamed-corn
1 (15 oz.) can kernel corn
Salt & pepper, to taste

Cut potato and ham into 1/2-inch cubes. Heat butter; add celery and bell pepper. Cook until tender. Stir in flour; heat until bubbly. Gradually add broth, milk and corn; whisk until blended. Add potatoes; bring to a boil. Reduce heat; cook, uncovered, 12 minutes. Stir in ham. Remove from heat. Optional: Top chowder with crisp crumbled bacon, chopped green onions and shredded cheese. Serve with bread or rolls and salad.

46

Corn Chowder

Pat Boler

3/4 c. chopped onion
2 T. butter or margarine
1 c. diced, cooked, peeled potatoes
1 c. diced, fully-cooked ham
2 c. fresh, frozen or canned sweet corn

1 c. cream-style corn
1 can cream of mushroom soup
2 1/2 c. milk
Salt & pepper, to taste
1 T. chopped fresh parsley

In a heavy saucepan, cook the onion in butter until tender. Add all remaining ingredients and bring to a boil. Simmer a few minutes to blend the flavors. So good on a cold day served with warm bread.

Corny Tomato-Dumpling Soup

Zach Hauser

1 Lb. ground beef
3 c. fresh or frozen corn
1 (28 oz.) can diced tomatoes
 (14 1/2 oz.) cans beef broth
1 c. chopped onion

1 garlic clove, minced
1 1/2 tsp. dried basil
1 1/2 tsp. dried thyme
1/2 tsp. dried rosemary, crushed
Salt & pepper, to taste

CORN DUMPLINGS:

1 c. all-purpose flour
1/2 c. cornmeal
2 1/2 tsp. baking powder
1/2 tsp. salt
1 egg

1/2 c. cornmeal
2/3 c. milk
1/2 tsp salt
1 c. fresh or frozen corn
1 T minced fresh parsley

In a large saucepan or Dutch oven over medium heat, cook beef until no longer pink; drain. Stir in corn, tomatoes, broth, onion, garlic and seasonings. Bring to a boil. Reduce heat; cover and simmer for 30 to 45 minutes.

Dumplings: Combine flour, cornmeal, baking powder and salt in a bowl. In another bowl, beat egg; stir in milk, corn, cheese and parsley. Stir into dry ingredients just until moistened. Drop by tablespoonfuls onto simmering soup. Cover and simmer for 15 minutes, or until a toothpick inserted in a dumpling comes out clean (do not lift cover while simmering). Yield: 8 servings (about 2 quarts).

Crock-Pot Chicken Tortilla Soup

Aymee Wilson

1 Lb. shredded, cooked chicken
1 (15 oz.) can whole peeled tomatoes, mashed
1 (10 oz.) can enchilada sauce
1 med. onion, chopped
1 (4 oz.) can chopped green chili peppers
2 cloves garlic, minced
2 c. water
1 (14.5 oz.) can chicken broth
1 tsp. cumin
1 tsp. chili powder
1 tsp. salt
1/4 tsp. black pepper
1 bay leaf
1 (10 oz.) pkg. frozen corn
1 T. chopped cilantro

Place chicken, tomatoes, enchilada sauce, onion, green chiles and garlic into a slow-cooker. Pour in water and chicken broth; season with cumin, chili powder, salt, pepper and bay leaf. Stir in corn and cilantro. Cover and cook on low setting for 6 to 8 hours, or on high setting for 3 to 4 hours.

Preheat oven to 400°. Lightly brush both sides of tortillas with oil. Cut tortillas into strips, then spread on baking sheet. Bake in preheated oven until crisp, about 10 to 15 minutes. To serve, sprinkle tortilla strips over soup.

Minestrone Soup with Ground Beef or Ground Turkey

Kerri Hauser

1 Lb. ground beef
1 sm. onion, chopped
1 Large celery stalk, sliced
1/4 sm. head green cabbage, thinly sliced   1 1/2 tsp. beef-flavor instant bouillon
1/2 tsp. dried basil leaves
1 (10 1/2 oz.) can garbanzo beans
1 (7 oz.) can whole kernel corn
1 med.-size zucchini, sliced
3/4 c. med.-sized shell macaroni
1 (14 1/2 to 16 oz.) can tomatoes

In a sauce pot over high heat, cook ground beef, onion, celery and cabbage, stirring carefully so meat stays in chunks, until all pan juices evaporate and meat and vegetables are lightly browned, about 10 minutes. Add tomatoes, garbanzo beans and corn (all with their liquid), zucchini, macaroni, bouillon, basil leaves and 2 1/2 cups water. Over high heat, heat to boiling, stirring to break up tomatoes. Reduce heat to low; cover and simmer soup 8 to 10 minutes, until macaroni and vegetables are tender. Yield: 6 servings. Serve with garlic bread or crackers.

Potato-Corn Chowder

Kay Hauser

1 Lb. or so red potatoes, diced
Com, fresh, frozen or canned cream-style
1 onion, chopped
2 or more cans chicken broth
Instant mashed potatoes, for thickening

Salt & pepper, to taste
Basil, to taste
1/2 c. or so celery, chopped
1/2 c. grated carrot
2 c. or so milk
1/4 c. butter

Cook the potatoes, onion and celery in water until potatoes are tender. Add remaining ingredients and stir in a little instant mashed potatoes until thickened slightly. Cut-up ham can be added to make it a yummy main dish. Measurements aren't exact, as this is my sister-in-law, Kay's, recipe and she is such a good cook that she just doesn't see the need. This is so good served with her homemade bread.

Rosemary Corn Soup

Claudia Hauser

2 c. chopped onions
1/2 c. diced carrots
1/2 c. diced celery
3 T. butter or margarine, divided
7 1/2 c. fresh or frozen corn, divided
6 c. chicken broth

1 T. minced fresh rosemary, or 1 tsp.
dried rosemary, crushed
2 garlic cloves, minced
1/4 tsp, cayenne pepper
1 med. sweet red pepper, chopped
1 c. half & half cream
Salt & pepper, to taste

In a large saucepan, saute onions, carrots and celery in 2 tablespoons butter until tender. Add 3 1/2 cups corn, broth, rosemary, garlic and cayenne pepper. Bring to a boil. Reduce heat; simmer, uncovered, for 30 minutes, stirring occasionally, Cool; process in batches in a blender or food processor until pureed. Return to the pan. In a small skillet, saute red pepper in remaining butter until tender. Add to corn mixture. Stir in cream and remaining corn; heat through, stirring occasionally. Season with salt and pepper. Yield: 8 servings.

Southwest Cream Of Pinto Bean Soup

Jennifer Fuller

1 - 16 Oz. Bag Of Pinto Beans, Cleaned And Sorted
3 T Butter
2 White Onions, Chopped

6 C Chicken Stock
2 C Heavy Cream
Coarse Salt & Ground Pepper, Tabasco To Taste

In Large Pot Quick Soak And Cook Beans According To Pkg. Drain. In Same Pot Melt Butter And Lightly Brown Onions. Add Beans And Mix Well. Add Chicken Stock And Bring To A Boil, Then To A Bubbling Simmer Until Beans Are Done, About 45 Min.

**Or Use 2 Cans Refried Beans And 1 Can Whole Pinto Beans Instead. You Can Also Use Half & Half. This Tastes Just The Same As The Dried Beans With Cream, But Takes Way Less Time. If Using Dried Beans - With A Hand Blender (Or Potato Masher) In Soup Pot, Puree Beans With The Stock. Leave Some Beans Whole. Add Cream And Mix Well. Add Salt, Pepper Etc. To Taste. Top With Salsa.

Taco Soup

Brenda Hauser

1 can kidney beans
1 can pinto beans
1 can whole kernel corn
1 can tomatoes & green chilies
1 Lb. turkey, chicken or beef, ground
1 sm. onion, chopped

1 can chicken broth
2 c. water
1 (12 oz.) can tomato sauce
1 pkg. taco seasoning
1 pkg. ranch dressing

Brown meat and onion in medium saucepan. Add remaining ingredients and simmer for 10 to 15 minutes. Serve with crushed tortilla chips.

Uncle Donald's Chili

Brenda Hauser

1 1/2 lb. ground beef
1 onion, chopped
1 green pepper, chopped
1 can tomatoes with green chilies

2 cans chili beans
2 Lg. cans diced tomatoes
1 or 2 pkg. chili seasoning

Brown beef and add onions and peppers. Saute a few minutes, then add remaining ingredients. Simmer, low and slow until vegetables are cooked and flavors have blended.
Note: You can make more or less by adding more or less ingredients. He always added more chili powder and used a chili brick, but I can't find that anymore.

Vinnie's Whole Meal Soup

Sara Malanca

1 T. butter
2 qt. hot water
1 c. finely-chopped celery
1 c. corn
2 c. shredded cabbage

2 lb. ground beef
2 c. diced potatoes
1/4 c. regular rice
1 c. diced carrots
2 diced onions
1 1/2 T. salt

Melt butter, then brown meat in butter. Add water; bring to a boil and add the other ingredients (except rice) and bring back to a boil. Then add rice and simmer 1 to 1 1/2 hours.

Wayne's Absolutely Fabulous Chicken Noodle Soup

Jennifer Fuller

This Makes About 5 Quarts Of The Best Chicken Noodle Soup You Will Ever Have.

1 Whole Chicken
3 Thighs With Drumsticks

4 Packages Grandma's Or Similar Frozen Noodles
1 Small Jar Chicken Bouillon
Pepper, Be Generous

Cover Chicken With Water In Pressure Cooker And Cook About 45 Minutes. Let Cool, De- Bone & Shred Chicken. Put Chicken Back In Pot With Noodles, Pepper And Liquid. Add Enough Liquid To Cover Noodles And Chicken. Cook Until Noodles Are Done. Stir Often While Serving Or Pepper Will Settle To The Bottom. You Can Also Use 2 Sam's Club Rotisserie Chickens And Save Yourself Some Time.

Salads

DICK AND BRENDA HAUSER

Bean Salad

Mary Hauser

1 can green beans
1 can wax beans
1 can kidney beans

1 red onion, chopped
1 bell pepper, chopped

DRESSING:

1 c. sugar
1/2 c. oil
1/2 c. vinegar

1 tsp. mustard seeds
1 tsp. celery seeds

Heat sugar, oil and vinegar together (just until sugar is dissolved). Add mustard and celery seed. Pour over beans, onion and celery. Let stand overnight.

Bean Salad

Bertie Lightfoot

1 can shoepeg corn
1 can peas (I use frozen, thawed)
1 can French-style green beans
1 c. green bell pepper, chopped
1 c. green onions, chopped

1 c. celery, chopped
1/2 c. sugar
1/2 c. vinegar
1/2 c. oil

Drain all liquid from canned vegetables. Mix all ingredients in a large bowl and chill about 6 hours. Note: Can be made a day ahead.

SALAD

Bok Choy Salad

Jennifer Fuller

1/2 C Margarine
2 T Sugar
2 (3 Oz.) Pkgs. Ramen Noodles (Uncooked & Broken Into Small Pieces)

1 (3 Oz.) Pkg. Sliced Or Slivered Almonds
1 Large Or 2 Small Heads Of Bok Choy
6-8 Green Onions (Sliced)

Dressing:

3/4 C Vegetable Oil
1/4 C Red Or White Wine Vinegar

1/2 C Sugar
2 T Soy Sauce

Melt Margarine In Skillet, Add Sugar, Almonds (Can Be Added Towards End Of Cooking Time) & Broken Noodles (Do Not Use The Seasoning Packets From The Noodles). Cook Until Brown - Being Careful Not To Burn. This Takes Quite A While. Drain On Paper Towels - It Will Become A Little Hardened. Store In An Uncovered Bowl Until Serving. Mix It Up Once In A While So It Doesn't Become A Clump. Combine All Dressing Ingredients And Shake Well. To Serve, Tear The Bok Choy Into Small Pieces, Toss With Noodles And Dressing Just Before Serving. May Be Made 3 Days In Advance With Bok Choy & Onions Together. Keep Dressing And Noodles Separate Until Ready To Serve. It's Good Even When It's Soggy -Left Over.

Broccoli-Cauliflower Salad

Suzanne Beeler

1 lg. head cauliflower
1 bunch broccoli

1 onion, cut in rings
1 Lb. bacon, fried & diced

DRESSING:

1 1/2 c. real mayonnaise
3 T. sugar

3 T. vinegar

Wash vegetables and cut into bite-size pieces. Add onions and bacon pieces. Mix dressing ingredients and pour over the vegetables and bacon. Mix well. Let stand in refrigerator for several hours or overnight.

Chicken Fruit Salad

Lori Hauser Hale

2 c. cooked, cubed chicken
1 c. diced celery
1 c. pineapple chunks

1 c. green grapes
1/2 c. toasted cashew nuts

DRESSING:

1/2 c. sour cream
1/2 c. Miracle Whip

Lemon juice, to taste

Add the nuts just before serving.

Chicken Salad

Teddy Whitaker

4 c. diced cooked chicken
1 c. diced celery
1 Lb. Thompson seedless grapes

1 (10 oz.) can sliced water chestnuts, drained
1 can pineapple chunks
1 c. pecans

Mix all ingredients together and fold in dressing.

DRESSING:

1 c. mayonnaise
1 T. soy sauce

1 T. lemon juice
Pinch of curry powder

Beat all ingredients well and fold into the chicken salad. Note: Make the salad the night before.

Chicken Salad

Brenda Hauser

2 (12.5 oz.) cans chicken breast, drained
1 (20 oz.) can crushed pineapple, drained
1 (4 oz.) bag slivered almonds
2/3 c. sour cream
2/3 c. mayonnaise
1/4 c. chives, dried (these are expensive, so I use the green part of the green onion)

1 med. apple, diced
1 to 1 1/2 c. grapes, halved (red or green or both)
Salt & pepper, to taste (this can be optional, as the other ingredients have salt - it's up to you)
2 T. lemon juice
2/3 c. chopped celery (opt.)

This makes 7 1/2 cups (packed) chicken salad. Put 1/4 cup of chicken salad on a mini or medium-size croissant. Note: This salad can be made the day before.

Cinnamon Apple Salad

JoAnn Larson

2 (3 oz.) pkg. lemon Jello
3 c. boiling water
1/2 c. red hot candies
2 c. applesauce

2 (3 oz.) pkg. cream cheese
2 T. mayonnaise
1/4 c. milk
1/2 c. chopped walnuts

Dissolve lemon Jello with boiling water. At the same time, add red hot candies. Stir in applesauce. Chill until partially set. Blend cream cheese with mayonnaise and milk. Add chopped walnuts and swirl cheese mixture through salad. Refrigerate.

Cold Corn Salad

Lois Baldwin

1 pkg. frozen corn, almost thawed
6 to 8 slices bacon, fried crispy & crumbled
2 to 3 fresh garlic cloves (more, to taste)
2 to 3 chopped fresh jalapeno peppers, with membrane & seeds removed
Chopped olives, black or green (opt.)
2 to 3 stems chopped green onion
1 c. grated Colby-Jack cheese, marbled
Original Hidden Valley Ranch dressing

In a large mixing bowl, combine all chopped vegetables with corn. Stir in enough dressing to coat vegetables (1/2 bottle will do). Then stir in grated cheese and crumbled bacon on top. If you are going to serve immediately, let the corn thaw completely. If you have a long way to go, mix the salad with the corn slightly thawed, so it will still be cold when you get there. This is a good replacement for potato salad at cookouts.

Colorful Corn Salad

Banning Cantarini

2 (10 oz.) pkg. frozen corn, thawed
2 c. diced green pepper
2 c. diced sweet red pepper
2 c. diced celery
1 c. minced fresh parsley
1 c. chopped green onions
1/2 c. shredded Parmesan cheese
2 tsp. ground cumin
11/2 tsp. salt
3/4 tsp. pepper
1/2 tsp. hot pepper sauce
1/8 tsp. cayenne pepper
3 T. olive or vegetable oil
2 garlic cloves, minced
6 T. lime juice

In a large bowl, combine the first 12 ingredients. In a microwave-safe dish, combine oil and garlic. Microwave, uncovered, on HIGH for 1 minute. Cool. Whisk in lime juice. Pour over the corn mixture and toss to coat. Cover and refrigerate until serving. Yield: 16 to 18 servings. For the record, we only use our own Hauser sweet corn, which we freeze and can in the summer.

Confetti Corn Salad

Pat Boler

2 c. fresh com kernels
3/4 c. water
1 (14 1/2 oz.) can black beans, rinsed & drained
1/2 c. sliced green onions
1/2 c. chopped red bell pepper
1 sm. cucumber, seeded & chopped
2 cloves garlic, minced

1/4 c. chopped fresh cilantro
1 tsp. sweet red pepper flakes
1/4 tsp. ground ginger
1/4 tsp. salt
2 T. com oil
2 T. rice vinegar
1 T. sesame oil
1 T. lime juice

Combine corn kernels and 3/4 cup water in a saucepan; bring to a boil. Cover, reduce heat, and simmer 7 to 8 minutes, or just until tender. Drain. Combine corn kernels and the next 6 ingredients in a large bowl. Whisk together red pepper flakes and the next 6 ingredients until blended; pour over corn mixture. Cover salad and chill at least 2 hours. Yield: 4 to 6 servings.

Country Coleslaw Dressing

Grandma Clara Ames Wall

1 (6 oz.) can evaporated milk
1/3 c. sugar
1/3 c. vinegar

1 egg
1 tsp. celery seed
1 tsp. salt

Blend dressing ingredients in blender until smooth, about 10 seconds. Pour into saucepan; cook and stir until thick. Chill; toss with crisp shredded cabbage and carrots. Yield: about 11/3 cups dressing.

Cranberry Coleslaw

Teddy Whitaker

5 c. shredded cabbage
1/2 c. almonds, toasted
1 1/2 c. dried cranberries
1/2 c. celery, diced

1/4 c. chopped green onions, white & green parts
1/2 c. chopped green bell pepper

DRESSING:

1/2 c. mayonnaise
1 T. sweet pickle relish
1 T. honey mustard

1 T. honey
Salt & pepper

Combine cabbage, almonds, cranberries, celery, green onions and green pepper in a large plastic bowl with a snap-on lid and refrigerate. Combine all dressing ingredients, adding salt and pepper to taste, and refrigerate until ready to serve. Pour dressing over slaw just before serving. Stir well.

Cranberry Salad

Grandma Clara Wall

1 Lg. can crushed pineapple
2 pkg. raspberry Jello
1 can whole-berry cranberry sauce

1 apple, chopped
2/3 c. walnuts

Drain pineapple, reserving liquid, and add water to make 3 cups. Boil mixture and add Jello. Dissolve well. Add cranberry sauce, apple and nuts. Chill. An easy salad for Thanksgiving.

Cranberry Salad

Gale Welshire

Cranberry Salad
1 Lb. fresh cranberries
1 1/2 c. sugar
1Lg. pkg. lemon Jello

3 sliced bananas
1/3 c. nuts, chopped

Wash cranberries and put enough water on them to cover, and when they pop open, put sugar on them and boil 5 minutes. Cool. Make gelatin per usual. Cool. Mix all together and refrigerate until firm.

Cranberry Salad

Kathy Hauser

1 Lg. pkg. raspberry Jello
1 1/4 c. boiled water
1 can whole cranberries

1 can crushed pineapple, drained
1/2 c. chopped walnuts

Mix Jello and water in a bowl. Cool. Add cranberries, pineapple and walnuts. Mix well and pour into a rectangular glass baking dish and refrigerate. When set, top with topping.

TOPPING:

1 (8 oz.) pkg. softened cream cheese

3/4 c. sour cream

Beat together until smooth and spread on top of Jello, Note: This recipe can be made a day ahead and keeps well in the refrigerator for a few days. Recipe can be doubled if you are serving a large crowd. Enjoy. You can sprinkle finely-chopped nuts on top of cream cheese mixture.

Creamy Corn Salad

Pat Boler

6 c. frozen corn, thawed
3 c. chopped seeded tomatoes
1 c. cubed avocado

2/3 c. julienned sweet red pepper
2/3 c. julienned green pepper
1/2 c. chopped onion

DRESSING:

1 c. mayonnaise
2 T. red wine vinegar
2 T. Dijon mustard

1 tsp. salt
1/8 tsp. pepper

In a large bowl, combine the corn, tomatoes, avocado, peppers and onion. In a small bowl, whisk the dressing ingredients. Pour over salad and toss to coat. Cover and refrigerate for 30 minutes, or until chilled. Yield: 12 servings.

Cucumber Salad

Lisa Runk

2 cucumbers, sliced
2 T apple cider vinegar
2 T apple cider vinegar

1/2 cup sour cream
1 onion, diced
1 T sugar, dissolved in vinegar

Combine and pour over a head of lettuce.

Easy Berry Relish

Hazel Fuller

1 (12 oz.) pkg. cranberries, fresh or frozen
2 1/2 c. sugar

1 2/3 c. ginger ale
3 oz. raspberry Jello
1/3 c. lemon juice

Combine the first 4 ingredient. Cook until berries pop (about 15 minutes). Remove from heat and stir in Jello. Chill overnight. An easy, make-the-night-before dish for holidays.

Easy Salad Dressing

Susan Welch

1/2 tsp. salt
Dash of pepper
2 T. sugar
2 T. vinegar (any kind)

1/4 c. oil
Dash of red pepper sauce
1 T. snipped parsley

Put all ingredients in a small jar and shake well.
Good over any combination of salad greens.

SALAD

Forever Fruit Salad

Betty Black

2 or 2 1/2 c. ginger ale
1 c. sugar
2 T. lemon juice, fresh or canned
2 cans mandarin oranges
1 can sliced peaches

1 Lg. pkg. frozen strawberries
3 bananas, cut up
3 apples, diced
1 can pineapple tidbits (juice included)

Mix ginger ale, sugar and lemon juice. Add fruits and refrigerate. This keeps for days and is wonderful served over angel food cake for a light dessert.

French Dressing

Arlene Hauser

3/4 c. sugar
1 T. prepared mustard
1 tsp. salt
1 onion, minced

1/2 c. vinegar
1/2 c. vegetable oil
1 can tomato soup

Beat with mixer until smooth. Store in refrigerator.
Note: Keeps for weeks.
We serve it on lettuce and raw apples.

Fresh Corn Salad

Pat Boler

8 ears fresh corn
1 tomato, chopped
1 zucchini, chopped
1 cucumber, peeled & chopped

1 red onion, chopped
1 red bell pepper, chopped
1/2 c. Italian-style salad dressing

Husk the com and slice the kernels from the cob. In a large bowl, mix together the com, tomato, zucchini, cucumber, onion and red bell pepper. Pour dressing over vegetables and toss to coat. Refrigerate until chilled, at least 1 hour.

Frog-Eye Salad

Lori Boyce

3/4 c. sugar
1 T. flour
1/2 tsp. salt
2/3 c. pineapple juice
1 egg, beaten
1 tsp. lemon juice
1 c. Acini de Pepe pasta

2 cans mandarin oranges, drained
1 (20 oz.) can chunk pineapple, drained
1 (20 oz.) can crushed pineapple, drained
1 ctn. Cool Whip
1 c. mini marshmallows

In a small saucepan, mix sugar, flour and salt. Stir in pineapple juice and egg. Cook over moderate heat, stirring constantly, until thickened. Add lemon juice. Set aside and cool. Cook Acini de Pepe according to package directions. Combine cooked mixture with Acini de Pepe. Cover and place in refrigerator until chilled. Combine remaining ingredients; stir lightly. Chill at least 1 hour before serving. Yield: 8 to 10 servings.

Frozen Cranberry-Banana Salad

Suzanne Beeler

1 (20 oz.) can crushed pineapple
5 med. firm bananas, sliced
1 (16 oz.) can whole berry cranberry sauce

1/2 c. sugar, or 4 pkg. Sweet 'N Low
1 (8 oz.) ctn. frozen whipped topping, thawed
1/2 c. chopped walnuts

Drain pineapple juice into medium bowl; set pineapple aside. Add bananas to juice. In a large bowl, combine cranberry sauce and sugar. Remove bananas, discarding juice, and add to cranberries. Stir in pineapple, whipped topping and nuts. Put into 9x13-inch pan. Freeze. Remove from freezer 15 minutes before cutting.

Fruit Salad

Mary Hauser

1 (8 oz.) pkg. cream cheese
4 T. pineapple juice
1/2 c. powdered sugar
1 Lg. ctn. Cool Whip

4 tsp. cherry juice (or more)
1 can chunk pineapple
1 med. jar maraschino cherries
1/2 pkg. mini marshmallows

Beat with mixer, the cream cheese, pineapple juice and powdered sugar until smooth. Fold in remaining ingredients and refrigerate.

SALAD

Grape Salad

Sharon Massey

7 lbs purple grapes (seedless)
1 8 oz package cream cheese
1 8 oz container sour cream

1/4 cup powdered sugar
1/2 cup brown sugar
1/2 cup pecans

Wash and de-stem grapes. Let dry. Mix cream cheese, sour cream and powdered sugar together. Blend into grapes and refrigerate. Before serving, mix 1/2 cup brown sugar with pecans and sprinkle on top.

Hot Chicken Salad

Suzanne Beeler

2 1/2 c. diced, cooked chicken
1 c. diced celery
1 c. sliced, fresh mushrooms
1 T. minced onion
1 tsp, lemon juice
1/4 tsp, pepper

1 can sliced water chestnuts, drained
2 c. cooked rice
3/4 c. light mayonnaise
1 can cream of chicken soup, undiluted

TOPPING:

3 T. butter or margarine
1/2 c. corn flake crumbs

1/2 c. slivered almonds

In a 2 1/2-quart casserole, combine the first 9 ingredients. Blend mayonnaise and soup; toss with chicken mixture. Spoon into the greased casserole. In a skillet, melt butter and combine with the corn flakes and almonds. Top casserole with crumb mixture. Bake at 350° for 39 minutes.

Lime Salad

Susan Welch

2 pkg. lime Jello, dissolved in 2 c. boiling water & chilled until partially set

Fold in:
1/2 c. chopped celery
1/2 c. chopped walnuts or pecans
1 sm. can chopped pimentos

2 c. small-curd cottage cheese
1 sm. can crushed pineapple, drained

When mixture is completely set, cover with 1 large package cream cheese, softened and mixed with 2 tablespoons lemon juice and 1 tablespoon mayonnaise. Garnish with cherries or parsley. I use a 9x13-inch baking dish.

Macaroni Salad

Brenda Hauser

8 oz. elbow macaroni, cooked per directions
3 or 4 c. smoked turkey, cubed
1 med. cucumber, chopped
1 c. sweet pickle relish
5 hard-boiled eggs
1 c. pecans, chopped
1 c. green onions, chopped
2 T. mayonnaise
1 c. green grapes
1 c. red grapes

Just put everything into a pretty bowl and chill. This is a wonderful, easy salad for luncheon. Just serve with crackers and a yummy dessert.

Mexican Gazpacho

Sharon Olson

2 c. tomatoes, peeled, seeded & chopped
1/2 c. diced cucumber
1/4 c. chopped red onion
1/4 c. chopped celery
1/4 c. chopped green pepper
1/4 c. chopped cilantro
3 T. chopped scallions
2 T. minced green chilies or jalapenos
2 T. chopped parsley
1 T. minced garlic
1 c. tomato juice
2 T. red wine vinegar
2 T. fresh lime juice
1 T. olive oil
1/2 tsp. salt
1/4 tsp. pepper

Combine all ingredients in a large bowl. Cover and chill thoroughly before serving. You can prepare all the vegetables in a food processor, but don't puree. It is best served chunky and with croutons on top.

Mississippi Cornbread Salad

Betty Black

1 (8 oz.) pkg. cornbread/muffin mix
1 (1 oz.) env. ranch dressing
1 c. sour cream
1 c. mayonnaise
1/2 c. red pepper, chopped
8 Lg. tomatoes, chopped
1/2 c. green pepper, chopped
1/2 c. green onion, chopped
2 (15 oz.) cans whole kernel corn
2 c. shredded cheese
10 slices bacon, cooked & crumbled
2 c. shredded lettuce

Prepare cornbread according to directions. Stir together salad dressing mix, sour cream and mayonnaise. Gently toss vegetables; crumble half of cornbread into a trifle bowl. Top with half each ingredient and repeat layers. Cover and chill.

Molded Cranberry Salad

Kerri Hauser

1 c. boiling water
1 (3 oz.) pkg. Jello
1 (10 oz.) pkg. cranberry-orange relish (frozen or in jar)

1 (8 3/4 oz.) can crushed pineapple
1 tart apple, chopped
1/2 c. chopped celery
1/3 c. chopped nuts

Put boiling water over Jello in bowl, stirring until dissolved. Add relish, pineapple, apple, celery and nuts. Pour into 4-cup mold. Chill until firm. Yield: 6 to 8 servings.

Orange Jello

Clara Ames Miller

1 qt. cottage cheese
1 sm. pkg. orange Jello, dry
1 sm. pkg. orange-pineapple Jello, dry

1 Lg. ctn. Cool Whip
1 can crushed pineapple, drained
1 can mandarin oranges, drained

Mix all ingredients and chill. Other fruits and Jellos can be substituted and nuts can be added for crunchiness.

Orange Jello Salad

Nettie Eurom

2 sm. pkg. orange Jello
2 c. boiling water
1 pt. orange sherbet

1 can mandarin oranges
1 sm. can crushed pineapple
2 sliced bananas

Dissolve Jello in 2 cups water and sherbet. Stir until dissolved. Let stand until partially set, then add fruit. Chill until set.

Orange Tapioca

Suzanne Beeler

1 can mandarin oranges
Juice + water to equal 3 c.
2 pkg. tapioca pudding

1 (3 oz.) pkg. orange Jello
1 ctn. Cool Whip

Drain oranges and put 3 cups water-juice in saucepan with tapioca pudding and Jello. Cook until thick. Cool and fold in oranges and Cool Whip. Suzanne and her family make and sell homemade ice cream at all local events. Yum.

Orange Yogurt

Bertie Lightfoot

2/3 c. cottage cheese
1/4 c. buttermilk
1 T. frozen orange juice
1 tsp. vanilla

4 tsp. sugar
3 drops yellow food coloring
1 drop red food coloring

Put all ingredients in a blender and blend until smooth. Tastes just like yogurt. Yummy.

Oriental Chicken Salad with Pineapple Dressing

Ruth Hunter

16 oz. cooked chicken
3 T. soy sauce
1 tsp. ginger
8 c. torn greens
4 c. assorted vegetables

2 green onions, sliced
1 pkg. Ramen Oriental noodles
2 tsp. sesame seeds
Pineapple Dressing (below)

PINEAPPLE DRESSING:

1/3 c. pineapple juice
1/4 c. rice vinegar
1 T. soy sauce

2 tsp. sugar
1 1/2 tsp. sesame oil
1/4 tsp, pepper

Combine in jar. Cover and shake well. Combine chicken, soy sauce and ginger. Set aside. Toss greens, vegetables and broken noodles together in a large bowl. (Don't use seasoning packet from noodles.) Pour all but 3 tablespoons dressing over greens and toss. Spoon greens onto large platter. Top with chicken. Drizzle with remaining dressing and sprinkle with sesame seeds. Yield: 4 servings.

Pink Stuff

Pat Boler

1 (21 oz.) can cherry pie filling
1 (20 oz.) can pineapple chunks, drained

1 (14 oz.) can Eagle Brand milk
1/2 c. chopped nuts
1 (26 oz.) ctn. Cool Whip

Mix together pie filling, pineapple, milk and nuts in a large bowl. Fold in Cool Whip. Mix until evenly pink. Refrigerate until ready to eat.

Rainbow Pasta Salad

Bonnie Nyce

1 (Lb.) pkg. tri-color spiral pasta
2 med. carrots, shredded
1 Large. red onion, chopped
1 med. green pepper, chopped
1/2 tsp, celery seed, or 2 celery ribs, chopped

1 can sweetened condensed milk
1 c. cider vinegar
1 c. mayonnaise
2 T. sugar
1 tsp, salt
1/2 tsp. salt

Cook pasta according to package directions. Rinse in cold water and drain; place in a large bowl. Add carrots, onion, green pepper and celery or celery seed. In another bowl, combine remaining ingredients. Pour over pasta mixture. Toss to coat. Cover; refrigerate 3 hours or overnight. Yield: 12 to 14 servings.

Seven-Layer Salad

Pat Boler

1 or 2 heads lettuce, shredded
1/2 c. celery, chopped
1 bell pepper, chopped
1 onion, chopped

1 pkg. frozen peas, cooked & cooled
3 T. sugar
1 T. salad dressing
1 or 2 c. shredded Cheddar cheese

In an 8x12-inch dish, layer lettuce, then celery, pepper, onion and peas. Mix the sugar with salad dressing and pour over entire salad, sealing edges well. Cover with cheese. Cover with plastic wrap and refrigerate overnight. Can add fresh com kernels to this, also.

Soda Cracker Salad

Ann Hileman

1/4 lb. soda crackers, crushed
1 c. mayonnaise
1/2 c. green pepper, chopped
1/2 c. onion. chopped

1/2 c. celery, chopped
1/2 c. sweet pickle relish
3 hard-boiled eggs, chopped

Mix all with a teaspoon or so of sugar. Store overnight in covered bowl in refrigerator. This tastes like potato salad, but is much easier and a great little side dish to use up bits of vegetables.

Strawberry Jello

Mary Hauser

2 sm. pkg strawberry Jello
2 c. boiling water
2 pkg. frozen strawberries

2 sm. cans crushed pineapple with juice
3 bananas
2 c. sour cream

Dissolve Jello in boiling water; add strawberries, pineapple and bananas. Pour half into a 9x13-inch cake pan. Let stand in refrigerator. (Doesn't take long.) Spread sour cream over first layer. Pour other half of the Jello mixture over sour cream. Let set. We have this at almost every family gathering.

Sumi Salad

Topsy Eitel

2 T. oil
1/4 c. sliced almonds
1/4 c. sesame seeds
8 green onions, finely sliced

1 head cabbage, finely sliced & chopped
2 (3 oz.) pkg. Ramen noodles, broken
Dressing

Heat oil in skillet and toast almonds and seeds until lightly browned. Combine with onions, cabbage, noodles and dressing. Cover and chill several hours for flavors to blend. Yield: about 10 1/2 cups.

DRESSING:

1/4 c. sugar
1 tsp. black pepper
1 tsp. salt

1 c. oil (I try to reduce the amount of oil)
4 T. rice wine vinegar
3 T. wine vinegar

Combine sugar, pepper, salt, oil and vinegar and mix well. Note: Reserve any flavor packet in noodle package for another use. By adding cooked chicken or cooked shrimp, you have a nice main dish salad.

Susie's Orange Pineapple Salad

Donna Alaura

2 (3 oz.) pkg. or 1 (6 oz.) pkg. orange jello, dissolved in 2 c. boiling water
1 pt. orange sherbet or vanilla ice cream

2 cans mandarin oranges
Lg. can crushed pineapple (save pineapple & orange juice - enough to make 1 c.)

Chill until firm in a 9x13-inch pan.

TOPPING:

1/2 c. sugar

Mix together in a medium saucepan.
Add: 1 egg, beaten

3 T. flour
1 c. juice

Cook and stir topping mixture over medium heat until thick. Add 2 tablespoons butter and let cool. Fold in 1 cup whipped topping. Spread over firm Jello and let set overnight. Note: Use a heavy saucepan for making topping, otherwise it may stick and burn.

Watergate Salad

Claudia Hauser

1 ctn. whipped topping
1 box instant pistachio pudding
Lg. can crushed pineapple

1 c. mini marshmallows
1 c. nuts, chopped

Fold dry pudding mix into topping. Add pineapple, marshmallows and nuts. Refrigerate.

Watermelon Salad

Kim Gould

1/2 large shilled seedless watermelon, cut into 1" cubes
1 small red onion, sliced
1 cup thinly sliced fresh basil leaves

1 cup chopped fresh cilantro
1/2 cup minced fresh mint leaves
2 limes
1 (4oz) package crumbled feta cheese
3 T balsamic vinegar
salt and pepper to taste

Gently toss all ingredients in a large bowl and enjoy!

Wild Rice and Cranberry Salad

Teddy Whitaker

1 c. (1/2 lb.) raw wild rice*
5 1/2 c. chicken stock or water
1/2 c. chopped green onion
1 c. shelled pecan halves
1 c. yellow raisins (I substitute dried cranberries)

Grated rind of Lg. orange
1 sm. can mandarin oranges, chopped
1/4 c. olive oil
1/3 c. fresh orange juice
1 1/2 tsp. salt
Fresh ground pepper, to taste

*1 mix white and wild rice. Wild rice takes a long time to cook, so they should be cooked separately.

Put wild rice in strainer and run under cold water; rinse thoroughly. Place wild rice in a medium saucepan. Add stock or water and bring to a rapid boil. Adjust heat to a gentle simmer and cook, uncovered, for 45 to 50 minutes. After 30 minutes, check for doneness. (I cooked for 50 minutes.) Drain in colander and put into a bowl. Add remaining ingredients to rice and toss gently. Adjust seasoning to taste. Let mixture stand for 2 hours to allow flavors to develop. Serve at room temperature.

NO FARMS
NO FOOD

Breads

HAUSER Family at the Barn 2019

Alice Bradford's Applesauce Bread

Dorothy Trammel

2 c. flour
1 tsp. baking soda
1/2 tsp. cinnamon
1/2 tsp. baking powder
1/4 tsp. allspice
1/4 tsp. salt

1 can applesauce
1 c. sugar
1/2 c. oil
3 eggs
3 T. milk

Mix all ingredients together in a large mixing bowl. Pour into greased and floured loaf pans. Mix 1/4 cup chopped pecans, 1/4 cup brown sugar and 1/2 teaspoon cinnamon. Spread on batter. Bake 1 hour at 350°. Apple Cinnamon Muffins

Apple Cinnamon Muffins

Brenda Hauser

2 c. cake flour, or 1 3/4 c. all-purpose flour
3/4 tsp. salt
1/4 c. sugar
2 tsp. baking powder

2 eggs
2 T. melted butter
3/4 c. milk
1/2 c. peeled, chopped apples

Sift dry ingredients and add eggs, butter and milk. Fold in apples. Do not try to beat out the lumps or your muffins will be tough. Pare and core cooking apples. Try to have them the same diameter as the tin. Cut them into 1 /2-inch slices. Dip them into mixture of 1 part cinnamon and 4 parts of sugar. Place an apple slice on top of each partially-filled muffin cup. Bake for 15 to 20 minutes at 425°. Remove from tins at once.

Anna's Illinois Biscuits

AnnaMae Hileman

2 c. self-rising flour
1 c. buttermilk

2 T. mayonnaise

Knead lightly on floured board. Cut into biscuits or can be dropped by large spoonfuls onto ungreased cookie sheet. Bake for 10 to 15 minutes at 450°.

Angel Biscuits

Hazel Pyle Fuller

5 C flour
3/4 c. shortening
1 tsp. baking soda
1 tsp. baking powder
1 tsp. salt

3 T. sugar
1 package of Yeast
1/2 c. luke warm water
2 c. buttermilk

Mix together dry ingredients; cut in shortening well. Add buttermilk
and yeast dissolved in water. Mix until all flour is moistened. Cover bowl
and put in refrigerator until ready to use. When ready to use, take as
much dough as needed. Roll out on floured board to 1/2- to 3/4-inch
thick. Cut. Bake at 400° for 12 minutes. Will keep in refrigerator for
several weeks.

Baked cheese bread

Christine Hauser

1 cup milk
1/2 cup mayo
1/2 cup sour cream
112 stick butter

Pinch of garlic
2 cups cheddar
1 loaf French bread

Set aside 1 cup of cheddar cheese for topping. Mix ingredients together. Cut
French into slices, spread mixture into
each slice. Spread remaining cheese on top and bake until golden.
325° -15 minutes.

Banana Bread

Kevin Hauser

1/2 c. butter or shortening
1 c. sugar
2 eggs
1/2 c. buttermilk
3 ripe bananas
1 tsp, vanilla

1/2 tsp. baking soda
1/2 tsp. baking powder
2 c. flour
1 tsp. salt
1/2 to 1 c. nuts, dried cranberries,
chocolate chips or raisins

Cream butter or shortening and add sugar, then bananas. Mix well with mixer. Add
eggs and vanilla, then mix in dry ingredients. Add whatever fruit or nuts and put into
4 (3 1/2 x 6-inch) or 2 (6x9-inch) bread pans. Bake at 350° for 30 to 45 minutes.
I used to mash the bananas with a fork, but it is much easier to mash them with the
mixer.

Beer Bread

Ashley Hollamon

3 1/2 c. self-rising flour
1/3 c. sugar
1 egg

12 oz. beer
2 c. Cheddar cheese, shredded
1/2 c. dried herb or vegetable blend

Mix all ingredients together and bake at 350° for 1 hour in regular-sized bread pan.

Bread Pudding with Rum Sauce

Teddy Whitaker

1 (about 25 oz.) loaf French bread
(several days old)
1 qt. milk
2 1g. cans Carnation milk (1 milk can
of water)
6 Lg. eggs
2 1/2 c. sugar

1 1/4 T. nutmeg
1/4 tsp. salt
1 1/2 T. vanilla
1 tsp. cinnamon
1 stick margarine, cut in pieces
1/2 c. raisins

RUM SAUCE:

1 box regular Jello vanilla pudding mix
1/2 c. milk

1/2 stick margarine
1 T. rum flavoring

Mix together 1 quart of milk, evaporated milk, 1 can water, margarine, sugar, salt and vanilla flavoring: heat until margarine is melted. Pull French bread apart in small pieces; sprinkle raisins over bread. Beat eggs, nutmeg and cinnamon in mixer for 1 minute. Mix milk mixture with egg mixture; mix well. Pour over bread and let stand about 10 minutes. Pour mixture into a 9x13-inch greased baking dish and bake at 350° for 45 minutes or 1 hour, or until knife blade comes clean.
Rum Sauce: Follow directions on pudding mix box, adding 1/2 cup more milk. After cooking, add 1/2 stick margarine and 1 tablespoon rum. Pour rum sauce over bread pudding and serve.

Bread Machine Super Cinnamon Rolls

Emily Hauser

DOUGH:

1 1/4 c. milk
1 egg
1/4 c. (1/2 stick) butter, cut in pieces
4 c. all-purpose flour

1 env. or 3 tsp. active dry yeast
1 tsp. salt
1/4 c. sugar
2 T. ground cinnamon

FILLING:

1/4 c. sugar
6 T. dark brown sugar

2 T. ground cinnamon
1/2 c. (1 stick) butter, melted

GLAZE

1 c. confectioners' sugar
1 tsp. vanilla

1/4 c. milk or cream, or 1 (3 oz.) pkg. cream cheese

Dough: Combine ingredients in order specified in your bread machine manual. Set machine for dough cycle. Remove dough at end of cycle and let rest for 10 minutes, covered, on a floured surface while you prepare the filling.

Filling: Stir together white and brown sugars and cinnamon. Brush a 9x13-inch pan or cookie sheet with sides with about 2 tablespoon of the melted butter. Roll the dough into a 12x20-inch rectangle, about 1/2 inch thick. Brush the dough generously with the remaining butter and sprinkle with the cinnamon-sugar mixture. Roll up, starting at short end to form a log about 12 inches long. Cut into 'l-Inch-wide rolls. Place the roll, cinnamon spiral on top, in the buttered pan. Drizzle on any remaining butter. Let rise, covered, for about 30 minutes, or until rolls are puffy and have reached the side of the pan and each other. Preheat oven to 375° and bake for about 30 minutes.

Glaze: Mix ingredients and drizzle over warm rolls. These are good or better than the ones you get at the airport or mall and a heck of a lot cheaper.

Carrot-Pineapple Muffins

Naoma Moore

1 c. whole wheat flour
1/3 c. sugar
1 tsp. baking powder
1 tsp. baking soda
1 tsp. cinnamon
1 tsp, nutmeg

1/4 tsp. salt
1 egg, beaten
1/4 c. oil
1 c. shredded carrots
1/2 c. crushed pineapple, drained
1 tsp. vanilla

Place paper baking cups in muffin tins. Mix flour, baking powder, baking soda, cinnamon, nutmeg, sugar and salt together in mixing bowl. Add remaining ingredients and mix well, but do not over mix. Fill muffin cups 3/4-full. Bake at 350° for 20 minutes, or until top springs back when touched lightly.

Cheesy Corn Spoonbread

Kevin Hauser

1 med. onion, chopped
1/4 c. butter or margarine
2 eggs
2 c. (16 oz.) sour cream
1 (15 1/4 oz.) can whole kernel corn, drained
1 (14 3/4 oz.) can cream-style corn
1/4 tsp. salt
1/4 tsp. pepper
1 (8 1/2 oz.) pkg. cornbread/muffin mix
1 med. jalapeno pepper, minced*
2 c. (8 oz.) shredded Cheddar cheese, divided

When cutting or seeding hot peppers, use rubber or plastic gloves to protect your hands. Avoid touching your face or eyes. In a skillet, saute onion in butter until tender; set aside. In a bowl, beat the eggs; add sour cream, both cans of com, salt and pepper. Stir in cornbread mix just until blended. Fold in sautéed onion, jalapeno and 1 1/2 cups of cheese. Transfer to a greased shallow 3-quart baking dish. Sprinkle with the remaining cheese. Bake, uncovered, at 375º for 35 to 40 minutes, or until a toothpick inserted near the center comes out clean; cool slightly. Yield: 12 to 15 servings.

Coconut Banana Bread

Ruth Hunter

1/2 c. sugar
2 eggs
1/2 c. vegetable oil
1 c. ripe mashed bananas (about 2 med.)
1/2 c. flaked coconut
1 3/4 c. self-rising flour
1/4 tsp. baking soda

POWDERED SUGAR FROSTING:

Mix all together:
1 c. powdered sugar
1 T. milk
Coconut

Preheat oven to 350°. Grease 2 (4 1/2 x 8 1/2 x 2-inch) loaf pans. Set aside. Beat together sugar, eggs and oil in a large bowl. Stir in bananas and coconut. Combine flour and baking soda. Add to banana mixture. Divide batter into 2 loaf pans. Bake for 35 to 40 minutes. Toothpick inserted in center should come out clean. Cool slightly. Remove from pan and pour frosting over top. Let cool completely.

Cranberry Mini Loaf Bread {Great for Christmas}

Kristi Hauser Bright

3 cups all purpose flour
1 T baking powder
1 T cinnamon
Pinch of Salt
2 lg eggs

2/3 cup butter, chilled
¾ cup brown sugar
¾ cup fresh chopped cranberries
¾ cup milk
1/3 cup confectioners sugar Water

Grease mini loaf pans. Preheat oven to 350 degrees F. Mix flour, baking powder, cinnamon and salt. Cut butter into thin slices and add to bowl. Break butter into mixture until crumbly. Stir in brown sugar. Add cranberries, milk and eggs. Batter should be thick, but not dry. If necessary, add milk, 1 T at a time if dry. Fill 3 mini loaf pans and bake for 1 hour. For icing, mix confectioners sugar and a small amount of water and drizzle over breads.

Cranberry-Pumpkin Bread

Teddy Whitaker

3 3/4 c. all-purpose flour
3 c. sugar
4 tsp. pumpkin pie spice
2 tsp. baking soda
4 eggs

1 (15 oz.) can solid-pack pumpkin
1/2 c. vegetable oil
2 c. fresh or frozen cranberries, thawed
1 c. chopped walnuts

In a large bowl, combine the flour, sugar, pumpkin pie spice, baking soda and salt. In another bowl, beat the eggs, pumpkin and oil; stir into dry ingredients, just until moistened. Fold in cranberries and walnuts. Spoon into 2 greased 5x9x3-inch loaf pans. Bake at 350° for 70 to 80 minutes, or until a toothpick inserted near the center comes out clean. Cool for 10 minutes before removing from pans to wire racks to cool completely. Yield: 2 loaves.

Dutch Apple Bread

Patty Hauser Ink

1/2 Cup Softened Butter (1 Cube)
1 Cup Granulated Sugar
2 Eggs
1/2 Cup Milk
1 Tsp. Vanilla Extract

2 Cups All-Purpose Flour
1/2 Tsp Salt
1 Tsp Baking Powder
1 1/2 Cups Diced Peeled Green Apples
1/2 Cup Chopped Walnuts Or Pecans

Cream Butter And Sugar In A Mixing Bowl. Add In Eggs And Vanilla. Stir To Incorporate. Mix Flour, Salt And Baking Powder. Fold In Apples And Nuts. Transfer Mixture To Baking Pan Sprayed With Cooking Spray Or Parchment Paper.

Topping:

5 Tbsp Cold Butter
1/3 Cup Flour
2 Tbsp Granulated Sugar

2 Tbsp Brown Sugar
2 Tsp Ground Cinnamon

Combine All Ingredients And Mix With A Fork Or Pastry Mixer Until Crumbly. Sprinkle Over Baiter In Pan. Bake For 55-60 Minutes Until Toothpick Inserted In Bread Comes Out Clean. Let Cool Remove From Pan And Drizzle Top With Vanilla Glaze

Vanilla Glaze:

1 Tbsp Melted Butter
1/2 Cup Powdered Sugar

1 Tbsp Milk
1/4 Tsp Vanilla Extract.

Green Chili Cornmeal Casserole

Connie Steyaert

1 c. yellow cornmeal
1/4 tsp. baking soda
1 tsp. salt
1 can cream-style corn
2 eggs

1/3 c. melted shortening or oil
3/4 c. buttermilk
1 (4 oz.) can green chilies, diced
2 c. grated Longhorn cheese

Beat well, except for chilies and cheese. Pour 1/3 of the batter into a greased casserole dish, then half of chilies and cheese. Then another 1/3 of batter, then remaining cheese and chilies. Top with final 1/3 of the batter. Bake for 40 to 45 minutes at 350°. This is good hot or cold, with salsa. A great potluck dish.

BREAD

Homemade Noodles

Brenda Hauser

3 egg yolks
1 whole egg
3 T. cold water

2 c. flour
1 tsp. salt

Beat egg yolks and egg until very light. Beat in cold water and salt. Stir in and work in with hands, the flour. Divide dough into 3 parts. Roll out each piece as thin as possible on lightly-floured board. Place between 2 towels until dough is partially dry. Roll up dough as for jellyroll. With a thin, sharp knife, cut into strips of desired width (1/8- to 1/2-inch). Shake out the strips and allow to dry before using or storing. A real family favorite.

Honey Whole Wheat Bread

Brenda Hauser

1/2 c. honey or molasses
1/2 c. margarine
4 tsp. salt
2 eggs, beaten
1 c. dry milk

4 c. hot water
2 T. yeast
1/3 c. warm water
6 c. whole wheat flour
6 c. white flour

Combine honey, margarine, salt, eggs, dry milk and warm water; mix until margarine is melted. In a small bowl, dissolve yeast in 1/3 cup warm water. When first mixture cools to lukewarm, add dissolved yeast mixture. Gradually stir in whole wheat flour, then white flour. Knead until smooth and elastic. Cover and let rise until doubled in size, keeping free from draft. Shape into 4 loaves or rolls and allow to rise again (about 40 minutes). Bake at 350° for 30 to 40 minutes.

Kay's Bread

Kay Hauser

1 c. milk (lukewarm)
1/4 c. margarine
4 c. warm water
3/4 c. sugar

2 heaping T. instant yeast
1 1/2 tsp. salt
5 Lb. flour

In a mixer with dough hook, mix the liquid, then add flour to a very soft dough and slightly sticky. Let rise about an hour. Make into desired bread or rolls. Let rise until double. Bake at 3750 until browned. Her secret to scrumptious bread is the big mixer and everybody eating it hot out of the oven. Yum!

Lemon Blueberry Bread

Patty Hauser Ink

1/3 cup melted butter
1 cup sugar
3 T. Lemon Juice
2 eggs
1 Y2 cup flour
1 tsp. Baking Powder
1 tsp Salt

1/2 C Milk
2 T Lemon Zest
1/2 cup chopped Walnuts
1 cup Blueberries, (Fresh or Frozen)

Grease loaf pan. Bake at 350° for 45-50 minutes

GLAZE:

1 T. Butter Melted

1 cup Powdered Sugar

While the bread is still warm brush on the glaze.

Molasses Sweet Bread

Betty Black

2 c. flour
2 tsp. baking powder
1/2 tsp. salt
1/3 tsp. baking soda
2 tsp. ginger

1 tsp, cinnamon
1/3 c. melted butter
1 c. molasses
3/4 c. buttermilk
1 egg

Mix with mixer or by hand until well blended. Pour into regular-size loaf pan. Bake at 350° for about 50 minutes. You can add nuts, raisins or chips, but it is good with butter.

Mother's Monkey Bread

Naoma Moore

1 1/2 c. scalded milk
2 T. margarine
1 egg
1 pkg. yeast

4 T. sugar
1 tsp. salt
4 c. flour

Scald milk, then cool to lukewarm. Mix yeast and sugar; add beaten egg and yeast-sugar mixture, then flour. Turn out on floured board. Roll 1/8~inch thickness. Cut into small squares. Melt 1 cube margarine and dip strips and put crisscrosses in bundt pan. Let rise 1 1/2 to 2 hours. Bake in 350° oven for 40 to 45 minutes. When done, turn out on tall cake stand and place in center of table. Guest just "pick" off a piece.

Oat Pancakes

Bertie Lightfoot

1 c. oatmeal
1 c. flour
2 T. sugar
2 tsp. baking powder
1 tsp, salt

2 eggs, slightly beaten
1 1/2 c. milk
1/4 c. vegetable oil

Whisk all ingredients together. Batter will be slightly lumpy. Cook on hot grill. Enjoy with butter and syrup.

Old-Fashioned Cinnamon Rolls

Brenda Hauser

4 3/4 to 5 1/4 c. all-purpose flour
1 pkg. active dry yeast
1 c. milk
1/3 c. butter
1/3 c. sugar

3 eggs
3 T. butter, melted
2/3 c. sugar
2 tsp. ground cinnamon
1 recipe Creamy Glaze (below)

In a large bowl, combine 2 1/4 cups flour and yeast. In a saucepan, heat and stir milk, 1/3 cup butter, 1/3 cup granulated sugar and 1/2 teaspoon salt just until warm (120° to 130°) and butter almost melts. Add to flour mixture; add eggs. Beat on low speed for 30 seconds, scraping bowl. Beat on high speed for 3 minutes. Stir in as much of the remaining flour as you can.

On a lightly-floured surface, knead in enough of the remaining flour to make a moderately-soft dough that is smooth and elastic (3 to 5 minutes total). Shape into a ball. Place in a greased bowl, turning once. Cover; let rise in a warm place until double in size (1 hour).

Punch down dough. Turn out onto a lightly-floured surface; divide in half. Cover; let rest 10 minutes. Lightly grease 2 (9 x 1 1/2-inch) round baking pans. Roll each half of the dough into an 8 x l2-inch rectangle. Brush with melted butter. Combine the 2/3 cup sugar and the cinnamon; sprinkle over rectangles. Starting from a long side, roll up each rectangle into a spiral. Seal seams. Cut each spiral into 12 slices. Place slices, cut- sides down, in prepared pans.

Cover dough loosely with plastic wrap, leaving room for rolls to rise. Chill for at least 2 hours or up to 24 hours. Uncover; let stand at room temperature for 30 minutes.

Preheat oven to 375° Break surface bubbles with a greased toothpick. Bake for 20 to 25 minutes, or until light brown. If necessary to prevent overbrowning, cover rolls loosely with foil for the last 5 to 10 minutes of baking. Remove from oven. Cool for 1 minute. Carefully invert rolls onto wire rack. Cool slightly. Invert again onto a serving platter. Drizzle with Creamy Glaze. Serve warm. Yield: 24 rolls.

Creamy Glaze: Mix 1 1/4 cups sifted powdered sugar, 1 teaspoon light-colored corn syrup and 1/2 teaspoon vanilla. Stir in enough half & half or light cream (1 to 2 tablespoons) to make of drizzling consistency. Rising time: 1 hour. Chilling time: 2 to 24 hours. Standing time: 30 minutes. Baking time: 20 minutes.

Sharon's Corn Rolls

Kay Hauser

1/2 c. cornmeal
1/3 c. sugar
1/3 c. oil
2 eggs, well beaten
5 to 6 c. flour

2 tsp, salt
1 1/2 c. milk
1 pkg. yeast
1/4 c. water
3/4 c. creamed corn

In a heavy pan, cook cornmeal, sugar, oil, salt and milk until thick. Cool until luke-warm and add creamed corn, eggs and the yeast, which has been dissolved in 1/4 cup water. Mix well. Add enough flour to handle well. Knead until smooth and elastic. Let rise until double; form into rolls and let rise a second time for about 30 minutes. Bake for 15 minutes at 400°. Yield: about 30 rolls.

Sopapillas

Naoma Moore

8 c. flour
2 T. baking powder
1/2 tsp, salt

1 tsp. sugar
1 egg
2 to 3 c. hot water

Heat 4 cups vegetable oil in a skillet until very hot. Mix all ingredients, except water, in a large bowl. Add water slowly, mixing well and using as much water as necessary, until dough forms a ball. Divide dough into 5 balls and roll out flat. Cut each flattened ball into 4 pieces and fry in hot oil until done. Can be served as a bread with meal, or as dessert with butter and honey, or sprinkled with cinnamon and sugar.

Zucchini Nut Muffins

Marlys Hauser

3 eggs
1 c. oil
1 tsp. vanilla
2 c. shredded zucchini
2 c. flour
1 c. sunflower seeds

1 1/2 tsp. baking soda
1 tsp. salt
1/4 tsp. baking powder
1 T. cinnamon
2 c. sugar

Mix all ingredients in a mixing bowl until well blended. Fill muffin tins 1/2-full and bake 18 minutes at 400°. Any combination of nuts or raisins can be added or substituted for the sunflower seeds.

Main Dishes

DICK, JIMMY, DONNY, PATTY, MARY HAUSER

4-H Corn Special

Mitchell Ferguson

1 Lb. ground beef
1 sm. onion, finely chopped
1 1/2 c. cooked rice
2 c. seeded, chopped fresh tomatoes, or 1 can diced tomatoes
2 c. fresh, frozen or canned sweet corn
Salt & pepper, to taste
1 T. Worcestershire sauce
1 c. crushed saltine crackers
1/4 c. butter or margarine, melted
Dash of red pepper sauce

In a large skillet, brown beef and onion; drain. Stir in rice, tomatoes, corn, salt, pepper, Worcestershire sauce and red pepper sauce. Pour into a greased 9x13-inch baking dish. Combine cracker crumbs and butter; sprinkle on top. Bake at 350° for 30 minutes.

Air Fryer Coconut Shrimp

Kristi Hauser Bright

1 pound fresh shrimp, shelled and deveined, leaving tail
Salt & pepper
½ cup flour
2 eggs
½ cup panko crumbs
½ cup flaked coconut
Olive oil

Season shrimp with salt and pepper. Mix panko crumbs and coconut together in a bowl. Whisk eggs in a bowl. Dip shrimp in flour, then egg, and finally the panko/coconut mixture. Put in a single row in air fryer and spray with olive oil or cooking spray. Set air fryer to 400 degrees F. Cook shrimp for approx. 3 minutes, turn over and cook an additional 3 minutes, or until golden brown and crispy. Serve with a sweet chili sauce.

MAIN DISH

83

Banning's Mississippi Mojo

Banning Cantarini

A tough cut of meat (wild game works too)
1 ranch dip mix packet
1 au jus packet
Stick of butter
Sliced Pepperoncini's
Potatoes

White onion
Leak
Celery
Carrots
Chicken stock
Flour

Pull out your slow cooker. Seer your meat until its brown on all sides. Add the meat into the slow cooker. Pour the contents of the ranch and au jus packet over the meat. Lay a stick of butter on top. Surround the meat with a heap of pepperoncini's (add some of the juice if you want a stronger flavor to your liquid). Chop and add your vegetables. Add enough stock to submerge everything. Set your cooker to HIGH for one hour, then reduce to LOW for 6 or 7 hours or until it looks ready. After everything is cooked, use a slotted spoon and remove all of the solids from the crock pot and set aside in a bowl. You can choose to chop up the cooked meat if you'd like. Take an immersion blender and blend the broth in the slow cooker. Add some flour to thicken the liquid to the consistency that you like (I prefer mine like a stew). Salt and pepper to taste. Then add your solids and meat back into the base. Serve and enjoy.

Barbecued pineapple

Tammie Dunn

1 fresh pineapple
1/4 cup rum
1/4 cup brown sugar
1 tbsp cinnamon

1/2 tsp ground ginger
1/2 tsp nutmeg
1/2 tsp ground cloves

Peel pineapple, leaving whole - cut into 8 rings. Remove core. Place in baking dish. In small bowl, mix ingredients together. Pour marinade over pineapple, cover and refrigerate 1 hour or overnight. Preheat grill on high heat. Lightly oil grate. Grill pineapple rings about 15 minutes, turning once or until outside is dry and char marked. Serve with ice cream and remaining marinade.

Beefy Cornbread

June Thompson

1 Lb. ground beef
1 sm. onion
2 or 3 jalapeno peppers, seeded & chopped
1 (8 1/2 oz.) pkg. cornbread mix
3/4 tsp, salt
1/2 tsp. baking soda

1 can creamed corn
1 c. milk
1/2 c. vegetable oil
2 eggs, beaten
3 c. shredded Cheddar cheese, divided

In a large skillet, brown beef, onion and peppers over medium heat until no longer pink. Drain and set aside. In a small bowl, combine cornbread mix, salt, baking soda, corn, milk, oil and eggs. Pour half into a greased 9x13-inch baking dish. Layer with half of cheese and all of beef mixture. Top with remaining cheese and CAREFULLY spread remaining batter over top. Bake, uncovered, at 350° for 40 to 45 minutes, or until a toothpick inserted comes out clean.

Beer-Braised BBQ Chicken

Aymee Wilson

4 lbs chicken thighs, drumsticks and wings
Salt and pepper to taste
4 T canola oil
2 onions, sliced 1/4 inch thick

1 1/4 cups lager-style beer
2 1/2 cups BBQ sauce
4 ears of corn, boiled until tender
Herb butter for serving

Season chicken with salt and pepper. In a Dutch oven over medium high heat, heat 3 T of oil. Working in batches, brown the chicken on all sides, about 3 minutes per side. Transfer to platter. Add remaining 1T oil to the pan along with onions. Cook for about 5 to 7 minutes. Stir in the beer and BBQ sauce and bring to a boil. Add chicken, reduce heat to low, cover and cook until tender, about 1 hour. Transfer the chicken, using tongs, to a baking sheet and let cool to room temp. Meanwhile, bring the sauce to a simmer over medium high heat and simmer until thickened, about 30 minutes. Preheat grill and brush chicken on both sides with sauce. Grill the chicken, turning once and brushing occasionally with sauce, about 3 minutes per side. Serve with corn and herbed butter.

BBQ Roast

Lisa Runk

1 deer roast or pork loin
2 liters root beer

Simmer on low in a crockpot for 8 hours. Pull apart and cover with bbq sauce.

MAIN DISH

Bev's Chicken Enchiladas

Georgia Reddell

1 (16 oz.) ctn. sour cream
1 sm. can green chilies, chopped
3 or 4 green onions, chopped
1 doz. corn tortillas

2 cans white meat chicken
1 can cream of chicken soup
2 c. or so grated Longhorn cheese

Mix all ingredients, except cheese, in a medium-sized mixing bowl. Dip tortillas in oil or hot water to soften. Put a few tablespoons of the sour cream mixture on each tortilla; top with cheese and place in cake pan or casserole dish. Top all with remaining filling and sprinkle generously with cheese. Bake in 350° oven a few minutes, or until cheese melts.

Big Pot Stew

Brenda Hauser

2 med. onions, quartered from stem to root
4 garlic cloves, mashed
1/2 T. seafood seasoning, such as Old Bay
Salt

1 lemon, halved
2 lb. sm. red potatoes
2 lb. kielbasa, cut into 16 pieces
8 ears com, husked & halved
2 (21- to 2S-count) shrimp
Lemon wedges & melted butter

Pour 3 quarts of water into a large, heavy-duty roasting pan set over 2 burners or into a very large kettle, such as a lobster or crab pot. Add the onions, garlic, seafood seasoning (yes, 1/2 cup is correct) and salt to taste. Squeeze lemon juice into the stock, then toss in the lemon halves. Bring to a boil over medium-high heat. Add potatoes and kielbasa; return to a boil. Cover pan with foil or partially cover pot with lid. Reduce heat and simmer, cooking until potatoes are just tender, about 20 minutes. Add com; increase heat to medium-high and cook, covered, until tender, about 5 minutes longer. Stir shrimp into hot broth; let stand, covered, until they are just cooked, about 2 minutes. Serve seafood, sausage and vegetables on 1 or 2 large platters, with lemon wedges and small bowls of melted butter.

Breakfast Casserole

Brenda Hauser

4 c. or so fresh bread cubes
2 lb. sausage links
1 Lb. Longhorn cheese, grated
10 eggs

Salt & pepper, to taste
Dry mustard, to taste
1 c. mushrooms, fresh or canned

WHITE SAUCE:

1/2 c. cube margarine
3 T. flour

2 c. milk, until smooth, thin sauce

Layer bread cubes in greased 9x13-inch pan, then cut up sausage links over bread, then a layer of cheese. Pour eggs and seasonings over cheese, then white sauce and mushrooms. Refrigerate overnight. Bake at 300° for 1 hour.

Breakfast Pie

Betty Black

4 slices bread, or 1 (9") unbaked pie crust
6 oz. mild Cheddar cheese, shredded
8 oz. sausage, cooked, drained & crumbled

4 eggs, beaten
3/4 c. milk
1/2 tsp. salt
1/4 tsp. pepper

Lay bread slices flat on bottom of 8-inch square dish or line pastry shell with half of grated cheese, then cooked sausage and remaining cheese.
Combine egg, milk, salt and pepper. Beat well. Pour over ingredients in pastry shell or bread-lined baking dish. Bake at 375° for 30 to 35 minutes, until knife inserted in center comes out clean. Note: Make the night before and refrigerate until morning. This recipe is from my wonderful cousin in North Carolina. We rarely get to see each other, but are connected by swapping recipes by mail and phone.

California Zucchini Bake

Sharon Massey

1 Lb. ground beef
1 c. chopped scallions
1 tsp. minced garlic
1 T. chili powder
2 tsp. salt

2 (4 oz.) cans chopped green chilies
3 c. cooked rice
1 c. sour cream
3 c. shredded Monterey Jack cheese
3 c. sliced zucchini

Preheat oven to 350°. Butter a 2 1/2-quart casserole. Saute ground beef with scallions and garlic. Drain excess fat. Add chili powder, salt, chilies, rice, sour cream and 1 cup cheese. Layer zucchini, meat-rice mixture and remaining 2 cups cheese in prepared casserole in thirds, ending with layer of cheese. Bake for 25 to 35 minutes, uncovered.

Carousel Burgers

Dianna Haywood

1 1/2 lb. ground beef
2 T. ketchup
1 tsp. vinegar
1 tsp. Worcestershire sauce
1 1/2 tsp. salt

1/8 tsp. pepper
1/3 c. carrots, grated
1 sm. onion, chopped
1 egg

Mix all ingredients and bake in a loaf pan at 350° for 1 hour. Or, make into patties, chill and fry. Or, bake on low for 6 hours in the crock-pot. We are beef producers here in Central Iowa and this is a favorite wherever it is served to family, friends, or even beef promotions.

MAIN DISH

Chalupa

Debbie Trammel

1 (3 lb.) chuck roast, trimmed well
2 lb. pinto beans
4 cloves garlic
1 tsp. cumin
1 tsp. oregano
2 (7 oz.) cans green chilies
2 T. chili powder
1 T. salt
2 sm. onions

Soak pinto beans overnight. Drain, cover with water, and bring to a boil. Trim all fat from the roast and cut into l-inch cubes. Add to beans. Mince garlic and onions. Add to cooking pot. Add remaining ingredients. Cook, uncovered, to thicken, at least 6 hours. Serve with warm tortillas or on crisp corn tortillas with shredded lettuce, chopped tomatoes, sour cream, guacamole, salsa and grated Longhorn and Monterey Jack cheeses.

Cheese Boats

Brenda Hauser

18 French rolls
I lb. Longhorn cheese, grated
3 sm. green onions, chopped
1 Lg. can pitted olives
2 T. vinegar
4 eggs, hard-boiled
1 sm. can green chilies
1 (8 oz.) can tomato sauce
1/2 c. oil

Slice top off roll and remove center. (Save for dressing or bread crumbs.) Mix cheese, onions, olives, eggs, chilies, tomato sauce, oil and vinegar in a large bowl. Fill cavity of roll and put top on. Wrap each in foil and freeze. Bake at 375° for 20 minutes or so. You really must try these. They are so good.

Cheesy Chicken & Rice Casserole

Ashley Hollamon

1 (10 3/4 oz.) can Campbell's cream of chicken soup
1 1/3 c. water
3/4 c. uncooked long-grain white rice
2 c. fresh or frozen vegetables
1/2 tsp, onion powder
4 skinless, boneless chicken breast
1/2 c. reduced-fat shredded Cheddar cheese

Stir soup, water, rice, vegetables and onion powder in an 8xl2-inch shallow baking dish. Top with chicken. Season chicken as desired. Cover. Bake at 375° for 45 minutes, or until done. Top with cheese. Yield: 4 servings.

Chicken Casserole

Kristi Hauser Bright

4 chicken breasts, cut up
1 pkg. frozen broccoli
1 can cream of mushroom soup
1 can cream of chicken soup
1 c. grated cheese
1 box Stove Top stuffing

Cook chicken breasts in boiling water for a few minutes. Drain and put into casserole dish. Put frozen broccoli on top, then soups, which have been combined, and grated cheese. Mix Stove Top stuffing as directed on package and pat on top. Bake at 350° for 40 minutes.

Chicken Enchiladas

Kayla Toth

18 corn tortillas
Canola oil
2 cans chicken or
2 cups cooked, shredded chicken
1 sm can green chilis
½ cup sour cream
1 can cream of chicken soup
2 cups cheese
1 can Green enchilada sauce

Heat oil in small saucepan and dip tortillas, one at a time, briefly. You want the tortilla soft, not hard. Stack on a plate with paper towels to soak up excess oil. Mix chicken, green chilis, sour cream and soup in a bowl. Pour a small amount of enchilada sauce in bottom of a 13 x 9 baking pan. Put about a half cup of chicken in a tortilla along with some cheese, roll up, and put in baking dish. Once finished with all tortillas, pour the remaining enchilada sauce over all enchiladas and top with a cup and a half of cheese. Back at 350 degrees for 35 to 40 minutes, until sauce is bubbling.

Chicken Fingers

Mitchell Ferguson

6 boneless, skinless chicken breasts
1 egg, beaten
1 c. buttermilk
1/2 tsp. garlic powder
1 c. flour
1 c. seasoned bread crumbs
1 tsp. salt
1 tsp, baking powder
Oil, for frying

Cut chicken into 1/2-inch strips. Combine egg, buttermilk and garlic powder; pour over chicken and refrigerate 2 to 4 hours. Drain. Combine in bag the flour, crumbs, salt and baking powder. Coat and fry in a little oil until golden brown. Drain on paper towels. Yield: 6 servings. Every kid's favorite.

MAIN DISH

Chicken Mornay

Teddy Whitaker

8 chicken breasts (I cube them for ease at the buffet)
1 (8 oz.) pkg. sliced Swiss cheese
1 can cream of chicken soup
1 can cream of celery soup
1/2 c. milk
1 pkg. Stove Top chicken stuffing mix with seasoning

Butter a 9x13-inch pan. Layer chicken breasts. Layer Swiss cheese on top of breasts. Mix soups and milk. Spread over chicken and cheese. Spread stuffing mix on top. Dot with butter; cover and bake for 1 1/2 hours at 300°.

Chicken Pot Pie

Cheryl Johnson

3 boneless, skinless chicken breasts
2 med. potatoes, peeled & cubed
1 c. chopped carrots
1 c. chopped broccoli
1/2 c. frozen peas
1 med. onion, quartered
2 cloves garlic
1/2 c. kernel corn
1 can cream of mushroom soup
2 Pillsbury all-ready pie crusts

Preheat oven to 450°. Place chicken in boiling water. Cook 15 minutes. Add onion, potatoes and carrots. When potatoes are almost done (10 to 15 minutes), add remaining ingredients, except for soup. Let stand for 2 minutes off of heat. Drain. Separate chicken from vegetables in a large bowl; add vegetables, chicken (cut up) and soup. Mix well. Put into pie crust. Put top crust over and seal crusts together. Bake for 20 to 25 minutes, until golden brown, and enjoy!
Variation: Instead of using the pie crust, place ingredients in skillet. Top with a can of biscuits and bake in oven until the biscuits are golden brown. (Bake at 400° for about 20 to 25 minutes.)

Chicken Spaghetti

Lisa Enright

2 chicken breasts
1 pkg. spaghetti
1 can cream of mushroom or chicken soup
1 stick margarine
Chopped green pepper (opt.)
Chopped onion, to taste
1/2 to 1 c. milk
1 pkg. shredded Cheddar cheese

Boil chicken until done; save broth to boil spaghetti in and drain. In a small pan, melt butter, add onions and peppers. Add soup to mixture. Place cubed chicken, spaghetti and above mixture into a 9x13- inch pan. Place cheese on top and bake at 350° for 30 to 40 minutes.

Chicken with Dumplings

Martha Vick

Boil hen or good-sized fryer until tender in salted water. Remove chicken from liquid and set aside to cool.

DUMPLINGS:

2 c. plain flour
3 T. shortening

1 tsp. Salt
2 buds garlic

Mix all ingredients, adding enough ice water to make a soft dough. Roll on floured board and cut into strips, 1 1/2 inches wide and desired lengths. Drop in boiling liquid (from boiling chicken) and let boil 1 to 2 minutes. Add boned chicken and 1 teaspoon black pepper, and heat well. Serve hot in casserole dish. Delicious reheated.

Chili Cheese Puff

Teddy Whitaker

12 eggs, beaten
1 pt. cottage cheese
1 Lb. Cheddar cheese, shredded

1 cube melted butter
1/2 c. Bisquick
1 can diced Ortega green chilies

Mix together all ingredients and pour into a 9 x 13-inch pan. Bake at 350° for 35 to 45 minutes. Insert knife to test. It is done when knife comes out clean. Let stand a few minutes, can be cut into squares for serving. Great for brunch.

Corn Stuffing

Pam Oxendale

4 strips bacon, diced
1/2 c. onion, diced
3 c. collard or mustard greens, stemmed & chopped (I use spinach)
2/3 c. fresh corn (I use 1 c.)
1/2 c. red bell pepper, diced

3 T. chicken broth
1 jalapeno, seeded & minced
1 c. purchased prepared cornbread, crumbled
1/4 tsp. cayenne pepper
Salt, to taste
4 chicken breasts

Saute bacon until crisp, about 10 minutes. Add onion and greens; cook until tender. Stir in bell pepper and jalapeno. Cook 2 minutes. Add corn and broth. Cook 2 more minutes. Off heat, add cornbread and spices. At this point, it can be cooled and saved for another day, or on a foil- wrapped baking sheet. Spoon stuffing into 4 mounds. Lay a chicken breast over each mound (I pound the breasts in a gallon Ziploc bag to 1/2-inch thickness to shorten cooking time.) Bake at 350° for 20 to 40 minutes, depending on thickness of chicken. Yield: 4 servings. It takes quite a bit of chopping, but otherwise is very easy and tasty.

Crock-Pot Stuffing

Nettie Eurom

15 c. dry bread cubes or crumbs
1 Lb. turkey sausage
1 1/2 c. chopped celery
1 c. chopped onion
1/2 tsp. poultry seasoning
2 (14 oz.) cans chicken broth

Put bread in crock-pot and crumble sausage on top. Mix rest of ingredients together and put on bread and mix well. Cook in crock-pot on high for 4 hours or oven bake at 350° for 50 minutes.

Crock-Pot Tex Mex Pork Stew

Leonor Nelson

1 onion, chopped
4 cloves garlic, minced
2 lb. boneless pork top loin
1/4 c. cornmeal
1/2 tsp. salt
1/8 tsp. white pepper
1/2 tsp. cumin seeds
1/2 tsp. dried oregano leaves
1 (15 oz.) can chili beans, in sauce, undrained
1 (14 oz.) can diced tomatoes with onions & garlic, undrained
2 c. chicken broth
2 c. frozen corn, thawed

In a 5- to 6-quart crock-pot, mix together onion and garlic. Cut pork into 1 1/2-inch cubes and place on top of onions. In a small bowl, mix cornmeal, salt, pepper, cumin and oregano. Sprinkle over pork cubes and mix to coat. Add undrained chili beans, undrained tomatoes and chicken broth to pork mixture. Cover crock-pot and cook on low for 8 to 10 hours, or until pork is thoroughly cooked. Add corn, cover crock-pot and cook on high for 15 to 20 minutes, or until stew is thoroughly heated. Yield: 6 servings.

Divine Waistline Potatoes

Ben Hauser

1/2 stick butter
2 T olive oil
2 T minced garlic
2 T flour
1/2 onion, diced
1 1/2 cup of milk
1 can cream of mushroom soup (I usually use 2)
1 can cream of chicken soup
1 Lb turkey or ham
1 Lb Mexican mix cheese

Put all ingredients in a pan and heat on medium high heat Add in slowly: milk, soup, chicken soup. Cook on medium heat until desired thickness. Add more milk if too thick.

In a baking pan, add: 3 - 5 pounds of sliced russet potatoes, depending on size of your pan 1 Lb turkey or ham, 1 Lb Mexican mix cheese. Pour sauce over potatoes and meat and mix in until they're all covered. Sprinkle cheese on top. Bake at 350 degrees F for 1 to 1 1/2 hours, until potatoes are soft.

Do-Ahead Brunch Bake

Teddy Whitaker

6 c. hash browns
1 c. chopped/cubed ham (you may leave out & use peppers)
2 c. grated Cheddar cheese (may substitute low-fat cheese)
2 c. milk (may substitute 1 % low-fat milk)

1 can cream of mushroom soup
6 eggs (may substitute Egg Beaters)
1 tsp. ground mustard
1/4 tsp. pepper
1/2 sm. onion, chopped

Spray a 9x 13 x 2-inch baking dish with nonstick spray. Place potatoes evenly in dish. Top with cubed ham, chopped onion and 1 cup grated cheese. Combine milk, soup, eggs, mustard and pepper, mixing thoroughly. Pour over potato mixture in pan. Cover and refrigerate overnight. Remove from refrigerator 30 minutes prior to baking. Bake at 350° for 1 hour. Uncover and sprinkle with remaining cheese. Bake 20 minutes longer. Casserole is done when toothpick comes out clean. Let stand 5 minutes before serving. You may also add chopped green chili or bell peppers. Also good with salsa spread on top when served.

Dolmathes - Greek Stuffed Grape leaves

Tammie Dunn

1 jar grape leaves
3 Lbs hamburger
3 eggs
2 cups rice
1/2 cup butter
2 small cans tomato sauce
1 tsp salt

1/2 tsp pepper
3 T mint flakes
1 T oregano
1 T parsley
1 tsp garlic salt
*Optional: 1 can diced tomatoes

Open grape leaves and pour the liquid into large stick pot. Remove leaves, cut off stems. In separate bowl, mix all ingredients. Once mixed, take about 1 table spoon full of mixture and place into grape leaf. Roll like a burrito. Place into stock pot. Repeat until mixture is gone. Add water to pot, enough to cover bottom layer of dolmathes. Simmer in stock pot for about 1 hour. Keep enough water in pot to cover bottom layer of dol mathes, sometimes the water will evaporate. Just add more if necessary. If you run out of grape leaves but still have hamburger mixture, just roll out golf ball sized balls and place on top of rolled leaves. Garnish with sour cream and lemon slices. *Optional: add 1 can diced tomatoes on top of dolmathes before simmering.

Easy Green Chile

Bertie Lightfoot

1 1/2 lb. pork (boneless shoulder), diced
1 c. all-purpose flour
3 T. vegetable oil
4 (4 oz.) cans whole green chilies, cut into 1" pieces
1 med. onion, chopped

1 (14 oz.) can crushed tomatoes
1 tsp. salt
1 tsp. garlic powder
1 c. water
1/2 tsp. ground cumin
1 tsp. chili powder
1/2 tsp. ground oregano

Add flour to pork and toss to coat. Heat oil in a large skillet and add coated pork. Brown well. Add remaining ingredients and simmer for 20 minutes. Serve wrapped in a warm flour tortilla. Yield: 4 servings.

Easy Lasagna

Dianna Haywood

1 1/2 lb. ground beef
1 onion
1 qt. tomatoes
8 oz. spaghetti sauce
2 c. water (or use 2 qt. homemade spaghetti sauce)

2 c. cottage cheese
1/4 c. Parmesan cheese
1 egg
12 oz. (or more) Mozzarella cheese
1 pkg. lasagna noodles, raw

Brown beef and onion; drain. Add the tomatoes, spaghetti sauce and water or homemade spaghetti sauce and simmer 15 minutes. Mix cottage cheese, Parmesan cheese and egg together. Grate Mozzarella cheese. In a 9x13-inch pan, layer meat mixture, uncooked lasagna noodles, cottage cheese mixture and Mozzarella cheese, ending with cheese on top. Make sure noodles are covered with sauce. Cover pan with foil and bake for 45 minutes at 350°. Take foil off with 15 minutes left. Note: May be prepared ahead of time and refrigerated or frozen. If frozen, add cheese after thawed. Suggestion: Cook the day before and warm up the day of serving. Stays together better.

Enchilada Casserole

Hazel Pyle Fuller

2 lb. lean ground beef
1 can cream of celery soup
1 can cream of mushroom soup
1 Lg. onion, chopped

2 cans diced green chilies
1 Lg can enchilada sauce
12 corn tortillas
2 c. or so grated Longhorn cheese

In a large pan, brown beef and add onions until soft. Add soups and chilies. Heat enchilada sauce in a small saucepan and dip each tortilla to soften. Place 4 in bottom of a 9x13-inch pan, pour half of meat mixture and cheese, 4 more tortillas, rest of meat and more cheese. End with 4 more tortillas and pour all of hot enchilada sauce over this. Top with cheese and bake for 20 to 30 minutes at 350°, or until bubbly.

Fajita Marinade

Jacob Gould

1 Lb chicken, shrimp or steak
4 - 6 T canola oil
2 T lemon juice
1 tsp salt
1 tsp dried oregano
1 tsp cumin

1 tsp garlic powder
1 tsp chili powder
1 tsp paprika (I use smoked paprika)
1 tsp red pepper flakes

Combine all ingredients in a large ziplock bag or container and marinate for 2 to 6 hours.

Fiesta Tamale Pie

Brenda Hauser

1 sm. onion, minced
1 clove garlic, minced
3 T. butter
3 T. olive oil
1 1/2 lb. ground beef
1 (No. 2 1/2) can tomatoes
1 (No. 2 1/2) can whole kernel corn

2 tsp. salt
2 tsp. chili powder
20 to 24 pitted ripe olives
1 c. cornmeal
1 c. milk
2 eggs, well beaten
1 1/2 c. grated American cheese

Heat oven to 350°. Saute onion and garlic in butter and oil until yellow. Add ground beef; cook until brown. Simmer tomatoes, corn, salt and chili powder in saucepan 20 minutes; add meat mixture. Pour into 7 1/2 x 11 1/2 x 1 1/2" pan. Press olives into mixture. Mix cornmeal, milk and eggs and cook until thick. Spread over filling. Sprinkle with grated cheese. Bake 1 hour. Yield: 8 to 10 servings.

Garlic & Lemon Chicken

Patty Hauser Ink

4 Tablespoons Olive Oil
2 Lemons. 1 Thin Sliced And 1 Juiced
4 Cloves Garlic Minced
1 Tsp Salt
1/4Tsp Pepper

3/4 Pounds Green Beans
8 Small Red Potatoes Quartered
4 Chicken Breasts

Bake At 400 Degrees. Coat Bottom Of Pan With Olive Oil, Arrange Sliced Lemons In Bottom Of Pan And Rest Ingredient's Cover And Bake Until Chicken Is Tender.

Goulash

Brenda Hauser

1 1/2 lb. hamburger, lean
1 onion, chopped
1 Lg. can tomatoes

1 can kidney, pinto or chili beans
1/2 pkg. elbow macaroni, cooked
Salt & pepper, to taste

Brown hamburger and onion; add tomatoes, beans, macaroni and seasonings. I also add 1 small can chopped green chilies. This is a generational favorite

Green Chile Burros

Patty Hauser Ink

2 T. oil
1 med. onion, chopped
1 can stewed tomatoes, drained (save liquid)
1 Lb. round steak, cut in chunks
2 c. water, tomato liquid included in water measurement

2 T. granulated bouillon, or 2 cubes
2 T. flour
Salt & pepper, to taste
1 clove garlic, or 1 tsp. garlic salt
Sprinkle of oregano, to taste
2 sm. cans green chilies

Saute meat and onion in oil. When brown, add tomatoes and pimentos. Mix bouillon and flour in water and tomato liquid. Stir. Add rest of ingredients. Simmer approximately 15 minutes, or until meat is tender. Yield: 12 burros. Note: Make Sure flour tortillas are room temperature when filling, otherwise, you will have broken burros. These can be made ahead of time, wrapped in foil, and refrigerated or frozen.

Green Chile Pie

Jennifer Fuller

1 1/2 C Pepper Jack, Shredded - This Is The Crust Spray Pam In Pie Pan And Spread Cheese In Pan.

2/3 C Canned Milk (Can Substitute Cream) & 1/3 C Regular Milk
1/4 Tsp Cumin
1/2 Tsp Salt
1/4 Tsp Pepper

1 C Cheddar, Shredded
3 Eggs, Beaten
4 Oz. Can Chopped Green Chiles

Mix All Together And Pour Over Pepper Jack Bake At 325 For 40 Minutes Or Till Center Is Done. Let Cool 5 Minutes Before Serving I've Accidentally Added The Cheese That's For The Crust To The Rest Of The Ingredients And Other Than It Takes Quite A Bit Longer To Bake It Turns Out Just Fine.

Green Chili-Corn Tamales

Teddy Whitaker

5 Lb. masa
1 lb. lard
1 stick butter
2 cans white kernel corn
2 cans white creamed corn
Salt

About 2 lb. finely-chopped roasted green chilies (depends on how hot it is)
2 to 2 1/2 lb. grated Cheddar & Monterey Jack cheese
1 pkg. corn husks (Hojas)
Deli wrap (the grocery store has it in the meat department)

Whip lard and butter until smooth and creamy. Add masa, a little bit at a time, adding creamed corn (depending on the size of you mixer, you may have to do 2 batches). Beat about 3 minutes. Transfer to a large bowl and add the 2 cans of the kernel corn. Mix well and add salt to taste. Add chili and cheese. Mix well. Corn Husk: Clean the corn silks off, then put them in warm water to clean them and this softens them so they are pliable; drain. You may want to do this before you do your dough. To Assemble: Take a husk and drop a heaping tablespoon of corn masa on the left side of the husk and roll to the right side and fold up the end. Wet the ends of the deli wrap; put the tamale on one corner and roll in, then fold the 2 corners in and roll to the end and the wet corner should seal the tamale in (hope this makes sense), then cook them or freeze in freezer bags. To Cook: Steam for about 45 minutes, or when you test one, that it is firm. If frozen, cook for about 11/2 minutes, or until done. I usually take them out of the freezer and let them thaw out some before cooking and it doesn't take as long. This batter can be refrigerated the night before and made the next day.

MAIN DISH

Green Chili and Rice Casserole

Lori Boyce

1 can sliced mushrooms, drained
1 c. onions
2 T. oleo
1 can cream of mushroom soup
1/2 c. milk
1 can chopped green chilies

1 tsp. salt
1/4 tsp. pepper
3 c. cooked rice
2 T. diced pimentos
1 1/2 c. grated Cheddar cheese

Saute onions in butter until transparent. Add remaining ingredients, reserving 1 cup of cheese. Turn into a greased shallow 2-quart casserole. Top with remaining cheese. Bake at 350° for 20 to 30 minutes.

Ground Meat Casserole

Carolyn Howell

1 Lb. ground beef or turkey
1 can chicken noodle soup
1 can cream of mushroom soup

1/2 c. uncooked rice
1 c. diced celery
Chopped onion, to taste

Brown meat with onion. May add a dash of Worcestershire sauce or a little sage (optional). Mix with rest of ingredients. I also add pepper~ but no salt. Put into a 2-quart casserole and bake in 350° oven for 1 hour, covered. This is a simple, easy-to-make dish that is quite good. Serve with a salad and a green vegetable. Should feed 4 to 6 people, depending on appetite. Enjoy.

Hawaiian Pork

Dianna Haywood

1 1/2 lb. lean shoulder pork (1" pieces)
1/4 c. shortening
1/4 c. water
2 T. cornstarch
1/4 c. brown sugar
1 c. pineapple juice

1/2 c. green peppers
2 1/2 c. pineapple chunks
1/2 tsp. salt
1/3 c. vinegar
1 T. soy sauce
1 med. onion, sliced

Brown pork in shortening. Add water; cover and cook for about 1 hour over low heat. Combine other ingredients, except peppers, onion and pineapple chunks, in a saucepan. Cook, stirring constantly, until slightly thickened. Pour sauce over hot pork. Allow to stand for 10 minutes. Stir in peppers, onion and pineapple. Cook for about 5 minutes. Serve over hot rice. Chunks of chicken may be substituted for the pork.

Hungarian Gulyas

Toth Family

2 lbs of beef stew cubes, diced into bite size
2 onions, diced
2 cups diced potatoes
6 Hungarian yellow peppers (substitute 6 small Mexican peppers)

3 Large tomatoes, skinned and diced
Vegetable oil
4 T Hungarian Paprika (sweet)
1 T caraway seed Salt
Parsley

Preparation:
Cook onions in oil until glossy. Add the meat, stir on high heat until the meat is browned. Take the pot off the fire, salt it and add the paprika. Stir and replace to fire on lower heat. This will prevent the soup from becoming bitter. Add warm water to cover the meat, then add the caraway seed and cover pot. When the meat is almost tender, add the potatoes, peppers and tomatoes. Add more salt as needed and cook until potatoes are tender. Remove several cooked potatoes and mash, then add back to soup. The last few minutes add parsley. Total cook time is about 2-3 hours.

Instant Pot Creamy Bacon Ranch Crack Chicken

Brenda Hauser

6 - 9 strips of bacon, chopped
1 cup chicken broth
1 pkg ranch seasoning
2 Lbs chicken breasts

8 oz light cream cheese, softened and cubed
1/2 cup Monterey jack cheese
4 green onions, chopped

Turn instant pot on to saute mode and cook the chopped bacon for 5 to 7 minutes until crisped. Scoop out bacon onto paper towel and drain grease from pot. Put bacon back in pan and add chicken broth, ranch seasoning and chicken. Seal the pot, press manual and set timer for 12 minutes. Since the pot has been sauteing for a bit and is already hot, it should only take around 5 to 7 minutes to reach pressure. When timer goes off, allow 5 minutes for natural pressure release, and then turn the valve to vent to quick release the rest. Remove chicken from pot and shred with 2 forks. Set the pot back to saute and add cream cheese, whisking for a few minutes until melted. Put shredded chicken back in the pot and stir to combine. Serve over rice or pasta. Top with shredded cheese and chopped green onions.

Instant Pot Hamburger Soup

Sherry Hauser

1 T olive oil
1 lb ground beef
2 T tomato paste
15 oz diced tomatoes
32 oz beef broth

15 oz frozen green beans
15 oz frozen peas
1 Lb (or more if you like) diced potatoes
1 T taco seasoning
1 tsp garlic salt
1 tsp Italian seasoning

Place the olive oil in the pot and add ground beef; add in seasoning and cook until brown. Mix in tomato paste and then add remaining ingredients. Add your favorite vegetables to this soup to make it your own. Cook on high pressure for 8 minutes and then once it is done, quick release the valve to "venting" and let the steam release before opening the lid.

Instant Pot White Chicken Chili

Sherry Hauser

1 Lb. boneless skinless chicken breasts
1 yellow onion, diced
2 cloves garlic, minced
24 oz chicken broth
2 (15 oz) cans great Northern beans, drained and rinsed
2 (4 oz) cans of diced green chiles
2 cups frozen sweet corn (best if you have fresh)

Toppings:

Sliced jalapenos
Sliced avocados

1 tsp salt
1/2 tsp black pepper
1 tsp cumin
¾ tsp oregano
1/2 tsp chili powder
1/4 tsp cayenne pepper
4 oz cream cheese, softened
1/4 cup half and half

Sour cream
Tortilla strips
Shredded Mexican cheese

Add chicken breasts to pressure cooker; add onion, garlic, chicken broth, beans, green chiles, corn, salt, pepper, cumin, oregano, chili powder, and cayenne powder. Stir. Cube the cream cheese and place on top of the chili. Cover and seal the lid, cook for 20 minutes on high pressure. Once it is done cooking, let it naturally release for 10 minutes and then switch the valve to "venting" before opening the lid. Remove the chicken and shred. Add the half and half and stir everything together and return the shredded chicken to the pot and mix in. Serve with your favorite toppings.

Jasmine Rice with Garlic, Ginger and Cilantro

Kristi Hauser Bright

3 cups jasmine rice
3 T vegetable oil
1/3 cup finely chopped peeled fresh ginger

3 large garlic doves, minced
½ cups low sodium chicken broth
¾ tsp salt
large bunch of fresh cilantro, coarsely chopped.

Rinse rice in colander under cold running water. Drain. Heat oil in heavy large saucepan over medium-high heat. Add ginger and garlic, stir until fragrant, about 30 seconds. Add rice and stir for 3 minutes. Stir in broth and salt. Sprinkle cilantro over and bring to boil. Reduce heat to medium low, cover and cook until rice is tender, about 18 minutes. Remove from heat. Let stand covered 10 minutes. Fluff rice with fork.

Layered Fiesta Casserole

Lois Baldwin

1 Lb. extra-lean ground beef
1 green pepper, chopped
1 red pepper, chopped
1 (16 oz.) jar chunky salsa
1 can diced tomatoes, undrained

1 pkg. (about 2 c.) frozen corn
12 corn tortillas
1 1/2 c. shredded Cheddar or Longhorn cheese

Preheat oven to 375°. Brown meat with peppers in a large skillet, stirring frequently; drain. Stir in salsa, tomatoes and corn; bring to a boil. Spoon 1 cup meat mixture onto bottom of a 9x13-inch baking dish. Top with 6 tortillas, overlapping as necessary. Spoon half of the remaining meat mixture over tortillas; top with 3/4 cup of cheese. Top with remaining 6 tortillas and meat mixture. Cover with foil. Bake for 25 to 30 minutes, or until heated through. Remove from oven; uncover. Sprinkle with remaining 3/4 cup cheese. Let stand 5 minutes, or until cheese is melted.

Louisiana Black-Eyed Peas

Leonor Nelson

1 LB. dried black-eyed peas
1 Lg. onion, chopped
1 stalk celery, sliced thin
1/2 bell pepper, minced
1 qt. water + 2 c. chicken stock
1/2 tsp. black pepper

1 c. ham, diced
Dash of chili powder
2 T. bacon drippings
2 cloves garlic, chopped fine
4 whole cloves

Saute vegetables in bacon drippings until wilted. Add all other ingredients and bring to a boil. Lower to a simmer and cook until peas are tender and sauce begins to thicken. Stir regularly, and if it begins to dry out before you have a thick sauce, add a little water. It is better to add water, a little at a time. Serve with steaming rice. Leonor is one of the few nurses who worked at the old hospital in Cottonwood and the new one, Verde Valley Medical Center.

MAIN DISH

Mama Jo's Cheeseburger Casserole | Pat "Mama Jo" McDonald

(Not to be confused with Beth's Cheeseburger Casserole)

1 (12 oz.) pkg. Stouffer's macaroni & cheese, defrosted	1 T. yellow mustard
8 oz. ground beef	1 T. dill pickle relish (opt.)
1/2 c. onion, chopped	1 T. dill pickle relish (opt.)
1/2 tsp. garlic powder	1 c. (1 med.) tomato, chopped
3 T. ketchup	1 (7.5 oz.) can refrigerated biscuit dough (enough for 10 biscuits)

Defrost macaroni and cheese in microwave on 50% POWER for 20 to 25 minutes. Place ground beef, onion and garlic powder in a medium skillet. Cook over medium heat, stirring occasionally, until beef is browned and fully cooked; drain. Combine fully-cooked beef mixture, ketchup, mustard and relish in a medium bowl; stir in tomato. Place half of defrosted macaroni and cheese in a 9-inch square baking pan; top with ground beef mixture, then remaining macaroni and cheese. Bake in preheated 400° oven for 25 minutes. Place biscuits around edge of pan. Continue baking for 20 to 25 minutes, or until biscuits are fully cooked and golden brown. Yield: 4 servings.

Meat Balls and Spaghetti | Teddy Whitaker

3 lb. ground beef	1/2 tsp. Basil
1 c. crumbs (Kellogg's bread crumbs is what I use)	1/2 tsp, oregano
1/2 doz. eggs (2 eggs to each lb. of meat	Salt & pepper
	Garlic powder
	Parmesan cheese

Mix and roll into balls and fry until browned. Drop into sauce about 15 minutes before sauce is done. (The reason for this is because the meat balls will absorb the sauce, then you won't have as much sauce.)

SAUCE:

2 (28 oz.) cans tomato puree	1 whole onion
2 (28 oz.) cans whole tomatoes	Chopped parsley or dried parsley
4 sm. cans tomato paste & 1 can of water for each can	Oregano

Simmer for several hours.

Mexican Seafood Enchilada Casserole

Jennifer Fuller

Blend Together And Set Aside:

1 Chopped Onion - Saute In 2 T Butter
3/4 Sliced Mushrooms - Saute With Onion
8 Oz Softened Cream Cheese

1/2 C Cottage Cheese
2 T Dried Basil
1-2 Shakes Cayenne

Combine And Mix With Above:

2 Cans Cream Of Mushroom Soup
1/3 C Half & Half
1/3 C Chicken Bouillon

1/4 to 1/2 C Salsa
1/2 C Diced Green Chiles
1/2 Chopped Jalapenos

Fold In:

8 Oz Lump Crabmeat
1 # Medium Cooked Shrimp
8 Oz Small Scallops (Optional)

1# Shredded Cheddar, Pepper Jack Or Colby Cheese
1 ½ C Grated Parmesan Cheese
6-8 Corn Tortillas

Preheat Oven To 350 And Put Some Tortillas On Bottom Of 9x13 Pan, Then Layer 1/3 Of Seafood Mixture, 1/3 Cheeses, Repeat 2 More Times Ending With Cheese. Bake For 30 Minutes Or Until Lightly Brown.

MAIN DISH

Noodles and Hamburger

Naoma Moore

1 pkg. egg noodles (1/4" size)
2 lb. ground beef
1 Lg. can tomatoes
1 can whole corn
1/2 lb. grated cheese
1 can black pitted olives
4 T. oil

1 chopped bell pepper
1 onion, chopped
4 cloves garlic
Dash of cayenne pepper
1 T. sugar
Salt & pepper

Cook noodles. Brown meat in half of the oil. Add tomatoes and simmer. Brown onion, pepper and garlic in the other half of the oil. Add com and simmer 1 minute. Combine all parts and add olives and juice and half of the cheese. Pour into a 9x13-inch pan. Sprinkle the rest of the cheese on top and bake at 350° until bubbly.

Not Your Mama's Meatloaf

Jennifer Fuller

1# Hamburger
1# Spicy Italian Or Hot Sausage
1 Egg, Beaten
2 Cloves Garlic, Minced
1/2 C Italian Bread Crumbs
1 C Crushed Stacy's Pita Chips, Fritos, Etc

1 Jalapeno, Minced
1 Onion, Minced
1/8 - 1/4 C Bell Pepper, Minced
1/2 C Green Chiles
1 Tsp Cayenne
A Little Salsa
1/2 Tsp Salt & Pepper

Combine All And Bake 400° For 1 + Hour Or Microwave For About 20 Minutes.

One Pot Wonder

Kristi Hauser Bright

16 cups water
1 lg onion
3 T seafood seasoning
2 medium lemons, halved
1 lb small red potatoes
1 lb smoked kielbasa or fully cooked hot links, cut into 1 inch pieces

4 medium ears of corn, cut into thirds
2 lbs uncooked medium shrimp, peeled and deveined
Seafood cocktail sauce
Melted butter

In a stockpot, combine water, onion, seafood seasoning and lemons. Bring to a boil. Add potatoes, cook, uncovered, 10 minutes. Add kielasa and corn, return to boil. Reduce heat and simmer, uncovered for 10 to 12 minutes or until potatoes are tender. Add shrimp, cook 2 to 3 minutes, until shrimp turn pink. Drain and transfer to a bowl. Service with cocktail sauce, butter and additional seafood seasoning.

Pesto

Christine Hauser

2 cups basil
1/2 cup parsley
4 garlic cloves
1/4 cup pine nuts

1/2 cup extra virgin olive oil
1/2 cup Parmigiano Reggiano
1/4 tsp salt

Combine all ingredients in a food processor, cover and puree until smooth. Can be refrigerated for several weeks or frozen in a tight container.

Pizza Casserole

Erma Westermeier

2 lb. ground beef
1 (15 oz.) can tomato sauce
1 c. water
2 (15 oz.) cans pizza sauce with cheese
1 c. onions, chopped
1 Lg. garlic clove
1 1/2 tsp. oregano
1 tsp. sweet basil
1 tsp. salt
1/2 lb. thinly-sliced, skinned pepperoni
3 c. shredded Mozzarella cheese
2 c. elbow macaroni (measured dry, then cooked)

Brown ground beef; drain. Saute onion and garlic; add to ground beef. Add tomato sauce, water, 1 can pizza sauce, oregano, basil and salt. Simmer for 30 minutes. In a 9x13-inch baking dish, place a layer of cooked macaroni, meat sauce, pepperoni and cheese. Repeat, pouring last can of pizza sauce over mixture, and top with a layer of cheese. Bake at 350° for 30 minutes, or until bubbly. Yield: 6 to 8 servings. Note: The secret to this recipe being extra good is using generous amounts of pepperoni and cheese.

Posse Stew

Kay Hauser

3 Lb. hamburger
1 Lg. onion, chopped
2 Lg. cans tomatoes
2 cans corn
2 cans green chilies
2 cans ranch-style beans
2 cans hominy
2 tsp. salt, or to taste
1 tsp. pepper, or to taste
2 tsp. garlic salt, or to taste

Brown hamburger in a large pan; add onions and cook until soft. Add rest of ingredients. This is a great winter dish. Easy and so good with crackers or cornbread.

MAIN DISH

Pozole

Kim Gould

1 T Canola Oil
2 (1 pound) pork tenderloins, cut into I-inch pieces
4 cups chicken broth (can use fat-free; low sodium)
1 ½ tsp ground cumin
1 T dried oregano
½ tsp fresh ground black pepper
¼ tsp ground cloves
1/8 tsp crushed red pepper
4 large garlic cloves, minced
2 (15.5 oz) cans white hominy, rinsed and drained
2 (4.5 oz) cans chopped green chiles, undrained
1 cup chopped cabbage (can use angel hair slaw)
½ cup thinly sliced radishes
3 limes, cut into wedges

Heat a large nonstick skillet over medium-high heat. Add oil to pan and cook pork 8 minutes on all sides. You can also cook the pork slowly in a crock pot. Combine pork, broth, spices, hominy and green chiles. Cook on low heat for 1 hour.
Top with cabbage, radishes and limes.

Red Beans and Rice

Leonor Nelson

1 Lb. dried red kidney beans
2 qt. cold water
1 meaty ham bone, or a thick slice of raw ham, cut into cubes
1/2 lb. hot sausage, sliced thick
1 bunch scallions, including green tops
1 green pepper
2 stalks celery
3 med.-sized onions
Lg. pinch of ground thyme
4 bay leaves
Cayenne pepper or Tabasco sauce
Salt & Pepper
White rice (not instant)

Rinse kidney beans twice. Discard any that look bad. Put beans in a big, heavy pot, at least 3-quart size (4-quart is better). Add water, ham and sausage. Set, uncovered, on a burner at medium heat. While the beans are soaking and warming, chop and add scallions, green pepper, celery and onions. Add thyme and bay leaves. When the mixture boils, reduce heat and cover. Stir every 20 to 30 minutes for 3 hours. Then, with a wooden spoon, mash about 1/4 of the beans against the side of the pot. If they don't mash easily, try again after 1/2 hour. Forty minutes after mashing the beans, taste and season with cayenne pepper or Tabasco sauce. (Don't use too much; this is supposed to be delicious, but subtly flavored.) Cook for another 1/2 hour while preparing white rice. Ladle beans and sauce over lice and serve. Yield: 6 servings.
It's hard to believe, but all the vegetables cook away to nothing. The mashed beans thicken the sauce to a creamy consistency, It's even more flavorful rewarmed after a night in the refrigerator.

Red Beans and Rice, Louisiana-Style

Ruth Hunter

1 lb. red kidney beans, soaked overnight
1 Lg. onion, chopped
2 cloves garlic, chopped
3 stalks parsley, chopped

2 bay leaves
1/2 lb. ham or sausage
2 T. bacon grease or cooking oil
1 1/2 c. raw rice
Salt & pepper, to taste

Heat bacon grease or oil and brown meat in it. Remove meat and saute onion. Cover beans with water in a large deep pot and cook for about 1 hour. Add meat, onion, rice and all seasonings. Cover and cook slowly for 2 hours, stirring now and then, and adding water if it gets too thick. Add salt and pepper to taste. Serve with Tabasco sauce or red pepper vinegar.

Red Chili

Manny Varela

1 beef roast, cooked and cubed - reserve the liquid

2 bags dried New Mexico red chili pods. (pop off tops and shake out seeds)

Bring reserved liquid to boil with 3 cloves of smashed garlic. Put chili pods in boiling liquid until tender, about 3 to 5 minutes. Pour into blender and puree. Put puree and roast back in pan and simmer for 1 to 2 hours. Serve with flour tortillas.

Red Chili with Shredded Beef

Brenda Hauser

1 (2 lb.) beef roast, any cut
1/2 onion, chopped
1/2 c. vegetable oil
1/3 c. flour

8 oz. New Mexico chili powder*
1/2 gal. cold water
1 tsp, garlic powder
1 1/2 tsp. salt, or to taste

Mojave brand in cellophane package, available at most grocery stores. This is pure-ground with no other spices. Cook roast and onions in crock-pot overnight. Remove meat from crock-pot and discard fat. Shred beef and set aside. Heat oil in a large pan and add flour, stirring until flour is golden brown. Whip together chili powder and water, using a wire whisk until smooth. Add to the oil and flour in pan, whipping until all mixed together well. Add shredded beef, garlic powder and salt; bring to a hard boil, stirring often, until thickened. Serve with tortillas or sopapillas.

Santa Fe Chicken and Dressing

Betty Black

3 c. cornbread stuffing mix
2 c. chopped chicken, cooked
1 can green chilies
1/2 jar roasted red bell peppers
1 can cream of chicken soup
1 can cream-style corn

1 c. sour cream
2 tsp. ground cumin, salt & pepper
1 c. shredded Monterey Jack cheese
Tortilla chips
Chunky salsa

Stir stuffing mix, chicken, chilies and peppers in a large bowl. Add soup, corn, sour cream and seasonings. Spread in a 2-quart baking dish. Bake, covered, at 350º for 25 minutes. Uncover, sprinkle with cheese, and bake 5 minutes more. Serve with chips and salsa.

Shepherd's Pie

Aymee Wilson

Beef and Vegetable Layer:

1 Lb ground beef
1 1/2 c chopped onion
3/4 c chopped carrots
1/2 c peas
1/2 c corn kernels
2 T butter

2 T flour
1 T fresh thyme leaves
1 clove garlic, minced
1 c beef stock
Salt and pepper

Mashed potato layer:

2 lb. Yukon Gold potatoes, peeled and cut into large cubes
1/2 c heavy cream

1/4 c milk
3 T butter, melted
1 c grated cheese
Salt and pepper

Brown beef in large skillet, until fully cooked, about 5 minutes. Add onion and carrot. Season with salt and pepper and cook for about 10 minutes. Add peas and corn and cook for 2 minutes. Add butter to the pan and stir in flour, thyme and garlic. Stir for 1 minute. Add beef stock and bring to a boil. Cook for a minute or two until broth thickens into a light sauce. Remove from heat and transfer mixture to an 8 x 8 baking dish. Preheat oven to 425º.
To make mash potatoes, place cubed potatoes in a pot of water and bring to boil. Cook for about 5 minutes, until potato cubes are fork tender. Drain and spread potatoes out on a sheet pan in single layer and let sit for a few minutes. Use a fork or potato masher to mash the potatoes, then stir in cream, milk, butter and cheese. Season with salt and pepper. Spread mixture on top of beef and vegetable mixture and bake for 20 - 25 minutes.

Short Ribs Burgundy

Pat Boler

3 lb. short ribs, cut 2" to 3" long, or
3 lb. country-style spare ribs
3 T. oil
1 med.-sized onion, chopped
1 T. Worcestershire sauce
1 tsp. dry mustard
1/2 c. celery, diced

2 tsp, salt
1/4 c. vinegar
2 T. brown sugar
1/2 c. tomato catsup
1/2 c. Burgundy or other red table wine

Trim excess fat off meat. Brown ribs in hot oil; drain off all fat. Add remaining ingredients. Cover and cook slowly, or bake at 350° for 1 1/2 hours. Yield: 4 or 5 servings.

Shrimp Scampi

Kristi Hauser Bright

4 garlic cloves, minced
¼ cup butter
¼ cup olive oil
1 pound fresh shrimp, peeled and deveined
¼ cup lemon juice
¼ tsp red pepper flakes

¼ tsp dried oregano
½ cup grated Parmesan cheese
¼ cup dry bread crumbs
¼ cup fresh parsley, minced Hot cooked angel hair pasta

Saute garlic in butter and oil until fragrant. Add shrimp, lemon juice, red pepper flakes, and oregano; cook and stir until shrimp turn pink. Transfer to small baking dish. Sprinkle with cheese, bread crumbs and parsley. Broil for 2-3 minutes until topping is golden brown. Serve over pasta and sprinkle with fresh parmesan cheese.

Southwest Fiesta Baked Dish

Clara Miller

1 lb. ground beef or turkey, browned
1 can ranch-style beans
1 can diced green chilies

1 c. grated cheese, any kind
1 pkg. tortilla chips, any kind
Black olives, for garnish

Crush tortilla chips on bottom of a I-quart casserole dish. Layer meat (seasoned with salt, pepper and garlic powder), beans and chilies. Top with cheese and olives. Bake at 375° for 20 minutes.

MAIN DISH

Spaghetti with Eggplant Sauce

Brenda Hauser

1/2 c. olive oil
1 eggplant, cut in 1" cubes
1/2 c. onion, chopped
1 clove garlic, crushed
2 T. parsley, chopped
1 can Italian-style tomatoes
1 can tomato paste

1/2 c. dry red wine, or 1/2 c. chicken or vegetable broth
1 can mushrooms
1 tsp. oregano
1 tsp. salt
1 tsp. sugar
1 lb. spaghetti
Grated Parmesan cheese

In a 4-quart Dutch oven, heat oil. Add eggplant cubes, onion, garlic and parsley. Cook until tender, 5 minutes or so. Stir in tomatoes, tomato paste, wine, mushrooms, oregano, salt and sugar. Break up tomatoes with fork. Reduce heat, cover, and simmer for 45 minutes. Serve over spaghetti. Sprinkle with Parmesan cheese.

Stuffed Bell Peppers

Kristi Hauser Bright

1 Lb. ground beef
1/2 lb. sausage, Italian (opt.)
1/2 c. chopped onion
1/2 tsp. garlic powder
1 T. basil
1 T. oregano

Salt & pepper
1 (16 oz.) can stewed tomatoes
1 (8 oz.) can tomato sauce
1/4 c. water
1 c. instant rice
2 oz. Mozzarella cheese, grated

Cut tops off peppers, remove seeds and membranes. Parboil 5 minutes and drain. Saute beef and onion and sausage in a large skillet until lightly browned. Add garlic powder, spices, tomatoes, 1/2 can tomato sauce, water and rice. Stir well. Bring to a boil; reduce heat and cook, uncovered, 20 minutes. Place peppers in a 2-quart casserole; stuff with meat mixture. Spoon remaining meat mixture around peppers; top with remaining tomato sauce. Cover; cook 30 minutes at 350°. Uncover; top with cheese. Cook 10 minutes. Yield: 4 servings.

Stuffing Balls

Lisa Runk

2 bags bread cubes
1 box stove top stuffing
1 T poultry seasoning
5 eggs, beaten

2 cans cream of chicken soup
2 cups milk
2 sticks butter, melted

Mix ingredients and shape into balls. Spray pan with non-stick spray. Bake covered for 40 minutes at 350 degrees, then uncovered for 20 minutes. These can be frozen.

Super Zuppa (Minestrone)

Brenda Hauser

2 T. olive oil
1 med. onion, diced
2 med. carrots, diced
1 celery stalk, diced
2 med. zucchini, diced
1 garlic clove, minced
3 med. potatoes (about 3/4 lb.),
unpeeled & diced
3 c. thinly-sliced Savoy cabbage
1 (15 1/2 oz.) can cannellini beans,
drained

1 (14 1/2 oz.) can diced tomatoes,
undrained
2 (14 oz.) cans low-sodium chicken
broth
3 c. water
1/2 tsp. dried rosemary
1/2 tsp. salt
1/2 tsp. pepper
Grated Parmesan cheese

Heat oil in a large stockpot over medium heat. Add onion; cook, stirring occasionally, 6 minutes, or until softened. Add carrots and celery; cook, stirring occasionally, 3 minutes. Add remaining ingredients, except cheese. Cover and bring to a boil; reduce heat and simmer gently 1 to 2 hours. Serve with Parmesan cheese. Yield: 6 servings.

Sweet and Sour Chicken

Kay Hauser

1 (8 oz.) jar Russian salad dressing
1 (10 oz.) jar apricot jam

1 env. Lipton onion soup
8 pieces chicken, skinned

Skin chicken (breasts and thighs work well) and bake in heavy, foil lined pan for about 1/2 hour at 375°. Drain excess liquid. Pour part of the sauce over chicken and continue cooking 1 to 1 1/2 hours at 350°. Add sauce as needed to keep chicken well basted. Serve with rice. Yield: 6 to 8 servings. Can be easily doubled or tripled.

Taco Casserole

Jerri Reddell

1 1/2 lb. ground beef
1 med. onion, chopped
2 tsp. salt
1/2 tsp. pepper
1 T. chili powder

1 (8 oz.) can tomato sauce
1 med. can enchilada sauce
1 doz. corn tortillas
1 can chopped black olives
1/2 lb. grated Longhorn cheese

Brown beef and onions, then add remaining ingredients, except tortillas, cheese and olives. Butter each tortilla and layer alternately with meat sauce, cheese and olives. Add 1 cup water. Cover and bake for 40 minutes at 400°.

Taco Crescent Bake

Brenda Hauser

1 (8 oz.) tube refrigerated crescent rolls
2 c. crushed corn chips, divided
1 1/2 lb. ground beef

1 (15 oz.) can tomato sauce
1 env. taco seasoning
1 c. (8 oz.) sour cream
1 c. (4 oz.) shredded Cheddar cheese

Unroll crescent dough into a rectangle; press onto the bottom and 1 inch up the sides of a greased 9x13x2-inch baking dish. Seal seams and perforations. Sprinkle with 1 cup of chips; set aside. In a large skillet, cook beef over medium heat until no longer pink; drain. Stir in tomato sauce and taco seasoning; bring to a boil. Reduce heat; simmer, uncovered, for 5 minutes. Spoon over chips. Top with sour cream, cheese and remaining chips. Bake, uncovered, at 350º for 25 to 30 minutes, or until crust is lightly browned.

Taco Eggs

Brenda Hauser

9 eggs
1/2 c. milk
1/8 tsp. salt
2 c. shredded Cheddar cheese
1 Lg. can diced tomatoes

1 sm. onion, chopped
1 tsp. minced garlic
2 canned jalapeno peppers, chopped
1 tsp. chili powder
1/4 tsp. cumin

Beat eggs, milk and salt together and put into a 9x12-inch baking dish. Meanwhile, simmer tomatoes, onion, garlic, peppers, chili powder and cumin in a saucepan for about 15 minutes. Pour salsa on top of egg mixture and top with cheese. Bake at 325º for 20 minutes. Teddy was a neighbor on Afton Lane while her house was being built. She taught me how to make many great dishes, like flour tortillas and tamales.

Tamale Pie with Elk Burger

Kristi Hauser Bright

1 T oil
1 0nion
1 Clove garlic
1 Green Bell Pepper
1 ½ pounds elk burger (or regular burger)
½ cups corn kernels (fresh or canned)

14.5 ounce can crushed tomatoes
2 T cumin
T Chili powder
2 tsp salt
1 cup shredded cheddar cheese

For the Cornbread Topping:

1 box or package of corn bread (I use Marie Calendars)

Preheat oven to 375 degrees.

To make the filling: In a large skillet over medium high heat, heat the oil and add the onion, green pepper, garlic and meat. Cook, stirring occasionally, breaking up the meat, until meat is brown, approximately 15 to 20 minutes. Stir in the corn, crushed tomatoes, and spices. Bring to a simmer on low and simmer for 20 minutes. Remove from heat and let sit while you prepare the topping. Prepare the topping per instructions on box or package to make a batter. Pour the filling into a 13 x 9 baking pan and top with corn bread batter. Sprinkle with cheese. Bake for 30 to 40 minutes, until top is golden brown. let rest for 15 minutes before serving.

Turkey Chili

Aymee Wilson

3 T vegetable oil, divided
1 lbs ground turkey
1 package taco seasoning mix
1 tsp ground coriander
1 tsp dried oregano
1 tsp chili pepper flakes
2 T tomato paste
1 (14.5 oz) can beef broth
1 (7 oz) can salsa

1 (14.5 oz) can crushed tomatoes
1 (7 oz) can chopped green chili's
1 med onion, diced
1 green bell pepper, diced
3 medium zucchini, halved lengthwise and sliced
1 bunch green onions, chopped
1 cup sour cream
1 cup shredded cheese

Heat 1 T oil in large pot over medium high heat. Cook ground turkey, taco seasoning mix, coriander, oregano, chili flakes and tomato paste until turkey is well browned. Pour in broth and simmer for about 5 minutes. Add salsa, tomatoes and green chilies and continue cooking for about 10 minutes. While chili is cooking, heat 1 T oil in large skillet over medium high heat. Cook onion and green bell pepper, stirring occasionally for 5 minutes. Add onion and bell pepper to chili and simmer on low. In same skillet, heat remaining oil over medium high heat and add the zucchini. Cook, stirring occasionally for about 5 minutes or until lightly browned. Add to chili and continue cooking for 15 minutes. Ladle chili into bowls and top with sour cream, green onions and cheddar cheese.

MAIN DISH

Un-Stuffed Cabbage Rolls

Patty Hauser Ink

1 Pounds Lean Ground Beef Or Turkey
1 Tablespoon Oil
1 Large Onion Chopped
1 Clove Garlic Minced
1 Small Cabbage Chopped
2 Cans (14.5 Ounces Each) Diced To-matoes

1 Can (8 Ounces) Tomato Sauce
1 Cup Water
1 Teaspoon Black Pepper
1 Teaspoon Sea Salt
(I Added 3 Or 4 Tablespoon Chopped Cilantro)

In A Large Skillet, Heat Olive Oil, Add Ground Beef, Onion And Cook. Stirring Until Ground Beef Is Don And Onions Are Tender. Add Garlic Cook 1 Minute, Add Cabbage Tomatoes, Tomato Sauce, Pepper And Salt Cover And Simmer For 20 - 30 Minutes, Or Until Cabbage Is Tender.

Vince's Green Chili

Kim Gould

4 pounds of pork - roast, loin, or boneless chops (with fat trimmed off)
12 large fresh green chilies - roasted with most seeds and veins removed - if you want it hotter - leave
more seeds
1 large onion - finely chopped
4 cloves fresh garlic - minced or finely chopped
2-3 tsp dried oregano

Salt & Pepper to taste
1 tsp ground cumin
1 pint or small can stewed tomatoes
½ to 3/4 cup masa
3 Tbsp chicken base mixed in 4 cups hot water (you can use already prepared chicken broth also)

Cube pork in ½ inch cubes and brown in skillet with 1 Tbsp bacon grease; 2 Tbsp canola oil, & ½ cup water. Add cumin, oregano, salt, & pepper. Chop together in food processor: garlic, onion, & tomatoes. Add to the meat as it browns. Add chopped green chilies. When meat is completely browned, sprinkle masa over a little at a time, mix well until all the meat is well coated. Pour chicken broth over the meat, simmer 60-90 minutes or cook all day in crock pot on low.

Zesty Chicken Wings

Krystal Hollamon

1/2 c. corn syrup
1/2 c. catchup
1/4 c. cider vinegar
1/4 c. Worcestershire sauce
1/4 c. Dijon mustard

1 sm. onion, chopped
3 garlic cloves, minced
1 T. chili powder
16 whole chicken wings (3 lb. or so)

In a saucepan, combine the first 8 ingredients. Bring to a boil. Reduce heat and simmer, uncovered, for 15 to 20 minutes. Meanwhile, cut chicken wings into 3 sections; discard wing tips. Place wings in a well-greased 10 x 15-inch baking pan. Bake at 375° for 30 minutes, turning once. Brush with sauce. Bake 20 to 25 minutes longer, turning and basting at least once. Serve with additional sauce. Yield: about 10 to 12 servings.

Ziti Bake

Kristi Hauser Bright

12 ounces uncooked ziti
2 pounds ground beef
1 jar (24 oz) prego traditional spaghetti sauce
2 eggs, beaten

1 carton (15 oz) ricotta cheese
2 ½ cups shredded mozzarella cheese, divided
½ cup grated Parmesan cheese

Cook pasta according to direction. Preheat oven to 350 degrees F. In a large skillet, cook beef over medium heat until no longer pink. Drain. Stir in spaghetti sauce. In a large bowl, combine eggs, ricotta cheese, 1 ½ cups mozzarella cheese and the Parmesan cheese. Drain pasta and add to cheese mixture. Stir until blended. Spoon a third of the meat sauce into a greased 13 x 9 baking dish. Top with half of the pasta mixture. Repeat layers. Top with remaining meat sauce. Cover and bake 40 minutes. Uncover, sprinkle with remaining mozzarella cheese and bake S to 10 minutes or until cheese is melted. Let rest for 15 minutes before serving.

Vegetables

POPPY HAUSER AND SOME GRANDKIDS

Bacon Wrapped Corn

Kristi Hauser Bright

8 ears sweet corn, husks removed
8 bacon strips, uncooked
2 T Chili powder

Wrap each ear of corn with a bacon strip. Place on a piece of heavy-duty foil. Sprinkle with chili powder. Wrap securely, twisting ends to make handles for turning. Grill corn, covered, over medium heat for 20 to 25 minutes, turning once.

Baked Beans

Teddy Whitaker

1/2 pound bacon
1 chopped onion
1/2 green bell pepper, diced
1/2 cup brown sugar
3 tablespoons Worcestershire sauce

2 (16-ounce) large cans of pork and beans
(16-ounce) can pineapple chunks
1 cup catchup

Simmer in crock-pot on low.

Baked Zucchini Chips

Aymee Wilson

2 med. zucchini, cut into 1/4" slices
1/2 c. seasoned dry bread crumbs
1/8 tsp. ground black pepper

2 T. grated Parmesan cheese
2 egg whites

Preheat the oven to 475°. In 1 small bowl, stir together the bread crumbs, pepper and Parmesan cheese. Place the egg whites in a separate bowl. Dip zucchini slices into the egg whites, then coat the bread crumb mixture. Place on a greased baking sheet. Bake for 5 minutes in the preheated oven, then turn over and bake for another 5 to 10 minutes, until browned and crispy.

Broccoli and Corn Bake

Pat Boler

1/4 c. cracker crumbs
2 T. melted butter or margarine
1 (10 oz.) pkg. frozen, chopped broccoli

1 can cream-style corn
1 egg, beaten
1 T. minced onion
2/3 c. shredded cheese

TOPPING:

1/2 c. cracker crumbs
2 T. melted butter

1/4 c. shredded cheese

Stir cracker crumbs into melted butter; set aside. Combine broccoli, corn, cracker mixture, beaten egg, onion and cheese; mix well. Pour into casserole dish. Cover with topping. Topping: Stir crumbs into melted butter. Add cheese. Sprinkle topping over casserole. Bake at 350° for 45 minutes. Yield: 4 to 6 servings.

VEGETABLE

Buttermilk Fried Corn

Brenda Hauser

2 c. fresh corn kernels
1 1/2 c. buttermilk
2/3 c. all-purpose flour
2/3 c. cornmeal

1 tsp. salt
1/2 tsp. pepper
Corn oil

Combine corn kernels and buttermilk in a large bowl; let stand 30 minutes. Drain. Combine flour and the next 3 ingredients in a large zip-top plastic bag. Add corn to flour mixture, a small amount at a time, and shake bag to coat corn. Pour oil to a depth of 1 inch in a Dutch oven; heat to 375°. Fry corn, a small amount at a time, in hot oil 2 minutes, or until golden. Drain on paper towels. Serve as a side dish or sprinkle on salads, soups or casseroles. Yield: 2 cups.

Copper Pennies

Sara Malanca

3 c. sliced parboiled carrots (still firm)
1/2 c. sliced raw bell pepper
1/4 c. oil
1/3 c. vinegar

1 tsp. salt
1/2 c. sliced raw onion
1 (8 oz.) can tomato sauce
1 tsp. dry mustard
1/2 c. sugar

Mix all your seasonings, sugar, vinegar, oil and tomato sauce together and stir well. Put marinade over vegetables and marinate overnight.

Corn Casserole

Deanna Vaux

1/2 stick butter or margarine
1 c. sour cream
1 can whole kernel corn
1 can cream-style corn

2 beaten eggs
1 box Jiffy corn muffin mix
Salt & pepper, to taste
1 T. chopped onion

350°. Adapts well to home-canned or frozen corn. Even the picky eaters in our family love this.

Corn Medley

Brenda Hauser

2 c. fresh-cut sweet corn (3 to 4 ears)
2 T. butter or margarine
1/4 c. chopped onion
1/4 c. chopped green pepper

1/2 tsp. salt (opt.)
1/4 tsp. ground cumin
1 Lg tomato, chopped & seeded
2 T. sugar or sugar substitute

Combine the first 6 ingredients in a medium saucepan; cook and stir over medium heat until butter is melted. Cover and cook over low heat for 10 minutes. Stir in tomato and sugar or sugar substitute; cook, covered, 5 minutes longer.

Corn Oysters

Sue Hauser

1 3/4 c. all-purpose flour
1 T. sugar
1 tsp. baking powder
1/2 tsp. salt

1 (17 oz.) can whole kernel corn, undrained
1 egg, beaten
2 T. milk
1 1/2 c. shortening

Combine flour, sugar, baking powder and salt; mix well. Combine corn, egg and milk; stir into dry ingredients. Heat shortening in a large skillet over medium heat to 375°; drop corn mixture by tablespoonfuls into skillet. Cook until golden, turning once. Drain on paper towels. Serve hot. Yield: about 2 dozen.

Corn and Zucchini Fritters

Brenda Hauser

1 1/2 c. all-purpose flour
1/2 tsp. baking powder
Coarse salt & freshly-ground pepper
2 T. unsalted butter, melted
2 Lg. eggs
1/2 c. + 2 T. milk
1/2 c. finely-chopped, cooked ham (opt.)

1 1/2 c. grated zucchini (about 8 oz.)
2 c. fresh corn kernels (3 to 4 ears)
Vegetable oil, for frying
Cooked bacon, sliced Cheddar cheese, avocado & tomato for serving (opt.)

Whisk together flour, baking powder, 2 teaspoons salt and 1/4 teaspoon pepper in a large bowl. In a separate bowl, stir together butter, eggs and milk; add to flour mixture and stir until just combined. Add ham (if desired), zucchini and corn; stir until well blended. Heat 1 inch of oil in a large cast-iron skillet over medium heat until it registers 350° on a deep-fry thermometer. Working in batches of 4 or 5, gently drop 2 tablespoons batter into skillet for each fritter, pressing gently with a spatula to flatten. Cook, turning once, until golden brown, about 2 minutes per side. Transfer with a spatula or slotted spoon to paper towels to drain. Season fritters with salt and pepper while still hot. Make sandwiches with fritters using bacon, cheese, avocado and tomato, if desired.

VEGETABLE

Crispy Brussel Sprouts

Kristi Hauser Bright

2 pounds brussel sprouts
2 T minced shallots Salt & pepper

3 T extra virgin olive oil
Seasoning of your choice. (I use Italian herbs)
½ cup parmigiana-reggiano cheese

Preheat oven to 400 degrees F. Combine olive oil and seasonings. Toss brussel sprouts and shallots in the olive oil and coat evenly. Place on baking sheet and add salt and pepper. Bake for 30 minutes. Add cheese and continue to bake another 5 minutes, or until desired crispiness.

Crispy Green Beans

Kristi Hauser Bright

2 cups Fresh Green Beans, washed and ends trimmed 2eggs
½ cup flour
¾ cup panko crumbs

¼ cup finely grated parmesan cheese
1 T Italian Seasoning (Mixture of basil and oregano)
Salt to taste

Preheat oven to 425 degrees. Mix panko crumbs, cheese and seasoning. Beat the eggs in a bowl. Dip green beans in flour, egg mixture, then crumb mixture and lay in a single layer on a parchment paper lined baking sheet, or a baking sheet sprayed with cooking spray. Bake for 10 to 12 minutes, or until coating begins to brown. Use your favorite dipping sauce if desired.

Crispy Smashed Potatoes

Kristi Hauser Bright

2 lbs small potatoes Yukon Gold or Small Red
A light spray of olive oil
3 tablespoons melted butter
4 cloves garlic, crushed

1 tablespoon fresh chopped parsley
Kosher Salt and Black Pepper to taste
2 tablespoons Parmesan Cheese

Pre-heat your oven to 425°.
Place potatoes in a large pot of salted water. Bring to the boil; cook, covered for 30-35 minutes or until just fork-tender. Drain well. Lightly grease a large baking sheet or tray with cooking oil spray. Arrange potatoes onto the sheet and use a potato masher to LIGHTLY flatten the potatoes in one piece (not too hard or they will end up mashed). Mix together the butter, garlic and parsley. Pour the mixture over each potato. Sprinkle with salt and pepper and lightly spray with olive oil spray. Bake until they are golden and crispy (about 30 minutes). Remove from oven, sprinkle over the Parmesan cheese and return to the oven until the cheese is melted. To serve, season with a little extra salt and parsley, and serve immediately.

Freezer Sweet Corn

Brenda Hauser

4 qt. fresh-cut sweet corn (18 to 20 ears)
1 qt. hot water

2/3 c. sugar
1/2 c. butter or margarine
2 tsp. salt

Combine all ingredients in a large kettle; simmer for 5 to 7 minutes, stirring occasionally. Pour into large shallow containers to cool; stir occasionally. Spoon into freezer bags or containers; freeze. Yield: 3 quarts.

Fried Green Tomatoes

Marlys Hauser

3 med.-sized green tomatoes
Salt & pepper

Cornmeal
6 T. (or so) vegetable oil

Slice tomatoes about 1/2-inch thick; sprinkle with salt and pepper and dredge in cornmeal. Heat oil in a heavy skillet over high heat. Brown well on each side. Great way to use up green tomatoes at season's end.

Garlicky Summer Squash

Lois Baldwin

2 T. olive oil
1/2 yellow onion, sliced
4 cloves garlic, minced
1/2 c. vegetable broth
1 ear corn, kernels cut from cob

2 c. sliced yellow squash
2 c. sliced zucchini
1 T. chopped fresh parsley
2 T. butter
Salt & pepper, to taste

Heat the oil in a skillet over medium-high heat and cook the onion and garlic until slightly tender. Mix in the vegetable broth and corn kernels and cook until heated through. Mix in the squash and zucchini. Cover and continue cooking 10 minutes, stirring occasionally, until squash and zucchini are tender.

Glorified Corn

Patty Fox

In a greased casserole, put:
3 eggs, beaten
Salt, to taste
1 can whole kernel corn
1 can cream-style corn
1 tsp. garlic salt

6 T. melted butter
1/4 c. cornmeal
1 can diced chilies
1 c. grated cheese

Top with more cheese. Bake for 45 minutes or more at 350°

VEGETABLE

121

Grilled Corn, The Hauser Way | Kristi Hauser Bright

Grilling corn in the husks is so easy. There's no need to remove the silk and tie the husk closed before grilling. Just soak the corn in water for about 30 minutes, grill, turning often, for about 30 minutes, and add your favorite flavored butter.

Herbed Corn

Claudia Hauser

12 c. frozen corn
1 c. water
1/2 c. butter or margarine, cubed
2 T. minced fresh parsley
2 tsp. salt

1 tsp. dill weed
1/2 tsp. garlic powder
1/2 tsp. Italian seasoning
1/4 tsp. dried thyme

In a large saucepan, combine corn and water. Bring to a boil. Reduce heat; cover and simmer for 4 to 6 minutes, or until corn is tender. Drain; stir in the remaining ingredients. Yield: 10 to 12 servings.

Hominy-Chili Casserole

Patty Fox

Combine:
2 (1lb. 13 oz.) cans white hominy, drained
4+ T. grated onion (I just use a handful of the dried grated onion)
1 1/2 c. sour cream

1 can cream of mushroom soup
2 c. grated yellow cheese
1 (7 oz.) can diced chilies
Salt

Top with crushed Fritos. Top that with 4 tablespoons melted butter, or mix the butter in with the hominy (that's what I do). Bake for 45 minutes to 1 hour at 350°. Yield: 12 servings.

Lazy Green Bean Casserole

Kris Runk

6 to 8 cups canned green beans (depending on size of family)
1 can Cream of Chicken Soup

1/2 Cup milk or half and half cream
Bag of French's fried onions

Mix all ingredients together except the fried onions, save those to sprinkle on last and bake at 350 degrees until warm and bubbling at edges (takes about 15 minutes in my oven). I make this when I'm short on time or 1eed to take a dish to a large gathering.

Mexican Rice

Sue Hauser

2 tsp. vegetable oil
1 c. Uncle Ben's converted brand rice
1/2 c. chopped celery
1/4 c. chopped green onion
1 Lg. clove garlic, minced

2 tsp. ground cumin
2 c. water
2 chicken bouillon cubes
1/2 c. tomato sauce

Add oil, rice, celery, onion, green pepper and garlic to 12-inch skillet. Saute over medium-high heat, stirring constantly, until rice is browned. Remove from heat. Combine water to bouillon in a medium saucepan. Bring to a boil. Add rice mixture; stir in tomato sauce. Heat just until mixture simmers. Cover and continue to simmer 20 minutes. Remove from heat. Let stand, covered, 10 minutes before serving.

Mom's Corn Soup

Ken McKnight

2 doz. ears of com (Hauser's of course)
1 can evaporated milk

2 or 3 c. whole milk
1 c. butter or margarine
Salt & pepper, to taste

Use slicer to cut tops of kernels, then scrape cobs with back of a knife to remove the corn. Place in large pan and add the evaporated milk and enough milk to make a soup consistency. Add butter or margarine, salt and pepper. Bring to a boil slowly, stirring frequently to prevent sticking. Boil 15 to 20 minutes, stirring frequently. Remove from stove and enjoy, or freeze for later use.

VEGETABLE

Papas Ole

Pat Boler

1 can cream of potato soup
1 can cream of celery soup
1 c. sour cream

1 (2 Lb.) pkg. O'Brien frozen potatoes
1 (4 oz.) can chopped green chilies
2 c. grated cheese

Mix soups with sour cream, potatoes and chilies. Pour into greased baking dish. Sprinkle cheese after the first 30 minutes of baking time. Bake at 350° until bubbly, about 1 hour. Yield: 10 to 12 servings. Variation: Can substitute regular frozen hash browns or other cream soups.

Pinto Beans

Brenda Hauser

5 c. pinto beans
1 whole onion
2 jalapeno peppers
1 T. granulated garlic, or 1 clove

Salt, to taste
1 ham bone or ham hock
Water

Clean beans: take out the bad beans and a little rocks. Put into a large bowl and cover with water; stir, then drain into a colander. Do this about 3 times. Put beans into a pot, then add the onion, peppers, garlic and ham bone. Cover with water and stir. Turn stove on high and let the water boil, then turn down to low. Stir every 30 minutes and cook until beans are tender. Add salt to taste and stir.

Ways to Serve Beans
As a Soup: Fresh out of the pot, pour some beans into a bowl. Add salsa to taste, grated cheese, and tear up a flour tortilla, or just serve with cornbread.
Refried: Into a frying pan, pour 2 to 3 tablespoons oil, then add beans. Don't add too much of the bean juice, as the beans will be soupy when mashed. When beans start to boil, mash with potato masher until consistency you like. Add Longhorn or Cheddar cheese. Stir. When cheese has melted, beans are ready to serve.
Ways to Use Refried Beans: They can be served as a side dish, bean burros, or by adding salsa they can be used as an appetizer.
Tostadas: Spread beans on a corn shell. Sprinkle with shredded lettuce; add chopped tomatoes, then grated cheese. Top with salsa. This recipe makes quite a lot. I freeze in containers. You can use less beans, but I figure if you are cooking beans, you may go ahead and cook that many, because that way you have something to serve as a quick meal.

Potato Casserole

Teddy Whitaker

8 to 10 med. potatoes
12 oz. sour cream

1 can Campbell's (only) cream of chicken soup

Set oven to 375°. Boil potatoes until soft, then slice. Mix sour cream and Campbell's soup together. Butter bottom of casserole dish. Put in a layer of potatoes. Put on a layer of sour cream and soup mixture. Continue with layers of potato and sour cream and soup mixture, ending with sour cream mixture. Top with any kind of grated cheese. (Marble cheese is good.) Bake until cheese is melted on top.

Salsa Corn Cakes

Brenda Hauser

1 1/2 c. all-purpose flour
1/2 c. cornmeal
1 tsp. baking powder
1 tsp. salt
2 (3 oz.) pkg. cream cheese, softened
6 eggs
1 c. milk

1/4 c. butter or margarine, melted
1 (15 1/4 oz.) can whole kernel corn, drained
1/2 c. salsa, drained
1/4 c. minced green onions
Sour cream & additional salsa

Combine flour, cornmeal, baking powder and salt; set aside. In a mixing bowl, beat cream cheese and eggs; add milk and butter. Add the dry ingredients just until moistened. Fold in the corn, salsa and onions. Pour batter by 1/4 cupfuls onto a greased hot griddle. Turn when bubbles form on top; cook until the second side is golden brown. Serve with sour cream and salsa. Yield: 6 to 8 servings.

Scalloped Potatoes

Brenda Hauser

4 or 5 Lg. potatoes
1 med. onion
1 stick butter
2 1/2 c. evaporated milk

1 c. sharp cheese, grated
1 tsp. salt
1/2 tsp. pepper

Preheat oven to 350°. Melt butter in a 9x13-inch baking dish. Peel and wash potatoes; slice them thin and place in melted butter in baking dish. Cover with peeled and thinly-sliced onions. Sprinkle with salt and pepper. Add milk. Bake for 35 minutes. Add grated Cheddar cheese and cook an additional 20 to 25 minutes.

VEGETABLE

Spicy Corn and Cabbage

Jane Moore

1 head cabbage
1 Lg. onion
1 or 2 jalapenos (or 1 red bell pepper if you don't like spicy)

3 ears corn (or 1 c. frozen)
6 to 8 cloves garlic
1/2 to 1 bunch cilantro
1 to 2 T. olive oil

You will need a large, deep skillet with tight-fitting lid. Cut onion in 1/4-inch slices; quarter the cabbage, then cut into 1-inch slices. Finely chop pepper and garlic; saute and stir for 1 to 2 minutes, then tum heat to medium and add 1 or 2 tablespoons of water (just enough to keep from burning) and put lid on. Cook a few minutes; add com and replace lid. Cook until all is tender-crisp, stir in cilantro and salt to taste. Serve! The combination of colors is fabulous.

Sweet Potato Casserole Kim Gould

The best sweet potato casserole recipe! This version has just the right amount of sweetness, an irresistible buttery flavor, and a crisp cinnamon pecan crumble on top. It's the perfect autumn side dish and a Thanksgiving staple.

4 lbs sweet potatoes
½ cup packed light-brown sugar
½ cup unsalted butter, melted
½ cup milk (anything but skim)
2 large eggs
1 tsp vanilla extract
Salt and freshly ground pepper

Topping:
½ cup all-purpose flour
½ cup packed light brown sugar
½ cup ground cinnamon
1 cup chopped or broken pecans
¼ cup unsalted butter, melted

Preheat oven to 400 degrees. Line a rimmed baking sheet with foil. Pierce each of the sweet potatoes twice on two sides. Place on baking sheet and bake until cooked thru and soft, about 60 - 75 minutes. Reduce oven temperature to 350 degrees. Peel potatoes and transfer to large mixing bowl. Mash potatoes with potato masher until well mashed. Let cool 10 minutes. Add in brown sugar, ½ cup melted butter, milk, eggs, vanilla and season with ½ tsp salt and ¼ tsp pepper. Using electric hand mixer blend mixture until well combined. Pour into a greased casserole dish and spread into an even layer. Set aside. For the topping, in a separate medium mixing bowls using a fork stir together flour, brown sugar, cinnamon and pecans. Pour butter into mixture and stir until mixture is evenly moistened. Sprinkle mixture evenly over sweet potato mixture in banking dish. Bake in preheated oven until heated through, about 40 minutes, while tenting with foil during the last 10 minutes to prevent excessive browning on topping.

Sweet Potato Casserole Brenda Hauser

Boil 3 or 4 good-sized sweet potatoes in jackets. Cool, peel and mash. Add:

1/2 stick butter or margarine
1/2 c. sugar
1/4 c. brown sugar
1/2 tsp. vanilla

1/4 c. evaporated milk
2 eggs, beaten
1/4 tsp. nutmeg
1 tsp. cinnamon

Put into casserole dish. Top with:

1 c. crushed corn flakes
1/2 stick melted butter or margarine

1/2 c. brown sugar
1/4 c. chopped pecans

Bake at 350° for 1 hour. This is another holiday favorite.

Texts Two-Step Medley

Aymee Wilson

1 med. onion, chopped
1/4 c. butter or margarine
2 med. yellow summer squash, sliced
2 garlic cloves, minced
2 T. canned chopped green chilies

1/4 tsp. salt
1/8 tsp. pepper
2 (11 oz.) cans Mexicorn, drained
3/4 c. shredded Co-Jack cheese

In a skillet, saute onion in butter until tender. Add the squash, garlic, chilies, salt and pepper. Saute until squash is crisp-tender, about 5 minutes. Add corn; cook and stir for 2 minutes. Sprinkle with cheese; cover and let stand until the cheese is melted. Yield: 4 servings.

VEGETABLE

Lester and Eva Hauser
December 3, 1935

Cakes & Pies

FOUR GENERATIONS OF HAUSER FARMERS

14-Carrot Cake

Paula Rubin

2 c. sifted flour
2 tsp. baking powder
1 1/2 tsp. baking soda
1 1/2 tsp, salt
2 tsp. cinnamon
2 c. sugar

1 1/2 c. salad oil
4 eggs
2 c. carrots, grated
1 (8 1/2 oz.) can crushed pineapple, drained
1 (3 1/2 oz.) can flaked coconut

Sift together flour, baking powder, baking soda, salt and cinnamon. Add sugar, oil and eggs. Mix well; add carrots, pineapple and coconut. Bake at 350° for 35 to 40 minutes. Frost with cream cheese frosting.
Note: Can be baked in a bundt pan or a 9x13-inch oblong pan. I don't put in the coconut, but it's good either way.

Apple Cake

Mary Hauser

1 c. oil
2 c. sugar
3 c. flour, sifted
1 tsp. baking soda
1 tsp. cinnamon

3 eggs
1/2 tsp. salt
3 c. fresh diced apples
1 c. nuts, chopped
1 tsp. vanilla

Beat eggs, oil and sugar until blended. Add flour, baking soda, spices and salt. Fold in apples, nuts and vanilla. Bake at 350° for 1 1/2 hours in oblong or angel food cake pan. Doesn't need frosting.

Applesauce Cake

Pat Boler

1/2 c. butter or margarine
2 eggs
11/2 tsp. baking soda
1 tsp. cinnamon
1/4 tsp. allspice
1/2 c. raisins or craisins

2 c. sugar
2 1/2 c. flour
1 tsp. salt
1/2 tsp. nutmeg
1 1/2 c. applesauce
1/2 c. chopped pecans

Cream butter and sugar until light. Add eggs, beating well. Mix dry ingredients and add alternately to creamed mixture with applesauce. Stir in raisins and nuts. Turn batter into a greased and lightly-floured 9x13x2- inch pan. Bake at 350° for 45 minutes, or until done.

Apple Stack Cake

Betty Frazee

1 c. sugar
1/2 c. shortening
1 egg
1 1/2 tsp. vanilla

1/4 tsp. salt
2 1/4 c. flour
3 tsp, baking powder
1 c. milk

Cream shortening and sugar. Add unbeaten egg and vanilla. Beat thoroughly. Sift flour, baking powder and salt; add alternately with milk to creamed mixture. Grease cake pans well and bake in 4 layers. I bake 2 (8- or 9-inch) layers at a time, then wash pans, grease, and bake 2 more layers. Bake at 375° for about 18 to 20 minutes.

Applesauce Frosting

3/4 to 1 teaspoon cinnamon
2/3 cup sugar

2 (15 oz.) regular cans of plain apple-sauce or 30-32 oz jar of plain apple-sauce

Stir cinnamon and sugar into plain applesauce. Frost each layer with the apple-sauce and use table knife to add to sides of cakes.

Bacardi Rum Cake

Susan Welch

1 pkg. yellow cake mix
1 c. pecans or walnuts
1 sm. pkg. vanilla instant pudding
4 eggs

1/2 c. cold water
1/2 c. oil
1/2 c. rum

Grease and flour bundt pan. Sprinkle nuts in bottom of pan. Mix (with mixer) the remaining ingredients and pour into pan. Bake at 325° for 1 hour. Remove from pan; prick holes in top of cake and drizzle on glaze.

GLAZE:

1/2 c. butter or margarine, melted
1/4 c. water

1 c. sugar
1/2 c. rum

Mix in medium saucepan and boil 5 minutes, stirring constantly. Pour while warm onto hot cake.

CAKES & PIES

Banana Split Cake

Bertie Lightfoot

1 1/2 c. graham cracker crumbs
1/2 c. butter, melted
8 oz. cream cheese
1 (1lb.) box powdered sugar
5 bananas, cut in half & sliced
lengthwise

1 can cherry pie filling
1 can chunk pineapple, well drained
(I cut each chunk in half)
1/2 c. nuts, chopped pretty fine (I use
walnuts or pecans)
1 (12 oz.) ctn. Cool Whip, for topping

Combine crumbs and melted butter and press in bottom of a 9x12-inch cake pan. (I put this in the refrigerator or freezer while getting rest of stuff ready, so that it sets up a bit.) Combine powdered sugar and cream cheese; spread on top of crumbs. Then layer bananas, cherry pie filling and pineapple chunks, in this order. Cover all with Cool Whip and top with nuts. Best if chilled for several hours, but doesn't always last that long before somebody gets into it. Ha!

Best Ever Carrot Cake

Jennifer Fuller

2 C sugar
4 eggs
1 ½ C oil
3 C grated carrots (be generous)

1 C chopped pecans
2 tsp. baking soda
1 tsp. salt
2 tsp. cinnamon
2 C sifted flour

Cream together sugar and eggs, slowly add oil. Add carrots and pecans to sugar mixture. Add in baking soda, salt, cinnamon and flour. Bake in greased & floured 9 x 13 pan or 2 - 8" round pans at 350 for 35 minutes or until toothpick comes out clean. It usually takes longer. This batter is so good you don't even need to bake it.

Cream Cheese Frosting

1 C white sugar
1 - 8 oz. cream cheese - softened
1/8 tsp. salt

1 ½ C whipping cream
1 tsp vanilla
1 tsp almond extract

Whip cream until stiff and set aside. Mix other ingredients and fold in whipped cream. This cake becomes totally lethal if you slice an 8" cheese cake in ¼" slices and use it as filling between the layers instead of the frosting, then frost as usual.

Best-Ever Chocolate Cake

Lynda Parker

3/4 c. butter
3 eggs
2 c. all-purpose flour
3/4 c. unsweetened cocoa powder
1 tsp. baking soda

3/4 tsp. baking powder
1/2 tsp. salt
2 c. sugar
2 tsp. vanilla
1 1/2 c. milk

Allow butter and eggs to stand at room temperature for 30 minutes. Lightly grease bottoms of 3 (8 1/2 x l-inch) round cake pans. Line bottoms of pans with waxed paper. Grease and lightly flour waxed paper and sides of pans. Set pans aside. **Preheat oven to 350°.** In a medium bowl, stir together the flour, cocoa powder, baking soda, baking powder and salt; set aside. In a large mixing bowl, beat butter with an electric mixer on medium to high speed for 30 seconds. Gradually add sugar, about 1/4 cup at a time, beating on medium speed for 3 to 4 minutes, or until well mixed. Scrape side of bowl; continue beating on medium speed for 2 minutes. Add eggs, one at a time, beating after each addition (about 1 minute total). Beat in vanilla. Alternately add flour mixture and milk to beaten mixture, beating on low speed just until combined after each addition. Beat on medium to high speed for 20 seconds more. Spread evenly into prepared pans. Bake for 30 to 35 minutes, or until a wooden toothpick inserted in the centers comes out clean. Cool cake layers in pans for 10 minutes. Remove from pans. Peel off waxed paper. Cool completely on wire racks. Prepare Chocolate Frosting; fill and frost cake layers. If desired, top with chocolate curls and candied nuts. Store cake in the refrigerator. Yield: 12 to 16 servings.

Chocolate Frosting

1 (12-ounce) package (2 cups) semi-sweet chocolate pieces
1/2 cup butter

1 (8-ounce container dairy sour cream
4 1/2 cups sifted powdered sugar (about 1 pound)

In a large saucepan, combine chocolate pieces and butter; heat over low heat until melted, stirring often. Cool for 5 minutes. Stir in sour cream. Gradually add sifted powdered sugar, beating on medium speed until mixture is smooth.

Better-Than-Sex Cake

Brenda Hauser

1 yellow cake mix
1 (15 oz.) can crushed pineapple with juice
1 c. sugar

1 pkg. vanilla instant pudding
3 bananas, sliced
Whipped topping
Chopped nuts

Mix the cake mix as directed on package. Pour into a greased and floured 9x13x2-inch baking dish and bake in a preheated 350° oven for 35 to 40 minutes. In a medium saucepan, combine the pineapple and sugar and boil 5 minutes. Pour onto hot cake. Cool. Prepare the pudding according to directions on the box and spread over pineapple mixture. Slice bananas over pudding mixture. Spread with whipped topping and sprinkle with chopped nuts. Refrigerate.
This recipe is slightly overrated.

Blueberry-Lemon Pound Cake

Teddy Whitaker

1 rectangular pound cake
1 can lemon pie filling

1 can blueberry pie filling
1 ctn. Cool Whip, thawed

Cut the pound cake lengthwise into 6 slices. Arrange 3 slices on the bottom of a glass baking dish. Spread lemon pie filling over pound cake. Add the last 3 slices of cake on top of lemon filling. Spread blueberries on top. Last, spread Cool Whip on top of blueberries. Refrigerate. It is best to make this dessert a day ahead for easy cutting.

Blueberry Pudding Cake

Brenda Hauser

2 c. blueberries
1 tsp. cinnamon
1 tsp. lemon juice
1 c. flour

3/4 c. sugar
1 tsp. baking powder
1/2 c. milk
3 T. oleo, melted

TOPPING:

3/4 c. sugar
1 T. cornstarch

1 c. boiling water

Toss fruit with cinnamon and lemon juice. Place in greased 8-inch square baking pan. In a bowl, combine flour, sugar and baking powder; stir in milk and oleo. Spoon over berries. Combine sugar and cornstarch. Sprinkle over batter. Slowly pour boiling water over all. Bake at 350° for 45 to 50 minutes, until done. Yield: 9 servings.

Candied Fruit Cake

Gene Hollamon

2 c. flour
2 tsp. baking powder
1/2 tsp, salt
1 Lb. candied cherries
1 Lb. candied pineapple

1 1/4 lb. pitted dates
4 eggs
1 c. sugar
8 c. pecans, or 4 c. pecans & 4 c. walnuts

In largest Tupperware bowl, mix flour, baking powder and salt. Add cherries, pineapple and dates. Beat together the eggs and sugar; add to fruit-flour mixture. Add nuts last. Put in 3 or 4 greased and floured loaf pans or 2 ring pans. Pack down tightly. Bake 1 hour at 275°. Check at 55 minutes. Be sure to put a pan of water on the lowest oven rack and bake cake on rack above it. Note: Leave nuts and fruit whole; don't chop any of it. Use hands for mixing.

Cherry Dumplin' Cake

Jennifer Fuller

1 (21 Oz) Can Cherry Pie Filling (Apple Works Well Too)
1 (14 Oz) Can Eagle Brand Sweetened Condensed Milk
1 Tsp Almond Extract
1/2 C Plus 2 T Cold Butter (Divided)

2 1/2 C Bisquick (Divided)
1/2 C Firmly Packed Brown Sugar
1/2 C Chopped Nuts (Pecans, Almonds, Walnuts)

Preheat Oven To 325. In Medium Bowl, Combine Pie Filling, Eagle Brand And Extract. In Large Bowl, Cut ½ C Butter Into 2 C Bisquick Until Crumbly. Stir In Cherry Mixture. Spread Into Greased 8"X8" Or 7"X12" Baking Dish. In Small Bowl, Combine Remaining ½ C Bisquick And 2 T Cold Butter Until Crumbly. Stir In Nuts. Sprinkle Evenly Over Cherry Mixture. Bake 1 Hour To 1 Hour 10 Minutes Or Until Golden Brown. Serve Warm With Ice Cream. Refrigerate Leftovers.

Choco-Holic Cake

Pat Boler

1 (18.25 oz.) pkg. chocolate cake mix
1 (3/4 oz.) pkg. chocolate instant
pudding & pie filling mix
1 c. milk
1/2 c. sour cream

4 Lg. eggs
1 c. chopped walnuts
2 c. (12 oz. pkg.) Nestle Toll House
semi-sweet chocolate morsels

GLAZE:

1 (2 oz.) bar Nestle Toll House
unsweetened chocolate baking bar
1 1/2 c. sifted powdered sugar

3 T. butter
2 to 3 T. water
1 tsp. vanilla extract

Preheat oven to 350°. Grease and flour a 12-inch bundt pan or other tube pan. Combine cake mix, pudding mix, milk, sour cream and eggs in a large mixer bowl. Beat on low speed just until blended. Beat on high speed for 2 minutes. Stir in morsels and nuts. Pour into prepared baking pan. Bake for 55 to 65 minutes, or until wooden pick inserted in cake comes out clean. Cool in pan for 20 minutes. Invert onto wire rack to cool completely.
Glaze: Melt baking bar and butter in a small heavy-duty saucepan over low heat, stirring until smooth. Remove from heat. Stir in powdered sugar alternately with water until of desired consistency. Stir in vanilla extract. Pour glaze over cake.

Coffeecake

Betty Black

1 sm. box vanilla pudding, not instant
2 c. milk

1 box Duncan Hines yellow cake mix
1 (12 oz.) bag butterscotch chips
1/2 c. nuts, chopped

In a large pan, cook pudding with the 2 cups of milk until bubbly. Add the cake mix (dry) to pudding. Pour into a greased 9x12-inch pan. Sprinkle nuts and chips on top. Bake at 350° for 30 minutes.

Connie's Chocolate Cake&Frosting

Connie Steyaert

2 c. flour
2 c. sugar
1 tsp. salt
1 tsp. baking soda
1/2 c. sour milk or buttermilk

3 eggs
1/2 c. margarine (1 cube)
3 sq. melted non-sweet chocolate
1 c. boiling water

Add dry ingredients together, except baking soda, and set aside. Cream margarine and add eggs, milk and chocolate. Combine dry ingredients to creamed mixture, mixing well. Add boiling water and baking soda. Bake at 350° for 40 minutes. Best made in 2 or 3 layers.

FROSTING:

1 1/2 c. sugar
1 c. canned milk
6 sq. melted unsweetened chocolate

3/4 tsp. vanilla
6 T. soft butter (real)

Place all ingredients in blender and blend until smooth and creamy. If runny, let set for a few minutes before frosting cake.

Corny Cake

Pat Boler

1 (17 oz.) can creamed corn
1/2 c. brown sugar
3/4 c. sugar
3 eggs
1 c. vegetable oil
1 T. baking powder

2 1/4 c. flour
1 tsp. baking soda
1 tsp. salt
1 tsp. cinnamon
1/2 c. raisins
1/2 c. nuts, chopped

CARAMEL FROSTING:

4 T. butter
1/2 c. brown sugar

1/4 c. milk
2 to 3 c. powdered sugar

In a mixing bowl, combine corn and sugars; add eggs and oil. Beat well. Combine dry ingredients; add to batter. Mix well. Stir in raisins and nuts. Bake at 350° for 30 to 35 minutes in a 9x13-inch pan. Frosting: Bring butter, sugar and milk to a boil, then stir in confectioners' sugar. Cool and frost cake.

137

Cream Puff Cake

Dee Orr

1 c. water
112 c. butter or margarine
1 c. flour
4 eggs

2 1/2 c. milk
9 oz. Cool Whip
2 sm. pkg. vanilla instant pudding
1 tsp. vanilla

FROSTING:

4 T. butter

3 oz. semi-sweet chocolate

Melt together. Add:

1 c. powdered sugar
1 tsp, vanilla

2 tsp. milk

Boil water and margarine; stir in flour. Mix well. Take off heat. Add eggs, one at a time; beat each one 30 seconds, until it sticks together, then add next egg. Spread dough on cookie sheet. Smooth - it is sticky. Bake at 400° for 45 minutes. Whisk together milk, Cool Whip, pudding and vanilla until smooth. Spread on cooled crust. Make frosting and drizzle over top.

Easy Pineapple Upside-Down Cake

Lisa Enright

1 pkg. yellow or pineapple cake mix
1/2 c. butter or margarine
1 c. brown sugar

1 can pineapple slices
1 sm. jar maraschino cherries

Preheat oven to 350°. Melt butter in a 9x13-inch pan. Sprinkle brown sugar evenly into pan. Arrange drained pineapple slices and cherry halves on the sugar mixture. Mix cake as directed on the box, except substitute pineapple juice for the water in the recipe. Pour batter over fruit. Bake at 350° for about 50 minutes, until it tests done with a toothpick. Wait 5 minutes before turning onto a pretty platter.

Fresh Peach Cake

Aunt Lucille Edwards

3/4 c. oil
1 1/2 c. sugar
1 1/3 c. mashed peaches
2 eggs

1 tsp. baking soda
1/2 tsp. salt
1 tsp. cinnamon
2 c. flour

Pour into greased and floured 9x13-inch pan. Bake at 350° for 40 minutes.

Fudgy Chocolate-Cherry Cake

Ruth Hunter

1 box devil's food cake mix
1 (21 oz.) can cherry pie filling

Eggs (use amount indicated on cake mix)

CHERRY CLOUD FROSTING:

1 (21 oz.) can cherry pie filling
1/2 c. powdered sugar

1 (12 oz.) ctn. nondairy topping, thawed

Heat oven to 350°. Grease and flour 2 (9-inch) cake pans. With electric mixer, beat cake mix, 1 can cherry filling and eggs. Do not add oil or water. Blend on low speed, then beat on medium speed for 2 minutes. Divide between 2 cake pans. Bake for 25 to 35 minutes. Cool 10 minutes. Remove from pans. Cool completely. To Frost: Stir all frosting ingredients until combined. Spread generously between layers and over top and sides. Refrigerate. Yield: 14 servings.

Grandmother Britton's 1937 Devil's Food Cake

Lynn Reddell

3 c. flour
3 tsp. baking soda
1 1/2 c. sugar
6 T. cocoa

1 c. warm water
1 1/2 c. Miracle Whip salad dressing (no substitutes)
1 1/4 tsp. vanilla

Mix flour, sugar and baking soda. Blend cocoa and water; mix into flour, sugar and baking soda. Add Miracle Whip and vanilla. Bake for 40 minutes at 350° in a 9x13-inch pan.

Honey Bun Cake

Lisa Enright

4 eggs
2/3 c. vegetable oil

1 c. sour cream
1 yellow cake mix

Mix the first 3 ingredients. Add cake mix and blend well. In a separate bowl, mix 1 cup brown sugar and 1 tablespoon cinnamon. Pour half of cake batter into greased 9x13-inch pan. Sprinkle sugar mixture on top and add rest of batter. Bake at 350° for 30 to 35 minutes. Mix 2 cups powdered sugar, 5 or 6 tablespoons milk and 1 teaspoon vanilla, and pour over cake while hot. Yum.

CAKES & PIES

Hot Fudge Pudding Cake

Ioelle Hauser

1 1/4 c. sugar, divided
1 c. flour
7T. cocoa
2 tsp. baking powder
1/4 tsp. salt

1/2 c. milk
1/3 c. oleo, melted
1 1/2 tsp. vanilla
1/2 c. packed brown sugar
1 1/4 c. hot water

Stir together 3/4 cup sugar, flour, 3 tablespoons cocoa, baking powder and salt. Stir in milk, oleo and vanilla; beat until smooth. Spread in ungreased 9-inch square pan. Stir together remaining 1/2 cup sugar, brown sugar and 4 tablespoons cocoa. Sprinkle evenly over batter. Pour hot water over top. Do not stir. Bake for 35 to 40 minutes, until set, at 350°. Let stand 15 minutes. Ioelle makes this in the crock-pot.

Ice Cream Cake

Sara Malanca

12 ice cream sandwiches
1 Lg. ctn. Cool Whip

ice cream topping

Line bottom of a 9x13-inch pan with ice cream sandwiches. Cut some sandwiches to make them fit. Layer on the topping (chocolate, fudge, caramel, or whatever). Put the cake in the freezer for a short time before applying the Cool Whip. Add nuts, if desired, then freeze.

Jello Pudding Cake

Kim Gould

1 yellow cake mix
1 sm. pkg. red Jello
1 ctn. Cool Whip

1 pkg. vanilla pudding, instant or regular, prepared as pkg. directs

Prepare cake mix as package directs and pour into a 9x13-inch greased and floured pan. When cake is finished baking, remove from oven and poke holes all over cake with large meat fork. Mix Jello, using 2 cups boiling water, and pour evenly over hot cake. Mix pudding and spread over top of cake. Cool in refrigerator and frost with Cool Whip when ready to serve.

Kahlua Cake

Norma Wombacher

3/4 c. cocoa
1 tsp. instant coffee
1 c. boiling water
1/2 c. + 2 T. Kahlua
1/2 c. margarine, softened
1/4 c. shortening
1 1/3 c. sugar

3 eggs
1 tsp. vanilla
2 c. flour, sifted
1 1/2 tsp. baking soda
1/4 tsp. baking powder
3/4 tsp. salt

In a small bowl, blend cocoa, coffee and water; stir in 1/2 cup Kahlua; cool. In a large bowl, beat butter, shortening, sugar, eggs and vanilla until light and fluffy. In a small bowl, combine flour, baking soda, baking powder and salt. Add flour mixture to butter mixture alternately with cocoa mixture, beating well after each addition. Line bottom of 2 (9-inch) pans with waxed paper; lightly spray with cooking spray. Bake in preheated oven at 350° for 25 to 30 minutes. Do not over bake. Kahlua

Frosting:

6 ounces chocolate chips
1/4 cup Kahlua

1/4 cup evaporated milk
1 cup margarine
4 1/2 cups powdered sugar

In a saucepan, combine chocolate chips, Kahlua, evaporated milk and margarine. Stir over medium heat until chocolate melts. Remove from heat and blend in powdered sugar. Beat until frosting is cool and holds its shape. Pan may be placed over ice water to hasten cooling. Norma shared recipes with me for at least 30 years. She was a joy.

CAKES & PIES

Lemon Chiffon Cake

Sue Hauser

7 eggs, separated
2 c. all-purpose flour
1 1/2 c. sugar
3 tsp. baking powder
1 tsp. salt

3/4 c. water
1/2 c. vegetable oil
4 tsp. grated lemon peel
2 tsp. vanilla extract
1/2 tsp. cream of tartar

LEMON FROSTING:

1/3 c. butter, softened
3 c. confectioners' sugar
4 1/2 tsp. grated lemon peel

Dash of salt
1/4 c. lemon juice

Let eggs stand at room temperature for 30 minutes. In a large mixing bowl, combine the flour, sugar, baking powder and salt. In another bowl, whisk the egg yolks, water, oil, lemon peel and vanilla; add to dry ingredients. Beat until well blended. In another large mixing bowl, beat egg whites and cream of tartar on medium speed until soft peaks form; fold into batter. Gently spoon into an ungreased 10-inch tube pan. Cut through batter with a knife to remove air pockets. Bake on the lowest oven rack at 325° for 50 to 55 minutes, or until top springs back when lightly touched. Immediately invert the pan; cool completely, about 1 hour. Run a knife around side and center tube of pan. Remove cake to a serving plate. In a small mixing bowl, combine frosting ingredients; beat until smooth. Spread over top of cake. Yield: 12 to 16 servings. I know this is labor intensive and uses 3 bowls, but it is so worth it when you have extra lemons or eggs. Good with orange juice & peel.

Lemon Jello Cake

Cody Cantarini

Cake:

1 pkg Lemon Jello
1 pkg Yellow cake mix

¾ cup oil
¾ cup water

Topping:

2 cups sifted powdered sugar
Juice of 2 lemons and zest

Mix cake ingredients together and pour into a 9 x 13 pan. Bake at 350 degrees F for 35 to 40 minutes. While cake is warm, poke holes in top with fork and spread topping over it.

Lemon Pudding Cake

Jacob Gould

5 eggs, separated
1/2 c. lemon juice
2 tsp. grated lemon rind
1 T. unsalted butter, melted

1 3/4 c. sugar
1 3/4 c. milk
3/4 c. flour
1/2 tsp. salt

Beat together egg yolks, lemon juice, rind, butter and 1 1/4 cups sugar in a bowl for 2 minutes, or until blended. Add milk, flour and salt; beat just until combined. Beat egg whites until soft peaks form. Beat in remaining 1/2 cup sugar and beat until glossy peaks form. Fold whites into lemon mixture until blended. Bake in 2-quart baking dish, greased, at 350° for 40 minutes, until done. Serve warm. Yield: 10 servings.

Magic Fruitcake

Erin Broadbent

1 Lb. candied cherries
1 Lb. candied pineapple
1 Lb.. pitted dates
1 Lb. shelled pecans (4 c. coarsely chopped)

4 oz. coconut (any kind)
1 can Eagle Brand milk (heat slightly in can - makes it come out & mix

Cut up all fruits, combine with Eagle Brand milk, mixing with hands or large wooden spoon. Pack into 2 greased and waxed-paper-lined loaf pans. Bake 1 hour at 300°.

Mrs. Wood's Quick Chocolate Cake

Sue Hauser

2 c. sugar
3 c. flour
1/2 c. cocoa
3 tsp. baking soda
1/4 tsp. salt

2 eggs
1 c. sour milk
1 c. shortening, melted in 1 c. hot water
1 tsp. vanilla

Put all ingredients in bowl and beat thoroughly. Nuts may be added. Bake at 350° until done (about 30 minutes).

FROSTING:

2 oz. chocolate (2 sq.)
1 1/2 c. sugar
7 T. milk
1 T. syrup

2 T. Crisco
2 T. butter or margarine
1 tsp. vanilla

Mix all ingredients in a medium saucepan and bring to a rolling boil. Boil 1 to 1 1/2 minutes. Stir well and spread on cooled cake.

Oatmeal Cake

Peggy Russman

1/2 c. butter or margarine
1 c. boiling water
1 c. brown sugar
1 c. white sugar
2 eggs

1 1/2 c. flour
1 tsp. cinnamon
1 /2 tsp. nutmeg
1/4 tsp. salt
1 tsp. baking soda

Put butter or margarine in a mixing bowl; add 1 cup oatmeal. Pour boiling water over this and let stand 20 minutes. Add brown sugar, white sugar and eggs. Mix well. Add flour, cinnamon, nutmeg, salt and baking soda. Mix well. Bake for 30 to 35 minutes at 350°.

Broiled Topping: In a saucepan, melt 1/3 cup butter. Add 1 cup brown sugar, 1 egg, 1 cup coconut, 1 cup chopped nuts and 3 teaspoons cream or milk. Mix and spread on hot cake, and broil until light brown.

Pineapple Dream Cake

Teddy Whitaker

3/4 c. flaked coconut, toasted
1 pkg. yellow cake mix
1 (20 oz.) can crushed pineapple in own juice
3/4 c. sugar

2 (3 1/2 oz.) pkg. instant vanilla pudding mix
3 c. milk
1 c. heavy cream
1/4 c. powdered sugar
1 tsp. vanilla

Spread flaked coconut in a rimmed jellyroll pan. Place pan in preheated 350° oven and toast for 10 to 15 minutes, stirring occasionally, until coconut is golden. Watch carefully - it toasts very quickly. With a wide spatula, remove coconut from pan to paper towels to cool. Store overnight in a paper-lined, tightly-covered container.
In a 9 x l3 x 2-inch baking pan, prepare and bake yellow cake mix according to package directions. Meanwhile, in a medium saucepan, combine pineapple with its juice
and 3/4 cup sugar; cook over medium heat, stirring occasionally, until thick and syrupy, about 20 minutes. When cake is done, remove from oven and pierce top of cake with a fork at 1-inch intervals. Pour pineapple mixture over top of cake, spreading evenly. Cool cake completely. In a medium bowl, combine pudding mix with milk; blend until thick. Spread over cake. In yet another medium bowl, beat heavy cream until soft peaks form. Add powdered sugar and vanilla; continue beating until stiff peaks form. Spread cream over cake. Refrigerate cake for 24 hours. Before serving, sprinkle top with reserved toasted coconut. Yield: 16 servings.

Pistachio Cake

Teddy Whitaker

1 pkg. white cake mix
1 sm. pkg. instant pistachio pudding
3/4 c. oil
1 c. + 2 T. club soda
3 eggs (beat 2 minutes)
1/2 c. walnuts, chopped

Beat all ingredients together and pour into a greased and floured bundt pan. Cook for 45 minutes in a 350º oven. Set on a wire rack and cool for 15 minutes. turn over on a plate. Cool completely.

FROSTING:

1 pkg. Dream Whip
1 pkg. instant pistachio pudding
1 1/4 c. milk

Beat well and spread all over cooled cake.

Pound Cake

Grandma Naoma Moore

5 eggs
3 c. sugar
2 cubes margarine
1/2 c. Crisco
1 c. milk
1 tsp. baking powder
Dash of salt
3 c. flour
1 tsp. vanilla

Cream margarine and Crisco; add sugar and eggs. Beat well on medium speed. Add remaining ingredients, mixing well. Pour into greased bundt pan and bake at 325º for 1 1/2 hours.

Pound Cake

Marie Schultz

1 lb. margarine
1 lb. powdered sugar
3 c. cake flour
6 eggs
1 tsp. lemon extract
1 tsp. almond extract

Cream margarine and sugar until creamy. Add flour, a little at a time, then 1 egg and repeat until all flour and eggs are used. Spray a large angel food pan with removable bottom or 2 bread-size loaf pans. Sprinkle chopped nuts into bottom of pan, then add batter. Bake at 350º for 1 to 1 1/4 hours. Freezes well. Be sure to use cake flour. I worked many years in a medical clinic and Marie shared so many recipes with us during that time, plus she provided us with wonderful crocheted dish towels.

Pumpkin Sheet Cake

Pat Boler

2 c. (or 16 oz. can) pumpkin
2 c. sugar
1 c. vegetable oil
4 eggs, lightly beaten
2 c. flour

2 tsp. baking soda
1 tsp. cinnamon
1/2 tsp. salt
1 tsp. vanilla

In a mixing bowl, beat pumpkin, sugar and oil. Add eggs; mix well. Combine flour, baking soda, cinnamon and salt; add to pumpkin mixture and beat until well blended. Blend in vanilla. Pour into a greased cookie sheet. Bake at 350° for 20 to 25 minutes, or until cake tests done. Cool. Frost with cream cheese frosting.

CREAM CHEESE FROSTING:

1 cube margarine or butter
1 (8 oz.) pkg. cream cheese
1 (1 lb.) pkg. powdered sugar

1 tsp. vanilla
1 c. chopped nuts

Cream margarine and cream cheese, then slowly add powdered sugar and vanilla. Beat until smooth. Frost cake. Sprinkle with nuts.

Punch Bowl Cake

Betty Hill

1 box yellow or white cake mix (bake as directed in two 8" or 9" pans)
1 sm. box vanilla instant pudding

1 Lg. can crushed pineapple with juice
1 can cherry pie filling
1 (9 oz.) ctn. Cool Whip

Line bottom of punch bowl with one cake layer, then instant pudding prepared with 2 cups milk. Add another cake layer, then pineapple. Another cake layer, then cherry pie filling. Top with Cool Whip. This is so good for baby or wedding showers or holidays. Keep refrigerated.

Red Velvet Cake

Pat Boler

2 1/2 c. flour
2 c. sugar
1/2 tsp. baking soda
1 tsp. baking powder
2 T. cocoa
1 c. salad oil

2 eggs
1 oz. red food coloring
1 tsp. vanilla
1 T. vinegar
1 c. buttermilk

In a large mixing bowl, combine dry ingredients. In a small bowl, beat eggs; add oil. Beat again. Add to dry ingredients and mix well. Add buttermilk and mix well. Add food coloring, vanilla and vinegar and mix well. Grease and flour cookie sheet. Bake at 350º for 30 minutes. Cool.

CREAM CHEESE FROSTING:

1 (8 oz.) pkg. cream cheese
1 cube margarine
1 tsp. vanilla

1 box powdered sugar
1 c. chopped pecans

Allow margarine and cream cheese to soften at room temperature. Cream cheese and margarine together. Add powdered sugar and beat well. Add pecans.

Sherrie's Texas Sheet Cake

Sherrie Nance

2 c. sugar
2 c. flour
1/2 tsp. salt
2 cubes margarine
1 c. water

4 T. cocoa
1/2 c. sour cream
2 eggs
1 tsp. baking soda

In a large bowl, combine Sugar with flour and salt. In a small saucepan, combine margarine, water and cocoa. Bring to a boil. Take from heat and add to large bowl. Add sour cream, eggs and baking soda. Pour into a 10 1/2 x 15 1/2-inch jellyroll pan (pan size important). Bake at 375º for 20 to 25 minutes.

Frosting:

1 cube butter or margarine
6 tablespoons milk
4 tablespoons cocoa

1 box powdered sugar
1 cup nuts
1 teaspoon vanilla

Cook until bubbly, butter or margarine, milk and cocoa (I use the same pan that the cake mixture was in); remove from heat. Add powdered sugar, nuts and vanilla. Mix until smooth and frost cake straight from oven.

Sour Cream Coffeecake

Brenda Hauser

1 1/4 c. sugar
2 sticks butter, softened
2 eggs
1 (8 oz.) ctn. sour cream
2 c. flour

1 tsp. baking soda
1 tsp. vanilla
1 heaping tsp. cinnamon, mixed with
2 heaping tsp. sugar

Preheat oven to 350° Grease a bundt pan very well. Sprinkle half of cinnamon and sugar mixture over the entire bundt pan until coated. Set pan aside. In a medium-size mixing bowl, cream together butter and sugar. Add eggs and sour cream. Mix well. Add flour, 1 cup at a time. Stir in vanilla and baking soda until evenly mixed. Pour half of the batter into the coated pan. Sprinkle remaining cinnamon-sugar mixture over batter. Spoon remaining batter into pan. Bake for 45 minutes. Turn cake out of pan onto a plate immediately. Spread 1 cup of chopped walnuts or pecans, along with the cinnamon and sugar mixture, over the first half of the batter. This coffee cake also is delicious with an icing glaze.

Swedish Nut Cake

Teddy Whitaker

2 c. sugar
2 c. flour
2 eggs
1/2 tsp. baking soda
1 (20 oz.) can crushed pineapple, including juice

1/2 c. chopped nuts
1 c. brown sugar
1/2 stick margarine, softened
Nuts, for topping

Preheat oven to 350• Mix sugar, flour, eggs, baking soda, pineapple and juice in a mixing bowl. Add 2/3 cup nuts and pour into a 9x12x2-inch greased baking pan. Bake for 40 minutes. Frosting: Mix brown sugar, margarine and cream cheese in a bowl. Spread on cake while it is hot. Sprinkle with nuts.
Note: Use a mixture of chopped walnuts, almonds and pecans for the crunch topping.

Two-Cherry Cream Cakes

Lori Boyce

1 white cake mix
2 (8 oz.) pkg. cream cheese
4 c. powdered sugar

1 pt. whipping cream (whipped), or
2 c. Cool Whip
1 tsp. vanilla
2 cans cherry pie filling

Mix cake as directed on box. Pour into 2 (8x13-inch) cake pans. Bake about 20 minutes. Cool. Beat cream to stiff peaks and add vanilla. Fold the 2 mixtures together. Spread half on each cake equally, then pour 1 can pie filling on each. Enjoy!

Upside-Down Cake

Reba Faulkner

1 c. pecans, chopped

1 c. shredded coconut

Mix German chocolate cake mix according to directions. Pour over coconut and pecans. Melt 2 sticks butter or margarine and 1 (8-ounce) package cream cheese. Mix with 1 box powdered sugar. Pour over cake batter. Bake at 350° for 50 minutes. Variation: Can use carrot cake mix for chocolate, if desired.

Pies

Ann's Pecan Pie

Naoma Moore

1/4 c. butter, melted
3 eggs, beaten
1 c. dark or light Karo syrup
1 T. flour
1/2 c. sugar

1/2 tsp. cinnamon
1 tsp. vanilla
1/2 tsp. salt
1 c. chopped pecans

Add butter, syrup, sugar ~ cinnamon, vanilla, flour, salt and pecans to the beaten eggs. Pour into an 8- or 9-inch pie shell and bake for 45 minutes at 350°, or until filling is set.

Aunt Bea's Fresh Strawberry Pie
Sue Hauser

1 qt. strawberries
1 c. water
1 c. sugar

2 T. cornstarch
2 1/2 T. strawberry Jello

Mix water, cornstarch and sugar; cook until it thickens. Add Jello, Allow to cool and pour over berries in baked 9-inch pie shell.

Buttermilk Pie
Juanita Johnson

1 cube margarine
1/2 c. sugar
3 eggs

1 1/2 T. flour
1 tsp. vanilla
1/2 c. buttermilk

Melt margarine; add rest of ingredients. Put into baked pie shell and bake at 375° for 20 to 30 minutes.

Chocolate Cream Pie
Kim Gould

3/4 c. sugar
1/3 c. cornstarch
2 sq. unsweetened chocolate, cut up
1/2 tsp. salt

2 1/2 c. milk
3 egg yolks, slightly beaten
1/2 tsp. vanilla extract
1 (9") baked pie shell

CREAM TOPPING:

1 c. heavy cream
2 T. confectioners' sugar

1/2 tsp. vanilla extract

In top of a double boiler, combine sugar, cornstarch, chocolate and salt; mix well. Gradually stir in milk. Cook over boiling water, stirring until mixture is thickened, about 10 minutes. Cook, covered, but stirring occasionally, 10 minutes longer. Gradually stir half the hot mixture into beaten egg yolks; return to double boiler. Cook over boiling water, stirring occasionally,S minutes. Remove from heat. Stir in vanilla. Pour chocolate filling into baked pie shell. Refrigerate at least 3 hours, until well chilled. Make Cream Topping 1 hour before serving.
Cream Topping: With rotary beater, beat cream with confectioners' sugar and vanilla until stiff. Spread over pie. Refrigerate. Yield: 6 to 8 servings.

Chocolate Pie

Nina Upton

1 sm. pkg. chocolate chips
2 T. sugar
3 T. milk
Whipped cream, for garnish

4 egg yolks
4 egg whites, stiffly beaten
1 baked pie shell

Melt chocolate chips in microwave; add sugar, milk and egg yolks. Cool. Fold into stiffly-beaten egg whites. Serve with whipped cream and nuts on top.

Chocolate Pie

Cody Cantarini

1 graham cracker crust
1 box (5 oz) Jello Chocolate cook & serve pudding mix

3 cups milk
1 carton cool whip

Stir mix into milk in a medium saucepan. Bring to a boil on medium heat, stirring constantly. Remove from heat and let sit for 5 minutes. Pour into graham cracker crust and refrigerate until set, about 2 hours. Top with cool whip.

Creamy Lemon Pie

Aymee Wilson

3 egg yolks
1 (14 oz.) can Eagle Brand sweetened condensed milk (NOT evaporated milk)
1/2 c. lemon juice

1 (8" or 9") baked pie crust or graham cracker crumb crust
Whipped topping or whipped cream
Lemon zest (opt.)

Preheat oven to 325°. Beat egg yolks in a medium bowl with rotary beater or fork; gradually beat in Eagle Brand and lemon juice. Pour into crust. Bake for 30 to 35 minutes, or until set. Remove from oven. Cool 1 hour. Chill at least 3 hours. Before serving, spread whipped topping or whipped cream over pie. Garnish with lemon zest (optional). Store leftovers, covered, in refrigerator.
Note: You will taste a burst of lemon flavor in every bite of this rich and smooth pie.

CAKES & PIES

Easiest Strawberry Pie

Debbie Hill

4 cups shucked strawberries
14 oz. pre-made strawberry pie glaze

1 package pre-made pie crust
1.5 cups crushed Lorna Doane Cookies
Fresh Mint
Lemon

Toss the cleaned strawberries in a bowl with the glaze, a bit of squeezed lemon and fresh mint snipped into small pieces to taste. Put into refrigerator to chill. Place uncooked pie crust in the 9" pie pan. Line the bottom and sides with crushed Lorna Doane cookies. Bake pie crust according to package directions. Cool. Place strawberry mixture into pie crust and chill for at least an hour. Serve with whip cream or ice cream.

Easy Key Lime Pie

Ruth Miller

1 (14 oz.) can sweetened condensed milk
1/4 c. frozen limeade concentrate, thawed

1 (8 oz.) ctn. frozen nondairy topping, thawed
2 to 3 drops green food coloring
1 (9") graham cracker crust

Combine milk, limeade and thawed topping until well blended. Add food coloring. Pour into crust and refrigerate until chilled or freeze until firm. Ruth used to bring 2 of these to our nurses get-togethers. Yum.

Easy Peach Pie

Diane Enright

1 (9") pie shell
3 c. peaches, sliced
2 eggs
1 c. sugar

1/4 c. flour
Salt
1 c. heavy cream
1 tsp. vanilla

Place peaches into pie shell. Blend rest of ingredients. Pour over peaches. Bake at 375° until done, 25 minutes. Serve warm or chill.

Gancache

Brenda Hauser

2 Cups Chocolate Chips

1 1/2 Cup Whipping Cream.

Combine both in a heated pan and combine until both are melted. Let it cool a little before putting on top of pie. If it is too thin, add more chocolate chips. Put back in freezer. This recipe makes more than you need for the pie but keeps well for other uses. Can also top with whipping cream instead of chocolate.

Alternate cookie crust:

1/2 C Melted Butter
1 C Flour

1/4 C Brown Sugar
2/3 C Chopped Nuts

Combine All And Pat Into Pie Pan. Bake at 350° for 10-15 Minutes or till done
Note: The original recipe uses chocolate frosting for topping Instead of Ganache.

Key Lime Mouse Pie

Jennifer Fuller

Graham Cracker Crust For 8" Pie
2 C Heavy Whipping Cream

1 (14 Oz.) Can Eagle Brand
1/2 C Key Lime Juice

Whip Cream Until Stiff Peaks Form. In A Separate Bowl, Whisk Together Eagle Brand And Lime Juice Until Smooth. Fold Lime Mixture Into Whipping Cream And Put In Prepared Pie Crust. Refrigerate 2 Or More Hours Before Serving.

CAKES & PIES

Lemon Meringue Pie

Grandma Naoma Moore

1/2 c. sugar
1/4 c. cornstarch
Pinch of salt
2 c. cold water

2 egg yolks, beaten
3 T. lemon juice
1 tsp. grated lemon peel
1 tsp, butter

MERINGUE:

3 egg whites
1/8 tsp. cream of tartar

6 T. sugar
Pastry for 9" single-crust pie, baked

In a large saucepan. Combine the sugar, cornstarch and salt. Stir in water until smooth. Cook and stir over medium heat until thickened and bubbly, about 2 minutes. Reduce heat; cook and stir 2 minutes longer. Remove from the heat. Gradually stir 1 cup hot filling into egg yolks; return all to the pan. Bring to a gentle boil; cook and stir for 2 minutes. Remove from the heat. Gently stir in lemon juice, peel and butter until butter is melted. Set aside and keep warm. Meringue: In a small mixing bowl, beat egg whites and cream of tartar on medium speed until soft peaks form. Gradually beat in sugar, 1 tablespoon at a time, on high until stiff glossy peaks form and sugar is dissolved. Pour filling into crust. Spread meringue over hot filling, sealing edges to crust. Bake at 350° for 15 minutes, or until meringue is golden brown. Cool on a wire rack for 1 hour; refrigerate for at least 3 hours before serving. Yield: 8 servings.

When my mom lived in Phoenix, she had lemon trees so we developed many ways to use and freeze lemons and juice. We missed her trees when she moved closer to Camp Verde.

Margaret's Chocolate Pie Filling

Margaret Eurom

FILLING:

1 c. sugar
2 T. cocoa
3 heaping T. cornstarch

2 c. milk
2 or 3 egg yolks

MERINGUE:

3 egg whites
1/2 tsp. cream of tartar

1/8 tsp, baking powder
Dash of Salt
4 T. (or so) sugar

Cook sugar, cocoa, cornstarch, milk and egg yolks over low heat until thick. With mixer on high, beat the egg whites, salt, cream of tartar and baking powder until holds stiff peaks. Gradually add sugar until dissolved. Spread over warm pie filling and bake 10 minutes at 400°. I swear, it even works for me.

Margarita Pie

Norma Wombacher

1/2 c. margarine
1 1/4 c. crushed pretzels
1/4 c. sugar
1 can Eagle Brand milk

1/3 c. ReaLime juice or can use fresh
2 to 4 T. tequila
1 c. whipped topping

In a small pan, melt margarine; stir in pretzel crumbs and sugar. Mix well. Press crumbs on bottom and up sides of buttered 9-inch pie plate. Chill. In a large bowl, combine Eagle Brand milk, lime juice and tequila. Mix well. Fold in whipped topping. Freeze or chill until firm, 4 hours in freezer or 2 hours in refrigerator. Garnish with lime wedges. To make pretzel crumbs, just put pretzels in blender. Don't leave any big chunks.

Mincemeat Pie

Sue Hauser

3 lb. beef or venison
6 lb. sour apples
6 Lb. raisins
1/2 lb. citron
1 T. cloves
1 tsp. cinnamon

1 tsp. mace
1 tsp. nutmeg
2 Lb. sugar
2 c. cider vinegar
2 c. molasses
1 T. salt

Simmer meat until tender. Cool. Grind meat and apples. Add remaining ingredients plus 2 cups of stock. Simmer 1 hour, stirring frequently. Pour into sterilized jars. Process as instructed in canning manual. Yield: 7 quarts.

Mock Apple Pie

Loretta Polston

6 c. zucchini (lg. zucchini are better)
1 1/4 c. sugar
1 1/2 T. flour
1 1/2 tsp. cream of tartar

1 1/2 tsp. cinnamon
Dash of salt
Dash of nutmeg
Dough, for double pie crust

Pare zucchini; wash and slice lengthwise. Remove seeds. Slice like apples. Add a little water and bring to boil in a large saucepan. Simmer for about 15 minutes, or until tender. Cool and drain well. Add rest of ingredients and place into an unbaked 9-inch pie crust. Cover with top pie crust and flute to seal edges. Cut slits into top of crust. Bake at 350° for 45 to 60 minutes. A wonderful Illinois cousin. Great cook, too.

Mother's Pie Crust

Naoma Moore

1 T. sugar
1/4 tsp. salt
4 c. flour
2 c. Crisco

1 T. vinegar
1 egg, beaten in measuring c. (finish filling with water to equal 1 c. liquid)

Mix all ingredients well until it forms a ball. Can be refrigerated for up to 2 weeks. She divides it into 6 portions, wraps it in Saran Wrap, and freezes. Just take out desired amount and pop into the microwave for 20 seconds or so. Rolls out perfectly.

Mountain Top Pie

Dollie Enright

1 Can Peaches
1 c. flour
1/2 c. sugar or honey
3/4 c. milk

Dash of salt
1 1/2 tsp. baking powder
1 cube margarine, melted in pan

Melt the margarine in an 8- or 9-inch iron skillet. Add 1 can peaches. Mix together the flour, sugar or honey, milk, salt and baking powder. Pour over top of peaches. This is an old recipe of my Grandma Dollie's. She used whatever fruit, fresh or canned, was available and it was always good. You can also use whole wheat flour, if desired.

N0- Weep Meringue

Teddy Whitaker

1/2 c. cold water
1 T. cornstarch
2 T. sugar

3 egg whites
Dash of cream of tartar
6 T. sugar

Cook water, cornstarch and 2 tablespoons sugar until thickened and let cool. Beat egg whites with cream of tartar until foamy. Add sugar, a little at a time, beating until soft peaks form. Add cooled cornstarch mixture and beat until well mixed. Spread on cooled pie and brown in 375° oven for 12 to 15 minutes.

Ohio Lemon Pie

Juanita Johnson

2 c. water
1 1/2 c. sugar
5 T. cornstarch

3 eggs
1/3 c. lemon juice
2 T. butter or margarine

Cook water, sugar and cornstarch until thick; add the eggs and lemon juice. Pour into baked pie shell and dot with margarine. Chill. Make a meringue, using 3 egg whites and 5 teaspoons sugar. Bake at 400° for 5 minutes.

Pecan Pie

Patty Fox

This was Number 1 at the ranch.

Cream 1/3 cup butter.
Add 1/2 cup brown sugar; cream well.
Blend in: 1 c. light corn syrup
Add: 3 eggs, slightly beaten

1 tsp. vanilla
1 c. chopped pecans

Pour into a 9-inch shell. Bake at 450° for 10 minutes. Turn down to 350° until set, about 25 minutes.

Pecan Pie

Mary Hauser

1 c. brown sugar
1/2 c. granulated sugar
1 T. flour
2 eggs

2 T. milk
1 tsp. vanilla
1/2 c. melted butter
1 c. pecans

Mix all ingredients. Add nuts. Bake in an 8- or 9-inch pie shell. Bake at 350° for 45 minutes.

Pete's Peanut Butter Pie

Jennifer Fuller

1-Cup Sugar
1 - 8 Oz. Pkg. Cream Cheese, Softened
1-Cup Peanut Butter (Smooth or Chunky)

1 T. Vanilla
1 T. Butter
1-Cup Heavy Cream (Whipping Cream)

Blend Together Sugar, Cream Cheese And Peanut Butter, Then Add Vanilla And Butter. Blend Some More And Add Heavy Cream, Blend A Little More And Put In Prepared 9" Graham Cracker Crust. Put In Freezer. After The Pie Is Solid Spread Ganache On Top And Freeze Again. Take Out Of Freezer A Little Before Serving So It will Be Softer.

Pumpkin Pie

Brenda Hauser

1 1/2 c. cooked pumpkin
1 c. milk
1 c. sugar
1/4 tsp. salt
1 T. butter, melted

1/4 tsp. nutmeg
1/2 tsp. cinnamon
2 eggs, slightly beaten
1 tsp. vanilla

Combine the above ingredients and mix well. Pour into unbaked pastry shell. Bake at 325° for about 1 1/2 hours. Test periodically with a dry knife after 1 1/4 hours. When knife comes out clean, pie is done. Serve with whipped cream or Cool Whip.

Sybil's Own Pecan Pie

Betty Frazee

1 1/2 c. chopped pecans (I left about 1/3 of them in halves)
1/2 cube oleo
3/4 c. white Karo syrup
1/4 c. maple syrup (I used Country Kitchen pancake syrup)

1 c. white sugar
1/4 c. brown sugar, packed
4 eggs, beaten
2 tsp. vanilla

Preheat oven to 350°. You need an unbaked pie crust in your pie pan (makes a 9- or 10-inch pie). Put pecans in bottom of unbaked pie crust.

Mix all other ingredients together well and pour over pecans. Bake for 50 minutes to an hour, until knife inserted into center comes out clean. Cool well before cutting. **Betty's Notes:** I baked it on the lowest rack in my oven (gas stove) so the pecans wouldn't get too brown. Things brown more in the stoves I have had when they are nearer the top of the oven. The knife comes out with clear syrup on it, but not clean like a pumpkin pie does. I baked mine the full hour. I left part of the pecans in halves just because I thought it would be prettier. Mine turned out great; I hope the next time it does. Sybil told me she got this recipe when she was taking care of a family in Oklahoma over 50 years ago, and that she made it many, many times and it never once failed her. I hope to be as lucky. I usually get the pecans too brown or it is too runny. Sure is a lot of sugar, but it tasted really good.

Walnut Applesauce Pie

Norma Wombacher

1 c. brown sugar, packed
1/3 c. sugar
1 T. flour
1 egg + 1 egg white
1/2 c. unsweetened applesauce

2 T. milk
1 tsp. vanilla
1 c. chopped walnuts
1 (9") unbaked pie shell

In a mixing bowl, combine sugar and flour; add egg, egg whites, applesauce, milk and vanilla. Mix well. Stir in walnuts. Pour into pie shell. Bake at 375° for 40 to 45 minutes, or until set.

Desserts

Apple Cobbler

Grandma Dollie Enright

FILLING:

5 c. sliced tart apples	1/2 tsp. cinnamon
3/4 c. sugar	1/4 tsp. salt
2 T. flour	2 T. butter or margarine
1 T. lemon juice	1/4 c. water
1 tsp. vanilla	

BATTER:

1/2 c. flour	1/4 tsp. salt
1/2 c. sugar	2 T. margarine
1/2 tsp. baking powder	1 egg, beaten

Filling: In a medium bowl, combine apple, sugar, flour, lemon juice, vanilla, cinnamon, salt and water. Tum into an 8x8-inch baking dish. Dot with 2 tablespoons butter or margarine. Preheat oven to 375°.

Batter: In a medium bowl, combine batter ingredients; beat with wooden spoon until smooth. Drop in 9 portions over filling, spooning evenly. Batter will spread during baking. Bake for 35 to 40 minutes, or until apple is tender and crust is golden. Serve warm with cream. Yield: 9 servings.

Apple Crisp

Kerri Hauser

3 med.-sized apples	1/2 c. flour
3/4 c. quick-cooking oats	1/2 c. butter or margarine
3/4 c. brown sugar	

Peel apples and remove cores. Slice into thin slices and put into lightly- greased round pie pan. In a bowl, mix oats, sugar and flour. Add butter or margarine and stir until mixture is crumbly. Put mixture on apples. Bake for 30 to 35 minutes at 350°. Yield: 6 servings. This is another one of Dick's favorites.

DESSERT

159

Apricot Cobbler

Loretta Polston

1/2 c. sugar
1 T. cornstarch
4 c. fresh or frozen apricots
2 T. water
1 c. Bisquick baking mix

1/4 c. milk
1/4 c. chopped nuts
1 T. sugar
1 T. butter, melted

Mix 1/2 cup sugar and cornstarch in a 2-quart saucepan. Stir in apricots and water. Heat to boiling, stirring constantly. Boil and stir 1 minute. Pour into ungreased 1 l/2-quart casserole. Stir together remaining ingredients until a soft dough forms. Drop dough by 6 tablespoonfuls onto hot apricot mixture. Bake at 425° for 15 minutes, or until golden brown. Serve with cream, if desired. Variation: You can use any fruit that you want.

Apricot Strudel

Teddy Whitaker

1 (8 oz.) pkg. cream cheese
2 sticks margarine
2 c. plain flour
1 jar apricot preserves

Brown sugar
Cinnamon
1 c. nuts (in blender)
Confectioners' sugar

Cream the cream cheese, margarine and flour; mix. Divide into 3 balls; wrap in aluminum foil and place in refrigerator overnight. Roll pastry thin and spread on preserves (1/3 jar for each ball). Sprinkle on brown sugar, cinnamon and nuts. Roll and close ends; place on cookie sheet and bake at 400° until browned. Let cool. Roll in confectioners' sugar and slice.

Aunt Glenna's Apple Dumplings

Betty Haywood

1 egg, beaten into
1 c. sour cream
2 tsp. baking powder
2 c. flour

1/4 tsp. salt
1/2 tsp. baking soda
1 1/2 T. sugar

Sift together flour, baking soda, baking powder, salt and sugar; blend with egg mixture. Roll dough into an oblong sheet. Spread with 4 large apples, peeled and cut into fine pieces. Sprinkle apples with 1/2 cup sugar and 1/4 teaspoon nutmeg. Dot with butter. Roll as a cinnamon roll. Cut into 'l-inch slices and place, cut-side up, into a greased baking dish.

SAUCE:

3/4 c. white sugar
3/4 c. brown sugar
2 T. cornstarch

1/2 c. sour cream
1/2 c. hot water

Mix well and pour over rolls. Bake in moderate oven until browned and sauce looks glazed

Banana bread brownies

Patty Hauser Ink

1 1/2 C. sugar
1 Cup sour cream
1/2 cup softened butter
2 eggs
1 3/4 Cup ripe bananas mashed (3 or 4)
2 tsp vanilla

2 Cups flour
1 Tsp soda
3/4 Tsp salt
1 Cup chopped walnuts

Mix well - bake at 375 degrees for 20-25 minutes

FROSTING

1/2 cup butter
1 1/2 tsp vanilla

3 T. Warm milk
4 Cups powdered sugar (approx) to spread consistency

Berry Cobbler

Tammie Dunn

5 cups berries
1.5 cups sugar
1 cup flour
1/2 cup butter

1.5 tsp baking powder
1/4 tsp salt
3/4 cup milk

Grease 2qt baking dish. Melt butter in dish while oven is preheating. Toss berries with 1/2 cup sugar. Add berries to baking dish over butter. Mix remaining sugar, flour, baking powder and salt. Add milk to dry mixture. Mix just until blended. Pour batter over berries. Bake at 350 approx 45 minutes until knife inserted comes out clean. Serve warm with whip cream or ice cream.

Best Banana Pudding

Brenda Hauser

1 1/2 c. sugar, divided
2 T. flour
1 1/2 c. evaporated milk
3 eggs
1 stick butter

1 tsp, vanilla
3 or 4 bananas
3/4 box vanilla wafers
1/4 tsp. cream of tartar

Mix 1 cup sugar and flour in a saucepan. Separate eggs. Beat egg yolks with a fork. Add milk in same cup as yolks. Slowly stir egg-milk mixture into sugar-flour mixture until blended. Put saucepan on low heat and allow to cook until a custard forms and thickens. Stir well. Remove custard from heat; add butter and vanilla and allow to cool. Line a quart- size dish (5x9-inch) with layers of vanilla wafers and bananas. Pour custard over wafers and bananas. In a small mixer bowl, add cream of tartar to the egg whites and beat until frothy, then add other 1/2 cup sugar and beat to stiff peaks. Bake at 375° in a preheated oven for 10 to 12 minutes, or until golden brown. Yield: 6 to 8 servings

DESSERT

Blueberry Torte

Grandma Sue Hauser

20 graham crackers, crushed
1/2 c. melted butter
1/2 c. brown sugar, packed
1 (8 oz.) pkg. cream cheese
1/2 c. white sugar

2 eggs
2 T. lemon juice
1 can blueberry pie filling
1 ctn. Cool Whip

Mix crackers with butter and brown sugar; pat firmly on bottom of a 9x13-inch cake pan. Mix cream cheese, white sugar and eggs until smooth. Add lemon juice. Pour over crust. Bake for 20 minutes at 350°. Cool and spoon pie filling over filling. Top with Cool Whip. Chill overnight. Cut into squares. Yield: 12 servings.

Bread Pudding

Naoma Moore

2 T. butter, softened
1 (12 oz.) loaf day-old French or
Italian-type white bread
1 qt. milk
3 eggs

1 c. sugar
1/2 c. raisins
2 T. vanilla extract
1/2 tsp. freshly-grated nutmeg
1/2 tsp. cinnamon

Preheat oven to 350°. Butter a 9x13x2-inch baking dish and set aside. Break bread into chunks, dropping them into a bowl. Pour milk over them. When bread is softened, crumble into small bits and let soak until all the milk is absorbed. In a small bowl, beat 3 eggs and 1 cup of sugar together with whisk or electric mixer until the mixture is smooth and thick. Stir in the raisins, vanilla extract, cinnamon and nutmeg, then pour the egg mixture over the bread crumbs. Stir until all the ingredients are well combined. Pour the bread pudding into baking dish. Place the dish in a large shallow roasting pan set in the middle of the oven. Add water to the roasting pan to a depth of about 1 inch. Bake 1 hour, or until a knife inserted in the center comes out clean.

SAUCE:

8 T. butter, cut into bits
1 c. sugar

1 egg
1/2 c. bourbon or brandy

Whiskey Sauce: Melt butter bits in top of double boiler set over hot (not boiling) water. Stir 1 cup of sugar and 1 egg together in a small bowl and add the mixture to the butter. Stir for 2 to 3 minutes, until the sugar dissolves completely or the egg will curdle. Remove the pan from the heat and let the sauce cool to room temperature before stirring in the bourbon. Serve the bread pudding at once and present the whiskey sauce separately. Yield: 8 to 10 servings.

Breakfast Apple Dumplings

Betty Black

4 Granny Smith apples
2 cans Pillsbury crescent rolls
1 cube butter or margarine

1 c. orange juice
1/2 c. sugar

Wash and quarter apples. Separate rolls and roll one crescent roll around each piece of apple. Line them in a 9x13-inch baking dish. Melt butter or margarine in a saucepan and add the orange juice and sugar. Bring to a boil and pour over apples. Bake at 350° for 30 to 35 minutes, until golden brown. I serve this and make-ahead egg casserole for an easy breakfast that serves a bunch.

Cherry Cake

Korki Walker

1 angel food cake
2 boxes instant vanilla pudding

2 cans cherry pie filling
1 pt. sour cream

Cut cake into squares about 1/2-inch thick. Line the bottom of a 9x13-inch cake pan. Pour both cans of cherry pie filling on top of the cake (except for 2 cherries). Put the remaining cake on top of the cherries. Mix pudding as directed on package, except omit 1 cup of milk and add 1 pint sour cream instead. Mix until smooth. Pour over the cake like frosting. Put the 2 cherries on top for decoration and chill for 1 hour.

Cherry Pudding

Kim Gould

3/4 c. sugar
3 T. butter
1 egg
1/8 tsp. salt
1 c. milk

2 c. flour
2 tsp. baking powder
3/4 c. sugar
1/2 c. hot water
2 c. cherries, drained

Mix sugar, butter, egg, salt, milk, flour and baking powder (as for a cake) and pour into a buttered baking pan, 8x10 inches. Mix cherries, hot water and sugar; pour over batter. Bake in 350° oven for about 30 minutes. Serve with Cool Whip.

DESSERT

163

Cherry Yum Yum

Claudia Hauser

2 c. flour
2 sticks margarine
1/2 c. pecans, finely chopped
1 (8 oz.) pkg. cream cheese

2 c. powdered sugar
2 c. Cool Whip
1 can cherry pie filling

Beat flour and margarine with mixer until smooth. Press mixture into a 9x13-inch cake pan. Bake for 20 to 25 minutes at 375°. Let cool. With mixer, beat cream cheese, powdered sugar and Cool Whip until smooth. Pour into cooled crust. Top with pie filling.

Classic Cheesecake

Kristi Hauser Bright

Crust:

1 ½ cups graham cracker crumbs
¼ tsp ground cinnamon
1/3 cup unsalted butter, melted

Filling:

4 (8 oz) packages cream cheese, softened
1 ¼ cups sugar
½ cup sour cream

2 tsp vanilla extract
5 large eggs

Topping:

½ cup sour cream
2 tsp sugar

Preheat oven to 475 degrees F. Place a large pan filled with ½ inch of water in oven.

Make crust: Mix graham cracker crumbs and cinnamon, add butter. Press crust onto bottom and part way up a 9" springform pan with the bottom lined with parchment paper. Wrap a large piece of foil around bottom of pan and just up the sides. Put in freezer until filling is prepared.

Filling: Mix cream cheese, sugar, sour cream and vanilla using electric mixer. Blend until smooth and creamy. Scrape down sides of bowl. Wisk eggs in a bowl and slowly add to cream cheese mixture, mixing on low just until eggs are incorporated.

Remove crust from freezer. Pour in filling. Place cheesecake into the pan with water, and bake for 12 minutes. Turn over down to 350 degrees and bake for SO to 60 minutes, until cheesecake top is golden. Remove to wire rack. Make topping by combining sour cream and sugar and spread over cake. Cover and refrigerate for a least 4 hours.

Crock-Pot Apple Crisp

Brenda Hauser

TOPPING:

1/2 c. flour
1/4 c. light brown sugar
1/4 c. granulated sugar
1/4 tsp, cinnamon
1/8 tsp. nutmeg

Pinch of salt
4 T. cold unsalted butter, cut into pieces
1/2 c. chopped pecans

FILLING:

3 T. granulated sugar
2 tsp. lemon juice
1 1/2 tsp. cornstarch
1/4 tsp. ground ginger

1/4 tsp. ground cinnamon
6 Lg. Granny Smith apples, peeled, cored & cut into slices

Coat a 2- to 4-quart slow-cooker bowl with nonstick cooking spray; set aside.
Topping: In a small bowl, mix together flour, sugars, cinnamon, nutmeg and salt. Add butter; work into flour mixture using a pastry blender or fingers until coarse crumbs form. Stir in pecans and set aside.
Filling: In a large bowl, whisk together sugar, lemon juice, cornstarch, ginger and cinnamon. Stir in apples; toss to coat. Spoon apple mixture into slow-cooker and sprinkle topping over it. Cover and cook on high for 2 hours or low for 4 hours, or until apples are tender. Serve with vanilla ice cream, if desired. Yield: 8 servings.

Delicious Brownies

Sherrie Nance

1 cube margarine
1 c. sugar
4 eggs, beaten
1 tsp. vanilla

1 (1 Lb.) can chocolate syrup
1 c. flour
1/2 c. nuts, chopped
1/2 tsp. baking powder

Cream the margarine and sugar; add rest of ingredients. Pour mixture into a greased large cookie sheet with sides and bake for 30 minutes at 350°.

TOPPING:

3 T. margarine
3 T. milk

3/4 cup sugar
1/3 cup chocolate chips.

Bring margarine, milk and sugar to a rolling boil and boil 1/2 minute. Remove from heat and add chocolate chips. Spread on while warm.

DESSERT

Dixie Cobbler
(Peach or Blackberry)

Loretta Polston

2 c. sifted Martha White self-rising flour

About 4 T. water
2/3 c. shortening

Put sifted flour into a bowl and cut half of the shortening in until particles are the size of big green peas. Sprinkle water over the mixture and stir with a fork until it cleans the sides of the bowl. Shape into a ball and wrap in waxed paper; let rise while making filling. Divide in half and roll out in 2 sections to fit a 2-quart dish, lining bottom and sides.

FILLING:

Sugar -about 1/4 c. for frozen fruit, 2 c. for fresh, but sweetened to taste - save 2 T. sugar to go on top.
2 T. cornstarch

2 T. cornstarch
4 c. fruit, fresh or frozen
1/2 tsp. almond extract, for peaches
1 tsp. lemon juice, for blackberries
1 stick or 1/2 c. butter or margarine

Heat oven to 375°; if using glass dish 350°. Combine sugar and cornstarch and mix thoroughly. Add fruit and flavoring. Pour mixture into a pastry-lined 2-quart dish. Dot with butter, saving 2 tablespoons for top. Bring pastry up over fruit, dot the top of the pastry with remaining butter (2 tablespoons) and sprinkle with 2 tablespoons sugar. Bake about 55 minutes.
Note: This cobbler may "juice-over" in baking; place a pan under it.

Empanadas (Turnovers)

Teddy Whitaker

3 c. flour
2 tsp. baking powder
3 T. sugar
1/2 tsp. salt

1/2 c. shortening
1/2 c. milk
1 egg
Use any pie filling

Mix and sift dry ingredients. Cut in shortening. Add enough milk to hold dough together (like pie dough). Make dough balls a little less than the size of a golf ball. Roll out dough on slightly-floured board to 1/8- inch thickness. Place 2 tablespoons fruit mixture in the center. Moisten edges with cold water and fold over and press edges together to seal. (Like a pie.) Bake 15 to 20 minutes at 375°.

Fruit Pizza Wheel

Suzanne Beeler

1/2 c. butter or margarine, softened
1/4 c. brown sugar
1 c. flour
1/4 c. quick-cooking oats
1/4 c. finely-chopped walnuts or pecans
1 (8 oz.) pkg. cream cheese, softened
1/3 c. sugar
1/2 tsp. vanilla

Assorted fruits like orange segments, strawberry halves, kiwi slices, banana slices, pineapple tidbits, blueberries, raspberries or seedless grapes, halved
1/2 c. orange marmalade, peach or apricot preserves
2 T. water

In a small mixing bowl, cream together butter and brown sugar. Work in flour, oats and walnuts. Press dough onto lightly-oiled or parchment- lined 12-inch pizza pan. Prick dough with fork. Bake in preheated 375° oven for 10 to 12 minutes, or until golden brown. Cool; leave crust on pizza pan or move to round cake plate or cardboard. In a medium mixing bowl, combine cream cheese, sugar and vanilla, beating until well blended. Spread over crust. Arrange fruit on cream cheese mixture. In a small bowl, combine marmalade and water. Brush over fruit to form a glaze. Chill. Cut into wedges with pizza cutter.

Fresh Peach Ice Cream

Norma Wombacher

3 c. fresh peaches, peeled
1 jar marshmallow creme

1 c. milk
1 tsp, almond extract

Puree peaches and add marshmallow creme, milk and extract to food processor. Put into ice cream maker, following manufacturer's directions. Easy and yummy.

Funnel Cake

Martha Vick

2 1/2 c. self-rising flour
1/3 c. sugar
1 1/3 c. milk

2 eggs, beaten
Vegetable oil, for frying

Put 1/4 cup oil in skillet and heat to 375°. Take a funnel and put your finger over the hole. Put in 1/4 cup batter. Let it out in hot oil and string it in circles and crisscross. Fry until browned and turn, about 1 minute. Do it like donuts. Sprinkle sugar, or can serve with jelly or syrup. These are served at every event in Southern Illinois. My great-Aunt Martha was a wonderful cook.

German Brownie Torte

Teddy Whitaker

1 1/2 c. sweetened flaked coconut
1 1/2 c. chopped pecans
1/2 c. firmly-packed light brown sugar

1/2 stick (4 T.) butter, melted
1 box family-style fudge brownie mix
2 c. heavy (whipping) cream
1/2 c. confectioners' sugar

Heat oven to 350°. Line a 10x15-inch rimmed baking sheet with heavy- duty foil, letting foil extend above pan on both ends. Coat with nonstick spray. Mix coconut, pecans, brown sugar and butter ill a bowl until well blended; set aside. Prepare brownie mix as package directs for cake-like brownies. Pour batter into prepared pan, spreading evenly. Top with coconut mixture. Bake for 25 minutes, or until a wooden pick inserted in center of cake comes out clean.

Cool in pan on a wire rack. Lift foil by ends onto a cutting board. Cut brownie crosswise in thirds. Beat cream and powdered sugar in a bowl with mixer on medi-um-high speed until moist, stiff peaks form when beaters are lifted.

To Assemble: Place 1 brownie layer, nut-side up, on a serving platter. Spread top with 1 cup whipped cream. Repeat with remaining layers and cream, ending with cake. Frost sides with remaining cream. Refrigerate at least 2 hours. To Serve: Cut with a serrated knife in I-inch slices; cut each slice in half. Yield: 20 servings.

Gooey Chocolate Dessert

Krystal Hollamon

1 c. flour
1 cube margarine
1/2 c. chopped nuts
1 c. powdered sugar

1 (8 oz.) pkg. cream cheese
1 Lg. ctn. Cool Whip
2 sm. pkg. chocolate pudding
3 c. milk

Mix flour and margarine until crumbly. Press into a 9x13-inch pan. Sprinkle with 1/2 cup nuts. Bake 15 minutes at 350°. Cool. Mix powdered sugar and cream cheese until smooth. Fold in half of Cool Whip. Spread on crust. Mix pudding with milk. Spread over first layer. Top with remaining Cool Whip and sprinkle with chopped nuts.

Grandma Foster's 1921 Gingerbread

Aunt Martha Vick

1/2 c. butter (I use margarine)
1/2 c. sugar
1 c. molasses
1 c. boiling water
2 1/2 c. flour
1 tsp, baking powder
1/2 c. raisins

1 tsp. baking soda
1/2 tsp. salt
1 tsp. ginger
1/2 tsp, cloves
1 tsp. cinnamon
2 eggs

There were no directions with this recipe, so I just mix everything in a large bowl and pour into a 9x13-inch pan. Bake for 40 minutes at 350°.

Grandma Wilson's Peach Pudding

Grandma Clara Wall

1/2 c. sugar
1/2 c. flour
1 heaping tsp. baking powder
1 egg
1 tsp. vanilla

Lump of oleo
1/2 c. milk
A little nutmeg
1/4 tsp. salt
1 Lg. can peaches

Mix sugar and oleo. Add egg, milk, then flour with baking powder, nutmeg, vanilla and salt. Now take peaches with all the juice and heat with 1/2 cup sugar and a little more nutmeg. Pour over batter and dot with butter. Bake at 350° until golden brown, about 30 minutes. Note: A lump of oleo is about a tablespoon.

CANDIES

Heavenly Hash

Pat Hauser Ink

1 ctn. Cool Whip
1 sm. pkg. strawberry Jello
3/4 c. sugar
1 pkg. frozen strawberries

1 angel food cake, broken in sm. pieces
1 c. mini marshmallows

Dissolve Jello in 1 cup boiling water; add sugar, strawberries, cake and Cool Whip. Let stand overnight in refrigerator.

Jam-Topped Mini Cheesecakes

Teddy Whitaker

1 c. graham cracker crumbs
3 T. butter, melted
1 (8 oz.) pkg. cream cheese, softened
1/3 c. sugar

1 tsp Vanilla extract
1 egg, lightly beaten
assorted jams, warmed

In a bowl, combine graham cracker crumbs and butter. Press gently onto the bottom of 12 paper-lined muffin cups. In a small mixing bowl, beat the cream cheese, sugar, egg and vanilla until smooth. Spoon over crusts. Bake at 350° for 15 to 16 minutes, or until center is set. Cool for 10 minutes before removing from pan to a wire rack to cool completely. Refrigerate for at least 1 hour. Remove paper liners; top each cheesecake with 1 teaspoon jam. Yield: 1 dozen.

Kay's Cheesecake Cupcakes

Dian Hauser

3 (8 oz.) pkg. cream cheese
5 eggs
1 c. sugar
1 1/2 tsp. vanilla
1 tsp. lemon juice

1 (8 oz.) pkg. sour cream
1/2 c. sugar
1 tsp. vanilla
1 can cherry pie filling

Mix the first 5 ingredients well and bake in cupcake tins lined with paper liners for 40 minutes at 300°. Mix sour cream, sugar and vanilla; put 1 teaspoon on top of each baked cupcake. Put cupcakes back in oven for 5 minutes. Remove and put 1 teaspoon (1 cherry) of pie filling on each cupcake. Refrigerate. Can be frozen.

Lemon Squares

Lucille Edwards

CRUST:

2 sticks margarine
2 c. flour

1/2 c. powdered sugar
1/3 tsp. salt

FILLING:

2 c. sugar
1/4 c. flour

1 tsp. lemon zest
6 T. lemon juice

Cream butter, flour, sugar and salt. Press into a 9x13-inch pan and bake 15 minutes at 350°. Mix filling ingredients and pour over crust while hot. Bake for 25 minutes more. While hot, sprinkle with powdered sugar. Cool and cut. My Aunt Lucille was the greatest cook ever! She used to mail me fudge.

Lunch Lady Peanut Butter Bars

Jennifer Fuller

2 C flour (a little more if above 3500')
2 C sugar
2 eggs, beaten
1 1/2 C peanut butter, divided

1 1/2 C butter, divided
1/2 C + 2 T milk, divided
1 t baking soda
1 t vanilla
1/2 t salt
4 C powdered sugar

Oven 400 line cookie sheet with parchment or foil, but don't grease Mix dry ingredients - flour, sugar, baking soda & salt. Set aside. Whisk Y2 C milk, vanilla & eggs. Set aside. In a saucepan melt 1 C butter & 1 C peanut butter. Bring to a boil. Remove from heat & add flour mixture followed by milk mixture. Mix well. Pour batter onto cookie sheet & spread evenly to edge. Bake 20 minutes or until toothpick comes out clean. Cool completely before frosting. In saucepan, bring 1 stick of butter & Y2 C peanut butter to a boil. Add 2 T milk & slowly add powdered sugar and combine. Add more milk or cream if too thick. Pour frosting over cake & spread to edges. Cool completely before cutting.
Note: I put butter, peanut butter & milk mixtures in a bowl to combine with the Flour mixture to combine instead of trying to do it in the pan.

Moist Brownies

Teddy Whitaker

2 1/2 c. flour
2 c. sugar
112 c. sour cream
1 tsp. salt
1 tsp, baking soda

2 eggs
2 sticks margarine
5 T. cocoa powder
1 c. water

Preheat oven to 350°. In a large bowl, stir together flour, sugar, sour cream, salt, baking soda and eggs. Bring margarine, cocoa and water to a boil in a saucepan. Stir this into flour mixture until smooth. Pour into a greased and floured llx20-inch jellyroll pan. Bake for 20 to 22 minutes.

FROSTING:

1 Lb. powdered sugar
1/2 c. walnuts, well chopped
1 stick margarine

1 tsp, vanilla
3 T. cocoa powder
6T. milk

Bring margarine, cocoa and milk to a boil in a medium-size saucepan. Remove from heat; add sugar, vanilla and nuts. Stir until smooth. Frost evenly over cooled brownies.

DESSERT

No-Bake Fruit Balls

Kayla Cantarini

2 c. Jet-Puffed mini marshmallows
2 c. Honey-Maid graham cracker crumbs
1/2 c. chopped red maraschino cherries
1/2 c. chopped green maraschino cherries

1 (14 oz.) can sweetened condensed milk
1/2 c. chopped Planter's pecans
3 c. Baker's Angel Flake coconut

Combine marshmallows, cracker crumbs, cherries, sweetened condensed milk and pecans; mix well. Shape dough evenly into 5 dozen balls, each about 1 inch in diameter. Roll balls in coconut until evenly coated. Refrigerate 3 hours or until firm. Store in airtight container in refrigerator.

Peach Cobbler, Cake-Style

Ruth Hunter

2 (24 oz.) jars Orchard Select sliced peaches, drained
1/4 c. brown sugar
1/2 c. + 1 T. butter
1 egg

1 c. white sugar
1/2 c. whole milk
c. flour
1 tsp. baking soda
1 tsp, vanilla

Heat oven to 350°. Put drained peaches in an 8-inch square baking dish. Sprinkle with brown sugar. Sprinkle thin slices of 1 tablespoon butter on peaches. Bake for 15 minutes, until bubbly and hot. In a bowl, mix 1/2 cup butter, egg, sugar, milk, flour, baking soda and vanilla for 3 minutes on high speed. Pour batter over peach mixture. Bake on middle rack for 40 to 50 minutes, or until top is golden brown. Yield: 8 servings. Note: Double recipe and bake in a 9x13x2-inch dish for 16 servings.

Pumpkin Roll

Betty Hill

3 eggs
1 c. sugar
3/4 c. flour
1 tsp. baking soda
1 tsp. nutmeg

1/2 tsp. ginger
1 tsp, cinnamon
2/3 c. pumpkin
1 T. lemon juice
1/4 c. ground pecans

FILLING:

8 oz. cream cheese, softened
4 T. margarine or butter

1 c. powdered sugar

Beat eggs until thick and light colored. Add the next 6 ingredients, beating well. Fold in pumpkin and lemon juice. Spread in jellyroll pan lined with parchment paper and sprayed with cooking spray. Bake 15 minutes at 375°. Dump out onto kitchen towel; spread liberally with powdered sugar. Roll up and let cool, then spread with filling and re-roll. Slice and enjoy.

Snow Ice Cream

Kay Hauser

1 egg
1/2 c. sugar
1 c. milk

1 1/2 T. vanilla
Dash of salt
Snow

Mix egg and add sugar, milk, vanilla and salt. Beat well. Add snow until thick and creamy. You can also add fruit juice concentrate (grape is good) to snow, or fruit-flavored Jello. Just mix and eat with a spoon. We don't get much snow in Camp Verde, but at least once a winter, someone will bring back a big ice chest full from the mountains. Yum.

Strawberry-Pretzel Dessert

Teddy Whitaker

2 c. pretzels, crushed
3 T. sugar
3/4 c. butter
8 oz. cream cheese
1 c. powdered sugar

8 oz. Cool Whip
6 oz. strawberry Jello
16 oz. frozen strawberries
3 c. hot water

First Layer: Mix and pat smooth in bottom of a 9x13-inch pan, the pretzels, sugar and butter. Bake 8 minutes in a 400° oven and cool.
Second Layer: Beat cream cheese, powdered sugar and Cool Whip.
Third Layer: Mix Jello, strawberries and water. Bake crust; let cool. Pour second layer onto cooled crust. Pour third layer onto second layer. Chill. Will keep several days.

Too Easy Peach Cobbler

Carolyn Howell

1 (29 oz.) can sliced peaches, drained
4 slices white bread
1 c. sugar
2 T. flour

1 stick margarine or butter, melted
1 tsp. cinnamon
1 egg, beaten

Preheat oven to 350°. Place fruit in an 8x8-inch baking dish. Cut crust from bread and cut each slice into 5 strips. Place strips over peaches. Mix sugar, flour, cinnamon, egg and margarine. Blend well. Pour over bread strips. Bake for 35 to 45 minutes, or until golden brown. Enjoy.

Vanilla Ice Cream

Grandma Sue Hauser

3 c. sugar
4 eggs, beaten
3/4 qt. cream

1 T. vanilla
2 qt. milk
1 sm. pkg. vanilla instant pudding

Beat well with mixer and freeze according to ice cream freezer instructions. This does not need to be cooked.

Candies

Bev's Fudge

Georgia Adams

5 c. sugar
2 cubes margarine
Dash of salt
1 can evaporated milk

2 (12 oz.) bags chocolate chips
1 jar marshmallow creme
1 tsp. vanilla

In a large saucepan, combine sugar, margarine, salt and milk. Put onto stove; stir and cook to boiling. Let boil for 9 minutes, without stirring, at low heat. Remove from heat and add chocolate chips, marshmallow creme and vanilla. Stir until cool and pour into large jellyroll pan or 2 regular-sized cake pans. Cut into squares.

Buckeyes (Peanut Butter Balls)

Kristi Hauser Bright

2 ½ cups sifted confectioners sugar
1 cup smooth peanut butter
6 T unsalted butter, melted
½ tsp pure vanilla extract

¼ tsp salt
8 ounces semisweet chocolate
1 tsp vegetable shortening

Line a baking sheet with parchment paper. Beat the confectioners sugar, peanut butter, vanilla and salt with an electric mixer, until well combined. Scoop 2 mounds and roll into balls. Arrange them on the prepared baking sheet and put in freezer for about 20 minutes.
In a double boiler, melt chocolate and shortening. Stick a toothpick in each peanut butter ball and dip in chocolate mixture and return the ball to the baking sheet. When all are finished, refrigerate until firm. I usually make these in bulk and freeze during holidays.

Buttery Almond Crunch

Kerri Hauser

1 T. + 1/2 c. butter (no substitutes), softened, divided
1/2 c. sugar

1 T. light corn syrup
1 c. sliced almonds

Line an 8-inch square pan with foil; butter the foil with 1/2 tablespoon butter. Set aside. Spread the sides of a heavy saucepan with 1/2 tablespoon butter. Add 1/2 cup of butter, sugar and com syrup. Bring to a boil over medium-high heat, stirring constantly. Cook and stir until mixture is golden brown, about 3 minutes. Stir in almonds. Quickly pour into prepared pan. Chill until firm. Invert pan and remove foil. Break candy into pieces. Yield: 10 ounces.

Caramel

Grandma Sue Hauser

2 c. sugar
1 1/2 c. syrup
3 c. cream

4 T. butter
2 T. vanilla

Cook sugar, syrup and 1 cup cream to soft ball stage. Add 1 cup cream and cook again to soft ball stage. Add last cup of cream and cook to very firm ball. Stir occasionally all during cooking. Add butter and vanilla; beat until smooth and thick. This is coating for the pecan log roll.

Cashew Caramel Fudge

Cody Cantarini

2 tsp. + 1/2 c. butter (no substitutes), softened, divided
1 (5 oz.) can evaporated milk
2 1/2 c. sugar
2 c. (12 oz.) semi-sweet chocolate chips

1 (7 oz.) jar marshmallow creme
24 caramels, quartered
3/4 c. salted cashew halves
1 tsp. vanilla extract

Line a 9-inch square baking pan with foil; butter the foil with 2 teaspoons butter. Set aside. In a large heavy saucepan, combine milk, sugar and remaining butter. Cook and stir over medium heat until sugar is dissolved. Bring to a rapid boil; boil for 5 minutes, stirring constantly. Remove from the heat; stir in chocolate chips and marshmallow creme until melted. Fold in caramels, cashews and vanilla; mix well. Pour into prepared pan. Cool. Remove from pan and cut into 1-inch squares. Store at room temperature. Yield: about 3 pounds.

CANDIES

Chocolate Caramel Candy Bars

Lois Baldwin

1 (14 oz.) pkg. caramel candies, un-wrapped
1 can evaporated milk, divided use
1 regular box chocolate cake mix

8 T. butter, room temp.
2 c. semi-sweet chocolate chips, divided use

Preheat oven to 350º and line a 9x13-inch baking pan with foil and spray with non-stick cooking spray. In a double boiler, gently heat unwrapped caramel candies with 1/3 cup evaporated milk. Stir often, until smooth. Remove from heat and cool to room temperature, but still liquid. In a large bowl, combine cake mix, butter and remaining 1/3 cup evaporated milk. Stir until smooth. Batter will be thick. Spread half of the cake mix batter into baking pan, smoothing to an even thickness. Bake 8 to 10 minutes. Sprinkle 1 cup of chocolate chips over hot bottom layer. Slowly pour melted caramel over chocolate chips. Drop teaspoonfuls of remaining cake batter over the top. Smooth the batter flat as possible. Return pan to oven and bake an additional 12 to 15 minutes. Distribute remaining 1 cup of chocolate chips evenly over the top of the hot cake, pressing slightly into the top to secure chips. Cool, then refrigerate 30 minutes before cutting into bars.

Chocolate Fudge

Aymee Wilson

Butter (to butter pan)
2 c. sugar
1/8 tsp. salt
3/4 c. evaporated milk
1 tsp, light corn syrup

2 (1 oz.) sq. unsweetened chocolate
2 T. margarine or butter
1 tsp. vanilla
1/2 c. chopped walnuts or pecans

Butter sides of a heavy 2-quart saucepan. Combine sugar, salt, evaporated milk, corn syrup and chocolate in pan. Cook and stir over medium heat until chocolate melts and sugar dissolves. Cook to soft ball stage (236°) without stirring. Remove immediately from heat. Add margarine without stirring. Cool to lukewarm (110°). Stir in vanilla. Pour into mixer bowl. Attach bowl and flat beater to mixer. Turn to Speed 2 and mix about 8 minutes, or until fudge stiffens and loses its gloss. Quickly turn to Stir Speed and add walnuts, mixing just until blended. Spread in a buttered 9x9x2-inch baking pan. Cool at room temperature. Cut into J-inch squares when firm.

Chocolate Peanut Clusters

Ben Hauser

1 pkg. chocolate pudding, not instant
1 c. sugar
1/2 c. evaporated milk

1 T. butter or margarine
1 c. small, salted peanuts

Mix all ingredients, except peanuts, in a heavy 1 1/2-quart saucepan. Cook and stir to full, all-over boil. Lower heat and keep stirring while mixture boils slowly for 3 minutes. Take off heat. Stir in peanuts, all at once. Beat until candy starts to thicken. With 2 teaspoons, drop mixture quickly onto waxed paper to form 24 clusters.

Chocolate Pecan Caramels

Zach Hauser

1 T. + 1 c. butter (not substitutes), softened, divided
1 1/2 c. coarsely-chopped pecans, toasted
1 c. (6 oz.) semi-sweet chocolate chips
2 c. packed brown sugar

1 c. light corn syrup
1/4 c. water
1 (14 oz.) can sweetened condensed milk
2 tsp. vanilla extract

Line a 9x13x2-inch baking pan with foil; butter the foil with 1 tablespoon butter. Sprinkle with pecans and chocolate chips; set aside. In a heavy saucepan over medium heat, melt remaining butter. Add brown sugar, corn syrup and water. Cook and stir until mixture comes to a boil. Stir in milk. Cook, stirring constantly, until a candy thermometer reads 248° (firm ball stage). Pour into prepared pan (do not scrape saucepan). Cool completely before cutting. Yield: about 21/2 pounds (6 3/4 dozen pieces).
Note: I recommend that you test your candy thermometer before each use by bringing water to a boil; the thermometer should read 212°. Adjust your recipe temperature up or down based on your test

Cocoa Box Fudge

Brenda Hauser

2 c. sugar
2/3 c. milk
2 sq. chocolate, or 1/3 c. cocoa
2 T. corn syrup

2 T. butter or margarine
1 tsp. vanilla
1 1/2 c. nuts

Cook sugar, milk, chocolate, syrup and salt to a soft ball stage. Remove from heat and add butter, vanilla and nuts. Beat with spoon until thick and creamy. Pour onto buttered pan. Dick's favorite.

Divinity

Brenda Hauser

3 c. sugar
3/4 c. light corn syrup
1/2 c. water

2 egg whites
1 tsp. almond extract
1 c. chopped walnuts or pecans

Place sugar, com syrup and water in a heavy saucepan. Cook and stir over medium heat to hard ball stage (248°). Remove from heat and let stand until temperature drops to 220° without stirring. Place egg whites in mixer bowl. Attach bowl and wire whip to mixer. Tum to Speed 8 and whip about 1 minute, or until soft peaks form. Gradually add syrup in a fine stream and whip about 2 1/2 minutes longer. Turn to Speed 4. Add almond extract and whip 20 to 25 minutes, or until mixture starts to become dry. Tum to Stir Speed and add walnuts, mixing just until blended. Drop mixture from measuring tablespoon onto waxed paper or greased baking sheet to form patties.

Fudge-Nut Balls

Emily Hauser

1 (6 oz.) pkg. semi-sweet chocolate pieces
3 T. corn syrup
1/2 c. evaporated milk

1 tsp. vanilla
1/2 c. powdered sugar
1 c. finely-chopped unsalted nuts
2 1/2 c. vanilla wafer crumbs

Heat the chocolate pieces in a 2-quart bowl over boiling water until melted. Remove bowl from water and stir in the corn syrup, milk and vanilla gradually. Add the sugar and mix until smooth. Stir in the nuts. Fold in the wafer crumbs, about 1/4 at a time, and mix well. Let stand at room temperature for 30 minutes. Shape into I-inch balls, and roll balls, one at a time, in additional powdered sugar. Chill. Yield: about 4 1/2 dozen.

Grandma Reddell's Caramels

Lynn Reddell

2 c. sugar
2 c. white Karo syrup
1/2 c. real butter

1/4 tsp. salt
2 c. Carnation canned milk
1 tsp. vanilla

Cook sugar, syrup, butter and salt until clear, then add milk. Cook to very firm ball stage, stirring constantly. Remove from heat and stir until almost cool. Pour into greased pan and let stand for 24 hours before cutting into squares. Grandma always wrapped each square in Saran Wrap and stored them in a covered tin.

Lucille's Cocoa Fudge

Aunt Lucille Edwards

2 c. sugar
3 T. cocoa
1 c. milk

2 T. white syrup
Pinch of salt

Mix cocoa and part of milk to make a paste. Add sugar and all of milk, except 1/4 cup. Add syrup and salt; wipe crystals from sides of pan. Bring to a full boil and stir in the remaining 1/4 cup milk. Let cook until it forms a soft ball when small amount is dropped in cold water. Remove from fire and add 2 tablespoons margarine and nuts, if desired. Set in cool water for a few minutes. Beat until thick enough to drop by spoonfuls onto waxed paper or pour into buttered pan.

Nutty Chocolate Marshmallow Cups

Jacob Gould

2 c. milk chocolate chips
1 (14 oz.) can sweetened condensed milk
1 (7 oz.) jar marshmallow creme

40 Lg. marshmallows
4 c. coarsely-chopped pecans (about 1lb.)

In a microwave or heavy saucepan, heat chocolate chips, milk and marshmallow creme just until melted; stir until smooth (mixture will be thick). With tongs, immediately dip marshmallows, one at a time, in chocolate mixture. Shake off excess chocolate; quickly roll in pecans. Place on waxed-paper-lined baking sheets. (Reheat chocolate mixture if necessary for easier coating.) Refrigerate until firm. Store in the refrigerator in an airtight container. Yield: 40 candies.

Toffee Butter Crunch

Naoma Moore

1/2 c. coarsely-chopped almonds or pecans, toasted
1 c. butter
1 c. sugar
3 T. water

1 T. light-colored corn syrup
3/4 c. semi-sweet chocolate pieces
1/2 c. finely-chopped almonds or pecans, toasted

Line a 9x13x2-inch baking pan with foil, extending foil over edges of pan. Sprinkle the 1/2 cup coarsely-chopped nuts in pan. Set pan aside. Butter sides of a heavy 2-quart saucepan. In saucepan, melt butter. Add sugar, water and corn syrup. Cook and stir over medium-high heat until mixture boils. Clip a candy thermometer to side of pan. Reduce heat to medium; continue boiling at a moderate steady rate, stirring frequently, until thermometer registers 290°, soft crack stage (about 15 minutes). Watch carefully after 280° to prevent scorching. Remove saucepan from heat; remove thermometer. Pour candy into the prepared pan. Let candy stand about 5 minutes, or until firm; sprinkle with chocolate. Let stand 1 to 2 minutes. When chocolate has softened, spread over candy. Sprinkle with the 1/2 cup finely-chopped nuts. Chill until firm. When candy is firm, use foil to lift it out of the pan; break into pieces. Store tightly- covered. Yield: about 1 1/2 pounds (48 servings).

179

1956

JOHN & MAMIE EUROM

IRA & PEARL HAUSER

Cookies

DICK HAUSER's 80TH BIRTHDAY CELEBRATION

Almond Joy Cookies

Patty Hauser Ink

1 Cup Butter
1 1/2 Cups White Sugar
1 1/2 Cups Brown Sugar
4 Eggs - Beat In One At A Time
3 Tsp Vanilla

4 1/2 Cups Flour
2 Tsp Baking Soda
1 Tsp Salt
4 Cups Chocolate Chips
2 Cups Sweetened Coconut
2 Cups Chopped Almonds

Bake At 375º on Greased Cooking Sheet 8 To 10 Minutes.

Ammonia Cookies

Jennifer Fuller

1 1/4 C Butter, Softened
1 C Solid Shortening (Butter Flavored Crisco)
2 1/2 C Sugar

3 C Flour
2 C Flaked Coconut (I Chop It A Little More)
2 Tsp Bakers Ammonia

Preheat Oven To 350º. Combine Butter, Shortening, Sugar, Coconut, Flour And Ammonia And Mix Well; Form Into Walnut Sized Balls. Flatten With A Fork And Place On Ungreased Baking Sheet. Bake 10 Minutes Until Light Brown. These Are Very Delicate And Really Good.

Ann's Oatmeal Cookies

AnnaMae Hileman

1 c. shortening
1 c. sugar
1 c. brown sugar
1 tsp. vanilla
2 eggs

3 c. oats
2 c. flour
1 tsp. baking soda
1 tsp. baking powder
3/4 tsp. salt

Cream shortening and sugars well with mixer. Add eggs and vanilla. Add flour, oats, baking soda, baking powder and salt. Mix well. It is very thick. Can add raisins, coconut or nuts, if desired. Bake at 350° for 10 to 12 minutes. Serve with milk.

Applesauce Cookies

Patty Hauser Ink

1/2 Cup Shortening
1 Cup Sugar
Cream Shortening And Sugar
Add: 1 Cup Strained Apple Sauce Unsweetened
2 1/4 Cup Flour

1 Tsp Salt
1/4 Tsp Cloves, Cinnamon, And Nutmeg.
1/2 Cup Raisins
1/2 Cup Nutmeats

Drop On Greased Cookie Sheet Bake At 400 Degrees For 10 -12 Minutes.

Apple Sauce Cookies

Tammie Dunn

Dry Ingredients:

4 cups flour
4 tsp cinnamon
1 tsp cloves
1 tsp nutmeg
2 tsp baking soda
2 tsp salt
2 cups sugar

Wet ingredients:

2 tsp vanilla
1 cup shortening
2 eggs
2 cups apple sauce

Mix dry ingredients. In separate bowl, mix wet ingredients except apple sauce. Mix dry and wet ingredients and then slowly fold in the applesauce. Spoon into lightly sprayed or oiled baking sheet. Bake at 350* for - 15 minutes.

Aunt Nettie Eurom's Caramel Cookies

Nettie Eurom

1/2 c. butter or margarine
1 1/2 c. brown sugar
2 eggs, well beaten
2 1/4 c. flour
1/2 tsp. salt

1 tsp, baking soda
1 c. sour cream
1 tsp. vanilla
2/3 c. walnuts (opt.)

Cream butter, sugar, eggs, vanilla and sour cream. Add the rest of the ingredients. Drop by spoon onto baking sheet. Allow room to spread.
Bake at 350° for 10 to 15 minutes.

Caramel Icing:

6 tablespoons butter
11/2 cups confectioners' sugar

1 teaspoon vanilla
4 tablespoons hot water

Melt butter (real) until golden brown. Blend confectioners' sugar, vanilla and hot water until icing is right consistency to spread. Frost cookies with Caramel Icing. These melt in your mouth.

COOKIES

183

Baby Ruth Cookies

Ruth Hunter

1/2 c. butter
3/4 c. sugar
1 egg
1/2 tsp. vanilla

1 1/3 c. flour
1/2 tsp. baking soda
1/2 tsp. salt
2 (21 oz.) Baby Ruth bars, chopped

Preheat oven to 350°. Beat butter and sugar together, then beat in egg and vanilla. Combine flour, baking soda and salt. Add to batter and stir in chopped candy. Drop teaspoons of batter 2 inches apart on a greased baking sheet. Bake for 10 minutes. Cool on wire rack. Yield: 4 dozen.

Butternut Balls

Banning Cantarini

1 c. butter, softened
3/4 c. powdered sugar
1 tsp. vanilla
2 1/3 c. flour

1/4 tsp. salt
Pecan halves
Chocolate kisses

Preheat oven to 400°. In a large bowl, combine butter and powdered sugar and mix well. Add vanilla and beat with mixer. Add dry ingredients and mix until a dough forms. Make into small balls and wrap each ball around a pecan half or chocolate kiss until covered completely. Place each ball on ungreased cookie sheet at 400° for 10 to 12 minutes. Cookies should not brown. Immediately drop into a bag or bowl full of powdered sugar and roll to coat well. Let cool on wire racks. When cool, roll in powdered sugar again.

Butterscotch Brickle Bars

Patty Fox

FIRST LAYER:

Combine and mix until crumbly:
1 1/2 c. flour
1/2 c. butter

3/4 c. brown sugar
1/4 tsp. salt

Press into a 9x13-inch pan and bake 10 minutes at 350°.

SECOND LAYER:

Combine in top of double boiler:
1 pkg. butterscotch chips
1/4 c. light corn syrup
2 T. salad oil

2 T. water
1/4 tsp. salt
2 c. pecans

Stir over hot water until smooth. Add 2 cups chopped pecans. Spoon over first layer. Bake about 10 minutes, or until bubbly.

Cherry Bars

Deanna Vaux

1 c. butter or margarine
1 3/4 c. sugar
4 eggs
1 tsp. vanilla

3 c. flour
112 tsp, salt
11/2 tsp. baking powder
1 can cherry pie filling

Cream butter, sugar and eggs. Add rest of the ingredients, except pie filling. Pat half of dough into a greased 9x13-inch pan. Top with pie filling. Drop remaining dough by teaspoon on top of pie filling. Bake for 35 to 45 minutes at 350°. If desired, top with powdered sugar glaze after cooled. Works well in jellyroll pan, too.

Chocolate Chip-Peanut Butter Cookies

Ashley Hollamon

3/4 c. butter or margarine
1 c. brown sugar
1 c. sugar
1/2 c. peanut butter
2 eggs

2 tsp. vanilla
2 1/2 c. flour
1 tsp. baking soda
1 tsp. salt
1 pkg. semi-sweet chocolate chips

Heat oven to 350°. Beat butter or margarine, sugars and peanut butter in a large bowl with mixer on medium speed until light and fluffy. Blend in eggs and vanilla. Mix in flour, baking soda and salt (I usually sift these together), just until blended, then add chocolate chips. Bake for 10 to 12 minutes, until slightly browned around the edges. Yield: about 4 dozen

Chocolate No-Bake Cookies

Kristi Hauser Bright

1/2 c. cocoa
1/2 c. milk
2 c. sugar

1/2 c. margarine
1/2 c. peanut butter
3 c. oatmeal

Boil the cocoa, milk, sugar and margarine for 1 minute. Immediately add peanut butter, oatmeal and vanilla. Drop quickly by spoonfuls onto waxed paper and cool.

Chocolate Surprise Cookies

Mitchell Ferguson

1/2 c. butter
1/2 c. shortening
1 c. light brown sugar
1/2 c. sugar
2 lg. eggs

1 tsp. vanilla
2 c. flour
1/2 c. cocoa
1/2 tsp. baking soda
1/2 tsp. baking powder

FILLING:

1/2 c. peanut butter

1/2 c. brown sugar

Cream butter, shortening and sugars; add eggs and vanilla. Beat well. Add dry ingredients, which have been sifted together gradually until light and fluffy. Chill dough for at least 1 hour. Drop chilled dough by spoonfuls (or small scoop) onto parchment-covered cookie sheet. With thumb, make indentation in center of each cookie. Fill with about 1/2 teaspoon peanut butter filling. Flatten small pieces of dough on top of each cookie. Bake at 350° for 15 minutes.

Coconut Cookies

Patty Fox

1 c. sugar
1 egg
1 1/2 c. flour
1/4 tsp. salt

1 stick butter
1 tsp. vanilla
1 1/2 tsp. baking powder
3 c. shredded coconut

Grease mini muffin pans well. Cream sugar with butter. Add: egg and beat well. Combine flour salt and mix into batter. Add 3 cups shredded coconut. Bake about 10 minutes in preheated 375° oven.

Coconut White Chocolate Cookies

Jennifer Fuller

Y2 C Butter, Melted And Browned
1 Large Egg
1/2 C White Sugar
1/4 C Packed Brown Sugar
2 Tsp Vanilla
1 C Sweetened Shredded Coconut,
Lightly Packed
1 1/4 C Flour

1 Tsp Baking Soda
1/2 Tsp Salt
1 C White Chocolate Chips Plus More
For The Tops

Brown the butter by cooking over medium heat in a medium saucepan until it's amber to brown in color, about 5 minutes, depending on the size of the pan. Butter will smell nutty and aromatic. Pour browned butter, and scrape out any brown bits from the pan, into a bowl of a stand mixer or large mixing bowl and allow to cool about 15 minutes. Add eggs and sugars to bowl and beat on medium for about 3 minutes or until creamed and slightly fluffed and smooth. Add vanilla and mix. Add coconut and beat. Add flour, baking soda, salt and beat just to blend, don't over mix. Then add in white chocolate chips. Using a medium cookie scoop, divide dough into 16 equal portions. This size and number of cookies works best. Place dough mounds on a large plate and cover with plastic wrap and place in freezer for 1 hour. You can also chill the mounds in the refrigerator for 3 to 4 hours instead. Preheat oven to 350, line a cookie/baking sheet with parchment paper or silicon mat. If you can get all 16 on your cookie sheet without crowding them, fine, otherwise do 8 at a time. Barely flatten the mounds with your hands and bake for 13 minutes or until cookies are done. Your time may differ, so watch your cookies more than the time. When done the tops will barely look like set and will be pale and loose looking, but will firm up as they cool. The bottoms will look slightly brown. Immediately top with a few chips. Allow cookies to cool on baking sheet for at least 10 minutes or until they are firm enough to move.

Cowboy Cookies

Brenda Hauser

1 c. shortening, or 2 sticks margarine
1 c. sugar
1 c. brown sugar, firmly-packed
2 eggs
1 tsp. vanilla
2 c. oatmeal

2 c. flour
1 tsp. baking soda
1/2 tsp. baking powder
1 tsp, salt
1 (12 oz.) pkg. chocolate chips
1 c. nuts, chopped (opt.)

Cream shortening or margarine and sugars well, then add eggs and vanilla. Mix until light and fluffy, then add dry ingredients. Mix and add chocolate chips and nuts. Drop by spoonfuls onto parchment-lined cookie sheet. Bake at 350° for 10 to 12 minutes.

Dishpan Cookies

Bertie Lightfoot

2 sticks margarine
1 c. sugar
1 c. brown sugar
1 egg
1 c. vegetable oil
1 c. rolled oats

1 c. crushed corn flakes
1 c. shredded coconut
1 c. pecans
3 1/2 c. all-purpose flour
1 tsp. baking soda
1 tsp. vanilla

Preheat oven to 350°. Cream margarine and sugar until light and fluffy. Add egg, mixing well after each addition. Add oats, corn flakes, coconut and nuts. Blend well. Form into balls the size of a walnut and place on ungreased cookie sheet. Flatten with the bottom of a glass dipped in sugar and bake until lightly browned, 10 to 12 minutes.

Ethel's Sugar Cookies

Brenda Hauser

3/4 c. soft shortening (I use margarine)
1 c. sugar
2 eggs

1/2 tsp. vanilla
2 1/2 c. flour
1 tsp. baking powder
1 tsp. salt

Cream shortening and sugar; add remaining ingredients. Chill dough for 1 hour. Roll out and cut into desired shapes. Bake at 400° for 6 to 8 minutes, or just until set, but not brown. Frost with powdered sugar frosting and decorate as desired. This is a family favorite for all holidays.

Five Chip Cookies

Donna Schwab

1 c. butter or margarine, softened
1 c. peanut butter
1 c. sugar
2/3 c. brown sugar
2 eggs
1 tsp. vanilla
2 c. flour
1 c. old-fashioned oats

2 tsp. baking soda
1/2 tsp. salt
2/3 c. milk chocolate chips
2/3 c. semi-sweet chocolate chips
2/3 c. peanut butter chips
2/3 c. vanilla chips
2/3 c. butterscotch chips

In a mixing bowl, cream butter, peanut butter and sugars. Add eggs, one at a time, beating well after each addition. Beat in vanilla. Combine flour, oats, baking soda and salt; gradually add to the creamed mixture. Stir in chips. Drop by rounded tablespoonfuls, 2 inches apart, onto ungreased baking sheets. (I use parchment paper.) Bake at 350° for 10 to 12 minutes, or until lightly browned. Yield: about 4 1/2 dozen yummy cookies.

Forgotten cookie (Vanilla meringues)

Kris Runk

4 egg whites
1 tsp vanilla

1 Cup Sugar
1/2 tsp cream of tartar

Preheat oven to 350.

1. Add vanilla to egg whites and beat Until just bubbly.
2. Add in the cream of tartar and beat until stiff peaks
3. slowly add in the sugar, beat until stiff peaks should form

At this time, fold in any chips if you'd like. I've used min: chocolate chips and white chocolate and liked them, or just go for plain Spoon mixture I to large ziploc bag and cut hole to pipe the cookies onto cookie sheet. You don't have to space them as far as they don't rise much. Make cookies about 2 inches wide. As soon as they're all piped, place tray into oven and SHUT OVEN OFF! forget about them overnight and enjoy the next morning. Or wait a few hours before opening the oven and indulging same day!

Fruit and Nut Bars

Marie Schultz

3 eggs
1 tsp. vanilla
1 c. sugar
1 c. sifted flour
1/2 tsp. salt

1 tsp. baking powder
1 c. chopped nuts
1 (8 oz.) pkg. pitted dates
1 (6 oz.) jar maraschino cherries, drained

Combine eggs and vanilla. Beat well. Add sugar and sifted dry ingredients; blend well. Stir in nuts and fruits. Bake in greased 10 1/2 x 15 1/2-inch jellyroll pan. Cool. Cut into squares. Sprinkle with powdered sugar while warm. Store in airtight container. Yield: 2 dozen. 325° 35 minutes.

German Fruit Cookies

Marie Schultz

1/2 c. shortening or butter
1/2 c. brown sugar
1/2 c. sugar
1/4 tsp. salt
1 tsp. baking soda
1/3 tsp. cinnamon
1/4 tsp. nutmeg

1 2/3 c. flour
1 egg
1 tsp, vanilla
1/2 c. mixed candied fruit
1/2 c. dates, chopped
1/2 c. raisins
1 1/2 c. nuts, chopped

Mix the fruits together and coat with 1 tablespoon flour. Cream together the shortening and sugars. Add egg and vanilla, mixing well. Add flour, salt, baking soda, cinnamon and nutmeg, which have been sifted together. Add fruit to mixture. Refrigerate a few hours or overnight. Shape into small balls and press flat on cookie sheet. Add 1/2 cherry on top. Bake at 350° for 20 minutes. **Note**: I use parchment paper to line the cookie sheet.

Holiday Sugar Roll-Out Cookies

Sharon Massey

1 1/2 c. sifted powdered sugar
1 c. margarine or butter
1 egg
1 tsp. almond flavoring or extract

2 1/2 c. flour
1 tsp. baking soda
1 tsp. cream of tartar

Cream sugar and margarine or butter. Mix in egg and flavorings. Stir dry ingredients together and blend into sugar-margarine/butter mixture. Refrigerate 1 to 2 hours. Take out of refrigerator and let stand until easy to handle and roll out dough on floured surface to 1/4 inch thickness. Use a variety of cookie cutters or a special holiday cutter. Place on ungreased cookie sheets, leaving enough room between so as they bake, they don't blend together. Bake at 375° for 12 to 15 minutes. Let cool on parchment paper or waxed paper until cool, then frost. .

Frosting:

Powdered Sugar
Melted margarine or butter

warmed milk

Frosting: Mix powdered sugar, melted margarine or butter and a small amount of warmed milk to make a consistency that spreads easily. Divide frosting into small cups or bowls and add food coloring to make different colors. Add sprinkles, Red Hots, sugar sparkles, etc., to decorate. I never make a single batch of this cookie dough - usually triple or quadruple the recipe to make a good many holiday cookies for family, friends, and for gift-giving

Iced Pumpkin Cookies

Sara Dunivin

2 1/2 c. all-purpose flour
1 tsp. baking powder
1 tsp. baking soda
2 tsp. ground cinnamon
1/2 tsp. ground nutmeg
1/2 tsp. ground cloves
1/2 tsp. salt
1/2 c. butter, softened

1 1/2 c. white sugar
1 c. canned pumpkin
1 egg
1 tsp. vanilla extract
2 c. confectioners' sugar
3 T. milk
1 T. melted butter
1 tsp. vanilla extract

Preheat oven to 350° Cookies: Combine flour, baking soda, baking powder, cinnamon, nutmeg, ground cloves and salt. In a separate bowl, cream together the 1/2 cup of butter and white sugar. Add pumpkin, egg and 1 teaspoon vanilla to butter mixture and beat until creamy. Mix in dry ingredients. Drop onto cookie sheet by tablespoon, flatten slightly, and bake for 15 to 20 minutes. Cool, then drizzle glaze with fork.
Glaze: Combine powdered sugar, milk, melted butter and 1 teaspoon vanilla. Glaze should be slightly runny, so add more milk if you need to.

M & M Cookies

Chance Hauser

1 c. brown sugar
1/2 c. granulated sugar
1 c. shortening
2 eggs
1 1/2 tsp, vanilla

2 1/4 c. flour
1 tsp, baking soda
1 tsp. salt
1 1/2 c. M&M's

Cream sugar and shortening; add eggs and vanilla. Add flour, salt and baking soda; mix well. Stir in 1/2 cup candies. Reserve remainder for decorating. Bake at 375° for 10 to 12 minutes.

N0-Roll Sugar Cookies

Arlene Hauser

2 cubes margarine
2 c. sugar
2 eggs
1 c. salad oil
1/4 tsp. salt

5 c. flour
2 tsp. baking soda
2 tsp, cream of tartar
2 tsp. vanilla

With mixer, cream margarine, sugar, eggs, oil and salt. Sift in dry ingredients and add vanilla. Roll into balls. Press down with a glass dipped in sugar. Bake at 350° for 10 minutes. I use the small ice cream scoop and dip the balls in different colored sprinkles for Christmas. This recipe makes lots of cookies.

Nut Diamonds

Kayla Cantarini

CRUST:

1 c. (2 sticks) unsalted butter, softened
3/4 c. granulated sugar
1 Lg. egg

1 tsp. vanilla extract
1/4 tsp. salt
3 c. all-purpose flour

TOPPING

1/2 c. (1 stick) unsalted butter, cut up
1 1/3 c. packed light brown sugar
2/3 c. honey

1/2 c. heavy cream
3 c. chopped nuts (pecans or cashews, both of which you have leftover)

Heat oven to 350°. Line a 10x15x1-inch jellyroll pan with foil extending over sides.
Crust: In a bowl, beat butter, sugar, eggs, vanilla and salt for 2 minutes. Beat in flour. With floured hands, press dough into pan. Bake at 350° for 20 minutes (edges brown slightly).

Topping: In a saucepan, melt butter, sugar and honey, then boil 4 minutes, without stirring. Remove from heat; stir in cream and nuts. Pour filling into crust. Bake in 350° oven for 25 minutes until bubbly. Let cool in pan. Lift cookie from pan. Cut 8 lengthwise strips 1 inch wide. Cut diagonal line lengthwise from opposite corner through center, but cut diagonally across strips at 'l-Inch intervals above and below first diagonal. Yield: 6 dozen

Oatmeal-Chocolate Chip Cookies

Mary Hamilton

1 c. shortening
3/4 c. white sugar
3/4 c. brown sugar
2 eggs
1 tsp. vanilla
1 1/2 c. flour
1/4 c. cocoa (opt.)

Salt
1 tsp. baking soda
1 tsp. hot water
2 c. Minute Quaker Oats
1 c. chopped nuts
1 (12 oz.) bag chocolate chips (2 c.)

Cream shortening and sugar; add eggs, one at a time, blending well after each addition. Add vanilla. Sift flour and salt; stir into creamed mixture. Finally, stir in hot water, oats, nuts and chocolate chips. Drop by teaspoons onto greased baking sheet. Bake at 350° for 10 to 12 minutes. These cookies have more body than the traditional chocolate chip cookie.

Peanut Blossoms

Kayla Cantarini

1/2 c. shortening
1/2 c. peanut butter
1/2 c. sugar
1/2 c. brown sugar, packed
1 egg
2 T. milk

1 tsp, vanilla
13/4 c. flour
1 tsp. baking soda
1/2 tsp. salt
1 pkg. candy kisses

Beat together shortening, peanut butter and sugars; add egg, milk and vanilla. Beat well. Add dry ingredients, which have been sifted together to wet ingredients. Shape by rounded teaspoonfuls into balls. Roll in sugar; place on ungreased cookie sheets (parchment lined). Bake at 375° for 8 minutes. Remove from oven and place a solid milk chocolate candy kiss on top of each cookie, pressing down so that the cookie cracks around the edges. Return to oven; bake 2 to 5 minutes longer. An oldie, but goodie.

Peanut Butter Cookies

Dorothy Trammel

2 cubes margarine
1 c. peanut butter
1 c. sugar
1 c. brown sugar
2 eggs

1 tsp. vanilla
2 1/2 c. flour
1 tsp. baking powder
11/2 tsp. baking soda
1 tsp. salt

Mix margarine, peanut butter, sugars and egg thoroughly. Blend all dry ingredients and stir in. Chill dough. Roll into balls the size of walnuts. Place 3 inches apart on cookie sheet. Flatten with fork dipped in flour, crisscross. Sprinkle a little sugar on top of each one. Bake for 10 to 12 minutes at 375°. Dick's favorite.

Potato chip cookies

Patty Hauser Ink

2 Cups brown sugar
2 cups white sugar
2 cups butter
4 Eggs
5 1/2 cups flour
1 tsp salt
2 Tsp soda

4 Cups crushed potato chips
2 cups chocolate chips
2 Cups chopped nuts

Mix all ingredients together. Bake at 350 degrees for 10 minutes

COOKIES

Power Cookies

Tammy Day

1/4 c. butter, softened
1/2 c. shortening (Crisco)
1 c. brown sugar
1 c. sugar
1 tsp. vanilla
2 eggs
1 tsp. salt

1 tsp. baking soda
11/2 c. flour
1112 c. oatmeal (not quick-cooking)
1/2 c. chocolate chips
1/2 c. coconut
1/2 c. raisins or craisins
1/2 c. nuts

Cream butter, shortening, sugar and add eggs and vanilla, mixing well with mixer. Add dry ingredients gradually, then chips, coconut, raisins and nuts. Bake at 350° for 8 to 9 minutes.

Pumpkin Cookies

Nicki Sprung

2 c. sugar
2 c. shortening or margarine
2 c. pumpkin, or 1 c. pumpkin & 1 c. applesauce
2 eggs
5 c. flour, sifted

2 tsp. baking soda
4 tsp. baking powder
1 tsp. salt
2 tsp. vanilla
2 tsp. cinnamon

Cream sugar and shortening with mixer; add pumpkin and eggs. Mix well. Slowly add dry ingredients, which have been sifted together. Drop by spoonfuls and bake at 400° for 10 to 12 minutes.

Frosting:

4 T. margarine
4 T. milk.

1 pound powdered sugar.
1 tsp. vanilla.

Frosting: Melt margarine; add milk. Remove from heat and beat in powdered sugar. Add vanilla. If too thick, add more milk until you are happy with it. Frost cookies while warm. This recipe was written for me by a neighbor in Scottsdale over 40 years ago. We still stay in touch.

Pumpkin Cookies

Jennifer Dutton

1 c. shortening
1 c. sugar
1 1/2 c. pumpkin
1 egg
2 c. flour
1 tsp. baking soda

1 tsp. cinnamon
1 tsp. salt
1 c. butterscotch chips
1 c. nuts
1 c. raisins

FROSTING:

3 T. butter
4 tsp. milk
1/2 c. brown sugar

1 c. powdered sugar
1 tsp. vanilla

Cream shortening and sugar. Add pumpkin and egg. Combine dry ingredients and mix into the creamed mixture. Stir in chips, nuts and raisins. Spoon dough onto ungreased cookie sheet and bake 10 to 12 minutes at 375°.

Frosting: Combine butter, milk and brown sugar in saucepan and cook until sugar dissolves. Let cool and stir in powdered sugar and vanilla. Frost cookies while they are hot. A wonderful fall treat and can be made with fresh pumpkin.

Raisin-Filled Cookies

Bertha Monroe

1 egg
1 c. sugar
1/2 c. shortening (Crisco)
1/2 c. milk or cream
1 tsp. vanilla

1 tsp. baking soda
2 tsp. baking powder
3 112 c. flour
1/2 tsp. salt

FILLING:

1 c. chopped raisins
1 T. flour
1/2 c. sugar

1/2 c. water
1/2 c. chopped walnuts

Cookies: Cream Crisco and sugar; add salt, egg (well beaten), milk, vanilla and flour sifted with baking powder and baking soda. Mix and turn out onto floured baking board. Dough should be soft. Roll very thin and cut out with cookie cutter. Spread half of cookies with filling, then place remaining cookies on top and press edges together. Place on greased tins and bake in 350° oven for 15 minutes.

Filling: Mix sugar and flour in saucepan; add raisins, nuts and water, then stir and cook until thick. Cool before using.

COOKIES

Scotcheroos

Cassidy Simms

1 c. sugar
1 c. light corn syrup
1 c. peanut butter

6 c. Rice Krispies
1 c. chocolate chips
1 c. butterscotch chips

Combine sugar and syrup in 3-quart pan. Cook over moderate heat, stirring frequently, until mixture begins to bubble. Remove from heat and stir in peanut butter; mix well. Add Rice Krispies and stir until well blended. Press mixture into buttered pan. Melt chips together over hot, but not boiling water, stirring until well blended. Remove from heat and spread evenly over Rice Krispies mixture. Cool until firm. Cassidy is an Iowa cousin, nurse, wife and mother, who resides in Iowa, but when she was a little girl, she spent lots of time in Camp Verde. She is a gem.

Snicker Doodles Cookies

Patty Hauser Ink

1 Cup Butter Softened
1 1/2 Cup Sugar
2 Eggs
2 3/4 Cup Flour
2 Tsp Cream Of Tarter

1 Tsp Soda
2 Tsp Salt
1 Tsp Cinnamon
2 Tsp Sugar

Cream Sugar Butter Add Eggs And Mix Well. Add Dry Ingredients. Shape Dough Into 1 inch Ball And 2 Tsp Sugar And 1 Tsp Cinnamon. Bake On Ungreased Cookie Sheet 8 To 10 Minutes At 350º.

Snickerdoodles

Sharon Massey

1 c. butter
1 tsp. vanilla
4 1/2 c. flour
2 c. sugar
1/2 tsp. baking soda

1/2 tsp. salt
2 eggs
4 tsp. baking powder
1 c. sour cream

Cream butter and sugar; add eggs, sour cream and vanilla. Mix thoroughly. Add dry ingredients and refrigerate for 1 hour. Dough will keep for 2 days, covered, in refrigerator. When ready to bake, drop by spoonful and roll in cinnamon and sugar mixture (mix to your liking). Bake at 350° for 10 to 12 minutes.

Soft Gingersnaps

Kim Gould

1 1/2 c. shortening or oleo
2 c. sugar
1/2 c. dark molasses
2 tsp. vanilla
2 eggs
3 tsp. baking soda

2 tsp. cinnamon
3 tsp. ginger
1 tsp. salt
1/2 tsp. nutmeg
1 tsp. cloves
4 c. flour (sift with last 6 ingredients)

Cream shortening, sugar, molasses, vanilla and eggs. Add dry ingredients and mix well. Roll in L-inch balls; roll in sugar. Place on baking sheet with room to spread. Bake for 15 to 20 minutes at 325°. Yield: 3 dozen small cookies.

Spritz

Kim Gould

1 c. soft butter or margarine
2/3 c. sugar
3 egg yolks

1 tsp. vanilla or almond extract
2 1/2 c flour

Mix thoroughly: butter, sugar, egg yolks and flavoring. Work in flour with hands. Force the dough through cookie press onto ungreased baking sheet in desired shapes. Note: Be sure to have cookie sheet cold for each batch.

Thin Mint Layers

Krystal Hollamon

1 (6 oz.) pkg. semi-sweet chocolate chips
3 T. butter, divided
1 c. powdered sugar

1/8 tsp. peppermint extract
3 drops green food coloring
4 tsp, milk

In a 2-cup measure, combine chocolate chips and 2 tablespoons butter. Microwave on HIGH for 45 seconds to 1 1/2 minutes, or until chips are soft. Stir until smooth. Spread in an 8x8-inch baking dish. Chill I hour. In a medium bowl, combine sugar, 1 tablespoon butter, peppermint extract and coloring. Beat with electric mixer, adding milk as needed until smooth and stiff frosting consistency. Spread on chilled chocolate layer. Chill 3 or 4 hours, or until firm. Cut into about 1 1/2-inch squares. Store in refrigerator, covered, no longer than 1 week. Yield: about 25 pieces.

NO FARMS
NO FOOD

Canning

COMBINING WITH THE HAUSERS

Apple Pie Filling

Hazel Pyle Fuller

10 c. water
4 1/2 c. sugar
1/4 tsp. nutmeg
5112 lb. peeled & sliced apples, or enough for 7 qt

1 c. cornstarch
3 tsp. cinnamon
1 tsp. salt

Cook water, sugar, nutmeg, cornstarch, cinnamon and salt until thick; add 2 or 3 drops yellow food coloring and 3 tablespoons lemon juice. Fill jars to the neck with apples and add thickened syrup. Put on lids. Process in hot water bath for 20 minutes.

Blue Ribbon Pickles

Rosa Gates

4 q. sliced cucumbers (not too thin)
6 med. white onions, sliced thin
3 cloves garlic, minced

1 green pepper chopped
1/3 c. salt

Cover with crushed ice.

3 c. distilled white vinegar
5 c. sugar
1 1/2 tsp. turmeric

1 1/2 tsp. celery seed
1 1/2 tsp. mustard seed

Let ice-covered cucumbers set for 3 hours in refrigerator, then drain. Combine the vinegar, sugar, turmeric, celery seed and mustard seed. Pour over cucumber mixture. Heat to boiling; put into jars and process 15 minutes in boiling water bath.

Calico Chow Chow

Mitchell Ferguson

7 c. shredded cabbage (about 1 sm. head)
4 c. fresh corn (about 5 ears)
4 c. cauliflowerets (about 1 sm. head)
2 c. diced sweet red pepper
1 c. diced green pepper
1 c. chopped onion
1/4 c. canning salt

7 c. water, divided
3 1/2 c. packed brown sugar
1/2 c. all-purpose flour
1/4 c. ground mustard
1 T. celery seed
2 tsp. ground turmeric
11/2 tsp. salt
5 c. vinegar

In a large bowl, combine the first 6 ingredients; sprinkle with canning salt. Add 6 cups water; cover and refrigerate for 4 hours. Drain and rinse well. In a large heavy saucepan or Dutch oven, combine the brown sugar, flour, mustard, celery seed, turmeric and salt. Stir in vinegar and remaining water until smooth. Bring to a boil; cook and stir for 5 minutes, or until thickened. Add vegetables; bring to a boil. Simmer, uncovered, for 8 to 10 minutes, or until crisp tender. Pack the hot mixture into hot jars, leaving 1/ 4-inch headspace. Adjust caps. Process for 15 minutes in a boiling water bath. Yield: 7 pints.

Cheryl's Corn Relish

Cheryl Eberhard

8 c. whole kernel corn
2 c. diced green peppers
2 c. diced sweet red peppers
4 c. chopped celery
8 to 10 sm. onions, chopped (3 med.)
1 c. honey

3 c. vinegar
1 c. lemon juice
2 tsp. celery seed
3 T. dry mustard
1 tsp. turmeric

Combine green peppers, red peppers, celery, onions, honey, vinegar, lemon juice and celery seeds in an enamel or stainless pot. Cover until mixture starts to boil, then simmer, uncovered, for 5 minutes. Mix mustard and turmeric. Add corn. Heat to boiling and simmer for 5 minutes. Process in boiling water bath for 15 minutes. Hauser sweet corn of course.

Chimichurri Sauce

Sharon Olson

1/2 c. olive oil
1/2 c. red wine vinegar
3 T. chopped fresh cilantro
3/4 c. chopped fresh flat-leaf parsley

6 garlic cloves, chopped
1 tsp. salt
1/4 tsp. cayenne pepper
1 tsp. freshly-ground black pepper

In a bowl, whisk together the parsley, cilantro, garlic, vinegar, olive oil, salt, cayenne and pepper. Use the sauce immediately, or cover and refrigerate for up to 4 hours. Bring to room temperature before serving.
Yield: 1 cup.
From Argentina, this packs a flavorful punch. It's found in virtually every Argentine dining table, where its culinary role is similar to that of ketchup in the USA. Primary ingredients are always fresh herbs, spicy chili, oil and vinegar. Delicious paired with grilled and toasted meats, as well as fish.

Cleaning Solution

Naoma Moore

2 T. vinegar
1 tsp. Borax

1 c. hot water
1/4 c. dishwashing liquid

Put into spray bottle and shake well. Use for all general cleaning.

Connie's BBQ Sauce

Pat Boler

1 can El Pato sauce
1 (8 oz.) can tomato sauce
1 T. vinegar

1 T. Worcestershire sauce
2 T. chopped onion
1/2 c. brown sugar

Heat in saucepan long enough to melt sugar and blend flavors. Can be used on any meats or fish.

Corn Chow Chow

Edith Jones

18 to 20 med. ears of Hauser's corn
11/2 qt. shredded cabbage 1/2 c. dry mustard
2 c. chopped sweet red pepper
5 T. canning salt
1 qt. white vinegar

3 T. mustard seed
2 T. celery seed
1 T. whole cloves, tied in cheesecloth bag
1 tsp. turmeric

Husk corn and remove silk. Blanch ears of corn 5 minutes in boiling water; plunge into cold water. Drain and cut corn from cob to about 2/3 of their depth to yield 2 quarts kernels. Put a layer of vegetables in an enameled pan, stone jar or glass bowl; sprinkle with salt. Repeat until all vegetables and 3 tablespoons salt are used. Let stand overnight. Drain well. Heat vinegar and all remaining ingredients (including 2 tablespoons salt) to boiling; add vegetables and cook slowly until tender, about 20 minutes. Pack hot, into hot jars, leaving 1/2-inch head space. Adjust caps. Process pints 10 minute and quarts 15 minutes in boiling water bath. Yield: about 6 pints.

Corn Relish

Grandma Naoma Moore

1 doz. ears corn, cut off cob
1 sm. head cabbage, chopped fine
1 bunch celery, chopped
2 med. onions, chopped
2 red peppers, chopped

2 c. sugar
1/4 tsp. salt
1 tsp. dry mustard
1 qt. apple cider vinegar

Boil all ingredients for 25 minutes and put into jars. Process in hot water bath for 15 minutes. We sometimes leave out the cabbage and dilute the vinegar if it seems too tangy.

Crisp Pickle Slices
(Bread-And-Butter Type)

Sharon Massey

4 qt. sliced unpared med. cucumbers
6 med. white onions, sliced (6 c.)
2 yellow or green bell peppers, sliced (1 2/3 c.)
3 cloves garlic
1/3 c. granulated pickling salt

5 c. sugar
3 c. cider vinegar
1 1/2 tsp. turmeric
1 1/2 tsp. celery seed
2 T. mustard seed

Combine cucumber, onion, bell pepper and whole garlic cloves. Add salt; cover with cracked ice. Mix thoroughly. Let stand 3 hours; drain well. Remove garlic. Combine remaining ingredients; pour over cucumber mixture. Bring to a boil. Fill hot jars to 1/2 inch from top; adjust lids. Process in boiling water bath for 5 minutes (start timing when water returns to boiling). Yield: 8 pints.

Crock-Pot Apple Butter

Sue Hauser

10 c. apples, cooked & mashed
5 c. sugar
1/4 c. cider vinegar

1 tsp. cinnamon
1/2 tsp, nutmeg

Cook on high crock-pot setting for 5 hours, covered, stirring occasionally. Uncover and cook about 2 hours, or until desired thickness. Add cinnamon and nutmeg to taste. Grandma Hauser's Note: I made 16 pints of this and is real good. It didn't stick one bit and I hardly stirred it at all. After I uncovered, I cooked about 11/2 hours. I think it depends on the crock-pot.

Della's Chili Sauce

Della Boler

4 doz. ripe tomatoes
6 green peppers
6 onions
1 c. sugar

4 T. salt
1/4 c. mixed pickling spices
2 c. vinegar

Scald and peel tomatoes; remove seeds and white fiber from peppers. Cut tomatoes, green peppers and onions into small pieces. Add vinegar, salt and sugar. Tie spices in cheesecloth. Cook 3 hours over medium-low heat. Put into jars and seal, using water bath time in calming book.

Grandma Dollie's Pear Preserves
Grandma Dollie Enright

Place in large bowl, pears that have been peeled and cut into small pieces. For each 2 cups of pears, add 1 cup of sugar. Let stand overnight, or long enough to make its own juice. Cook on low heat for 2 to 3 hours. Will turn honey-colored. While still hot, place in sterilized jars and seal.

Horseradish Pickles

Hazel Fuller

2 qt. baby dill pickles (Vlasic)
Drain slice and put back into jar.

Boil together:
2 c. sugar
2/3 c. vinegar

1/3 c. water

Put 5 ounce prepared horseradish on top of pickles. Pour the boiling- hot sugar-vinegar mixture over the pickles. Refrigerate and let stand a couple days before enjoying them

CANNING

Hot Sauce

Brenda Sheldon

8 c. tomatoes, mashed
1 c. chili peppers, chopped
1/2 tsp. oregano
1 clove garlic, chopped

1 or 2 c. onions, chopped
1/3 c. vinegar
1 T. salt

Heat to boiling in large saucepan and put into pint jars. Process in boiling water bath for 30 minutes. Pour the tomatoes into a strainer to drain off excess juice so sauce won't be watery.

Oven-Cooked Corn for Freezing

Brenda Hauser

22 c. fresh corn, cut off cob
Salt & pepper

1 Lb. Butter (we use 1/2 Lb.
1 qt. half & half

Mix all together in large oven proof pan and bake at 3250 for 1 hour. Cool well and put about 2 cups in freezer bags or containers. This is so good straight from the freezer and into the microwave.

Peaches for Freezing

Betty Haywood

10 lb. or so peaches (the recipe says 1 lug)

1 Lg. can frozen orange juice concentrate, mixed with amount of water called for on can)
6 to 8 c. sugar

Dissolve sugar in orange Juice and put peeled, sliced peaches into liquid. Freeze in pint or quart freezer bags and label. Your peaches will not turn dark and are so yummy.

Quick Corn Relish

Betty Haywood

1 can whole kernel corn, undrained
2 T. onion, chopped
3 tsp. sugar
3 T. pimentos, chopped

1 T. mustard seed
1/4 tsp. mustard seed
1/4 tsp. salt
1/4 tsp. dry mustard

Combine all ingredients, except corn, and cook for about 3 minutes. Add corn and cook 3 minutes more. Pour into jars and refrigerate. Yield: 1 pint.
Betty is Dick's Iowa cousin and such an inspirational cook. Her Mom used to make pies for a little restaurant in Union, Iowa.

Quick Frozen Corn

Brenda Hauser

15 c. corn (whole kernel - do not scrape cob)
3/4 c. sugar

1/4 c. salt, or to taste
5 c. ice water

Mix this all together. Pack in freezer bags and freeze immediately. When you prepare it for the table, remember it is already seasoned. May need a little more water as it cooks. Tastes almost as good as fresh.

Raspberry Jalapeno Jelly

Sara Malanca

1 c. fresh or frozen raspberries
1/4 c. chopped jalapeno pepper
3/4 c. apple cider vinegar

1/2 c. chopped green bell pepper
3 c. granulated sugar
2 oz. liquid pectin

In a saucepan, combine the raspberries, bell pepper and jalapeno peppers with the sugar and cider vinegar. Bring to a boil over medium- high heat, and boil rapidly for 1 minute. Remove from heat and let stand for 5 minutes. Stir in the liquid pectin, and run the mixture through a strainer to remove bits of peppers. Pour the strained liquid into 6 ~ sterilized 8-ounce jelly jars with lids, and seal. Store in a cool dark place. Refrigerate after opening.

Refrigerator Pickles

Colleen Patterson

4 c. sugar
4 c. vinegar
1/2 c. salt
1 1/3 T. turmeric

8 or more 19. cucumbers, sliced
1 1/2 T. mustard seed
3 onions, sliced thin

Mix together; do not heat. Place some onion slices in bottom of jar. We use quarts. Layer onion and cucumbers. Press down. Pour liquid over and put on lid. Refrigerate. They are ready to eat in 5 days. This is not a recipe for canning, only works in the refrigerator.

Spiced Pear Jam

Grandma Dollie Enright

10 c. cooked, mashed pears
1 seeded & blenderized orange & lemon
2 pkg. pectin

5 c. sugar
1/2 tsp. cloves & ginger
1 tsp. cinnamon

Mix all together in large pan and simmer for 30 minutes. Pour into sterilized jars and process for 15 minutes in boiling water bath

CANNING

Sweet Pickles (Made From Dill)
Naoma Moore

1 (32 oz.) jar whole dill pickles
2 1/2 c. sugar
1/2 c. vinegar

1 tsp. celery seed
1 tsp. mustard seed

Double recipe if you use the gallon jar. Mix sugar and remaining ingredients and pour over drained pickles. Let set out on kitchen counter. Stir frequently. Refrigerate after a day or two. Make sure all sugar is dissolved. These are crisper than any sweet pickle I've ever made.

Shemwell's BBQ Sauce (Cairo, Illinois)
Donna Wood

2 qt. cider vinegar
2 qt. water
1 c. sugar
1/2 c. salt

1/2 c. flour
2 oz. red pepper
1/2 cube margarine

Combine all but butter. Cook 1 hour, stirring often. Add butter while cooling. Pour into desired jars or containers. Refrigerate. Note: Will keep a long time in the refrigerator. Can cut recipe in half or double for more. Donna and 1 were neighbors in Cairo, Illinois, until we moved to Arizona in 1955. We are still BFF's.

Tomato Relish
Susan Welch

2 qt. ripe tomatoes, chopped
1/2 green pepper, chopped
1/2 c. onion, chopped

1/4 c. salt
1 tsp. Tabasco sauce (opt.)

Prepare vegetables (I use food processor) and sprinkle salt over all. Stir and let stand overnight. The next day, drain and mix in 11/2 cups sugar, 1/2 cup vinegar and 1 tablespoon mustard seed. Stir well and let stand for 4 hours, stirring occasionally. Put into jars (I sterilized mine in boiling water, but recipe doesn't call for that) and refrigerate. Note: This will keep a long time in the refrigerator and is as good as catchup.

Watermelon Pickles
Grandma Sue Hauser

4 c. sugar
3 c. water

1 tsp. allspice
1 tsp. cloves
1 19. stick cinnamon

Cover rind with brine made of 4 tablespoons salt to 1 quart water. Let stand 3 hours. Drain and rinse in cold water. Add rind to syrup, enough to cover. Boil 10 minutes. Let stand overnight. Boil slowly until rind is clear. Process in boiling water bath after filling pint jars.

Zucchini Chow Chow

Aunt Edith Jones

10 c. ground zucchini
4 c. ground onions
2 bell peppers, chopped
5 T. salt
2 qt. vinegar
7 c. sugar

1 tsp. nutmeg
1 tsp. turmeric
1 tsp. dry mustard
1 tsp. cornstarch
2 tsp. celery seed

Combine zucchini, onions, peppers and salt. Let stand overnight, covered. Rinse with cold water and drain extremely well; press firmly to get water out (this is important). The next day, add vinegar, sugar, nutmeg, turmeric, dry mustard, cornstarch and celery seed. Bring to a boil. Simmer 30 minutes. Put into prepared jars and seal. Yield: approximately 14 pints.

Zucchini Pickles

Naoma Moore

4 or 5 zucchini (about 2 lb.)
1/2 c. coarse salt
1/2 c. sugar
11/2 c. white vinegar

3 T. dry mustard
1 T. ground ginger
1 T. curry powder
6 peppercorns

Rinse unpeeled zucchini and cut into 1/2-inch slices. Layer with salt in a large bowl. Cover bowl with towel and let stand overnight. The next morning, drain, rinse in cold water and place in heavy kettle. Combine sugar, vinegar and spices in heavy pan. Heat to boiling and boil for 5 minutes. Pour over vegetable mixture and boil 5 more minutes, or until tender. Spoon hot mixture into sterilized jars and seal. Process in boiling water bath for 5 minutes.

Hauser Family Cookbook Index

INDEX

209

Sumi Salad	67
Susie's Orange Pineapple Salad	68
Watergate Salad	68
Watermelon Salad	68
Wild Rice And Cranberry Salad	69
Breads	**70**
Alice Bradford's Applesauce Bread	71
Apple Cinnamon Muffins	71
Anna's Illinois Biscuits	71
Angel Biscuits	72
Baked Cheese Bread	72
Banana Bread	72
Beer Bread	73
Bread Pudding With Rum Sauce	73
Bread Machine Cinnamon Rolls	74
Carrot-Pineapple Muffins	74
Cheesy Corn Spoonbread	75
Coconut Banana Bread	75
Cranberry Mini Loaf Bread	76
Cranberry-Pumpkin Bread	76
Dutch Apple Bread	77
Green Chili Cornmeal Casserole	77
Homemade Noodles	78
Honey Whole Wheat Bread	78
Kay's Bread	78
Lemon Blueberry Bread	79
Molasses Sweet Bread	79
Mother's Monkey Bread	79
Oat Pancakes	80
Old-Fashioned Cinnamon Rolls	80
Sharon's Corn Rolls	81
Sopapillas	81
Zucchini Nut Muffins	81
Main Dishes	**82**
4-H Corn Special	83
Air Fryer Coconut Shrimp	83

Banning's Mississippi Mojo	84
Barbecued Pineapple	84
Beefy Cornbread	85
Beer Braised BBQ Chicken	85
BBQ Roast	85
Bev's Chicken Enchiladas	86
Big Pot Stew	86
Breakfast Casserole	86
Breakfast Pie	87
California Zucchini Bake	87
Carousel Burgers	87
Chalupa	88
Cheese Boats	88
Cheesy Chicken and Rice Casserole	88
Chicken Casserole	89
Chicken Enchiladas	89
Chicken Fingers	89
Chicken Mornay	90
Chicken Pot Pie	90
Chicken Spaghetti	90
Chicken with Dumplings	91
Chili Cheese Puff	91
Corn Stuffing	91
Crock-Pot Stuffing	62
Crock-Pot Tex Mex Pork Stew	92
Divine Waistline Potatoes	92
Do-Ahead Brunch Bake	93
Domathes-Greek Stuffed Grape Leaves	93
Easy Green Chili	94
Easy Lasagna	94
Enchilada Casserole	95
Fajita Marinade	95
Fiesta Tamale Pie	96
Garlic and Lemon Chicken	96
Goulash	96
Green Chile Burros	96
Green Chile Pie	97
Green Chili-Corn Tamales	97

INDEX

211

Cakes	**129**
14-Carrot Cake	130
Apple Cake	130
Applesauce Cake	130
Apple Stack Cake	131
Bacardi Rum Cake	131
Banana Split Cake	132
Best-Ever Carrot Cake	132
Best-Ever Chocolate Cake	133
Better-Than-Sex Cake	134
Blueberry-Lemon Pound Cake	134
Blueberry Pudding Cake	134
Candied Fruit Cake	135
Cherry Dumplin' Cake	135
Choco-Holic Cake	136
Coffeecake	136
Connie's Chocolate Cake & Frosting	137
Corny Cake	137
Cream Puff Cake	138
Easy Pineapple Upside-Down Cake	138
Fresh Peach Cake	138
Fudgy Chocolate-Cherry Cake	139
Grandmother Britton's 1937 Devil's Food Cake	139
Honey Bun Cake	139
Hot Fudge Pudding Cake	140
Ice Cream Cake	140
Jello Pudding Cake	140
Kahlua Cake	141
Lemon Chiffon Cake	142
Lemon Jello Cake	142
Lemon Pudding Cake	143
Magic Fruitcake	143
Mrs. Wood's Quick Chocolate Cake	143
Oatmeal Cake	144
Pineapple Dream Cake	144
Pistachio Cake	145
Pound Cake (2)	145

Pumpkin Sheet Cake	146
Punch Bowl Cake	146
Red Velvet Cake	147
Sherrie's Texas Sheet Cake	147
Sour Cream Coffeecake	148
Swedish Nut Cake	148
Two-Cherry Cream Cakes	149
Upside-Down Cake	149
Pies	**149**
Ann's Pecan Pie	149
Aunt Bea's Fresh Strawberry Pie	150
Buttermilk Pie	150
Chocolate Cream Pie	150
Chocolate Pie (2)	151
Creamy Lemon Pie	151
Easiest Strawberry Pie	152
Easy Key Lime Pie	152
Easy Peach Pie	152
Gancache	152
Key Lime Mouse Pie	153
Lemon Meringue Pie	154
Margaret's Chocolate Pie Filling	154
Margarita Pie	155
Mincemeat Pie	155
Mock Apple Pie	155
Mother's Pie Crust	156
Mountain Top Pie	156
No-Weep Meringue	156
Ohio Lemon Pie	157
Pecan Pie (2)	157
Pete's Peanut Butter Pie	157
Gancache	157
Pumpkin Pie	157
Sybil's Own Pecan Pie	158
Walnut Applesauce Pie	158
DESSERTS	159

INDEX

213

Forgotten Cookie (Vanilla Meringues)	189
Fruit and Nut Bars	189
German Fruit Cookies	190
Holiday Sugar Roll-Out Cookies	190
Iced Pumpkin Cookies	191
M&M Cookies	191
No-Roll Sugar Cookies	191
Nut Diamonds	192
Oatmeal-Chocolate Chip Cookies	192
Peanut Blossoms	193
Peanut Butter Cookies	193
Potato Chip Cookies	193
Power Cookies	194
Pumpkin Cookies (2)	194,195
Raisin-Filled Cookies	195
Scotcheroos	196
Snicker Doodles Cookies	196
Snickerdoodles	196
Soft Gingersnaps	197
Spritz	197
Thin Mint Layers	197
Canning	199
Apple Pie Filling	200
Blue Ribbon Pickles	200
Calico Chow Chow	200
Cheryl's Corn Relish	201
Chimichurri Sauce	201
Cleaning Solution	201
Connie's BBQ Sauce	201
Corn Chow Chow	202
Corn Relish	202
Crisp Pickle Slices	202
Crock-Pot Apple Butter	203
Della's Chili Sauce	203
Grandma Dollie's Pear Preserves	203
Horseradish Pickles	203

Hot Sauce	204
Oven-Cooked Corn for Freezing	204
Peaches for Freezing	204
Quick Corn Relish	204
Quick Frozen Corn	205
Raspberry Jalapeno Jelly	205
Refrigerator Pickles	205
Spiced Pear Jam	205
Sweet Pickles (Made From Dill)	206
Shemwell's BBQ Sauce	206
Tomato Relish	206
Watermelon Pickles	206
Zucchini Chow Chow	207
Zucchini Pickles	207

Hauser Cookbooks can be found on our web site
www.hauserandhauserfarms.com

or through Glorybound Publishing in Camp Verde
www.gloryboundpublishing.com

or ordered directly from *Amazon.com*

Kristi's family. Left to right: Banning, Britt, Cody, Chris, Kayla, Kristi and Ron